Veranilo

George Gissing

Alpha Editions

This edition published in 2024

ISBN : 9789362922007

Design and Setting By
Alpha Editions
www.alphaedis.com
Email - info@alphaedis.com

As per information held with us this book is in Public Domain.
This book is a reproduction of an important historical work. Alpha Editions uses the best technology to reproduce historical work in the same manner it was first published to preserve its original nature. Any marks or number seen are left intentionally to preserve its true form.

Contents

CHAPTER I THE VANQUISHED ROMAN ....- 1 -
CHAPTER II BASIL'S VISION ....- 8 -
CHAPTER III THE DEACON LEANDER ....- 17 -
CHAPTER IV TO CUMAE ....- 26 -
CHAPTER V BASIL AND VERANILDA ....- 37 -
CHAPTER VI THE EMPEROR'S COMMAND ....- 47 -
CHAPTER VII HERESY ....- 54 -
CHAPTER VIII THE SNARE...- 63 -
CHAPTER IX CHORSOMAN..- 70 -
CHAPTER X THE ANICIANS...- 80 -
CHAPTER XI SEEKING..- 89 -
CHAPTER XII HELIODORA ....- 100 -
CHAPTER XIII THE SOUL OF ROME........................- 112 -
CHAPTER XIV SILVIA'S DREAM................................- 121 -
CHAPTER XV YOUNG ROME.....................................- 130 -
CHAPTER XVI WHISPERS ....- 137 -
CHAPTER XVII LEANDER THE POLITIC ....- 144 -
CHAPTER XVIII PELAGIUS ....- 151 -
CHAPTER XIX THE PRISONER OF PRAENESTE ..- 158 -
CHAPTER XX THE ISLAND IN THE LIRIS ....- 168 -
CHAPTER XXI THE BETRAYER BETRAYED ....- 180 -
CHAPTER XXII DOOM..- 192 -
CHAPTER XXIII THE RED HAND ....- 199 -
CHAPTER XXIV THE MOUNT OF THE MONK.......- 207 -
CHAPTER XXV THE ABBOT'S TOWER ....- 217 -
CHAPTER XXVI VIVAS IN DEO..................................- 224 -

CHAPTER XXVII THE KING OF THE GOTHS ....- 231 -
CHAPTER XXVIII AT HADRIAN'S VILLA ....- 240 -
CHAPTER XXIX ROME BELEAGUERED................- 252 -
CHAPTER XXX * * * *..- 257 -

CHAPTER I
THE VANQUISHED ROMAN

Seven years long had the armies of Justinian warred against the Goths in Italy. Victor from Rhegium to Ravenna, the great commander Belisarius had returned to the East, Carrying captive a Gothic king. The cities of the conquered land were garrisoned by barbarians of many tongues, who bore the name of Roman soldiers; the Italian people, brought low by slaughter, dearth, and plague, crouched under the rapacious tyranny of governors from Byzantium.

Though children born when King Theodoric still reigned had yet scarce grown to manhood, that golden age seemed already a legend of the past. Athalaric, Amalasuntha, Theodahad, last of the Amal blood, had held the throne in brief succession and were gone; warriors chosen at will by the Gothic host, mere kings of the battlefield, had risen and perished; reduced to a wandering tribe, the nation which alone of her invaders had given peace and hope to Italy, which alone had reverenced and upheld the laws, polity, culture of Rome, would soon, it was thought, be utterly destroyed, or vanish in flight beyond the Alps. Yet war did not come to an end. In the plain of the great river there was once more a chieftain whom the Goths had raised upon their shields, a king, men said, glorious in youth and strength, and able, even yet, to worst the Emperor's generals. His fame increased. Ere long he was known to be moving southward, to have crossed the Apennines, to have won a battle in Etruria. The name of this young hero was Totila.

In these days the senators of Rome, heirs to a title whose ancient power and dignity were half-forgotten, abode within the City, under constraint disguised as honour, the conqueror's hostages. One among them, of noblest name, Flavius Anicius Maximus, broken in health by the troubles of the time and by private sorrow, languishing all but unto death in the heavy air of the Tiber, was permitted to seek relief in a visit to which he would of his domains in Italy. His birth, his repute, gave warrant of loyalty to the empire, and his coffers furnished the price put upon such a favour by Byzantine greed. Maximus chose for refuge his villa by the Campanian shore, vast, beautiful, half in ruin, which had been enjoyed by generations of the Anician family; situated above the little town of Surrentum it caught the cooler breeze, and on its mountainous promontory lay apart from the tramp of armies. Here, as summer burned into autumn, the sick man lived in brooding silence, feeling his strength waste, and holding to the world only by one desire.

The household comprised his unwedded sister Petronilla, a lady in middle age, his nephew Basil, and another kinsman, Decius, a student and an invalid;

together with a physician, certain freedmen who rendered services of trust, a eunuch at the Command of Petronilla, and the usual body of male and female slaves. Some score of glebe-bound peasants cultivated the large estate for their lord's behoof. Notwithstanding the distress that had fallen upon the Roman nobility, many of whom were sunk into indigence, the chief of the Anicii still controlled large means; and the disposal of these possessions at his death was matter of interest to many persons—not least to the clergy of Rome, who found in the dying man's sister a piously tenacious advocate. Children had been born to Maximus, but the only son who reached mature years fell a victim to pestilence when Vitiges was camped about the City. There survived one daughter, Aurelia. Her the father had not seen for years; her he longed to see and to pardon ere he died. For Aurelia, widowed of her first husband in early youth, had used her liberty to love and wed a flaxen-haired barbarian, a lord of the Goths; and, worse still, had renounced the Catholic faith for the religion of the Gothic people, that heresy of Arianism condemned and abhorred by Rome. In Consequence she became an outcast from her kith and kin. Her husband commanded in the city of Cumae, hard by Neapolis. When this stronghold fell before the advance of Belisarius, the Goth escaped, soon after to die in battle; Aurelia, a captive of the Conquerors, remained at Cumae, and still was living there, though no longer under restraint. Because of its strength, this ancient city became the retreat of many ladies who fled from Rome before the hardships and perils of the siege; from them the proud and unhappy woman, ever held apart, yet she refused to quit the town when she would have been permitted to do so. From his terrace above the Surrentine shore, Maximus gazed across the broad gulf to the hills that concealed Cumae, yearning for the last of his children. When at length he wrote her a letter, a letter of sad kindness, inviting rather than beseeching her to visit him, Aurelia made no reply. Wounded, he sunk again into silence, until his heart could no longer bear its secret burden, and he spoke—not to Petronilla, from whose austere orthodoxy little sympathy was to be expected—but to his nephew Basil, whose generous mettle willingly lent itself to such a service as was proposed. On his delicate mission, the young man set forth without delay. To Cumae, whether by sea or land, was but a short journey: starting at daybreak, Basil might have given ample time to his embassy, and have been back again early on the morrow. But the second day passed, and he did not return. Though harassed by the delay, Maximus tried to deem it of good omen, and nursed his hope through another sleepless night.

Soon after sunrise, he was carried forth to his place of observation, a portico in semicircle, the marble honey-toned by time, which afforded shelter from the eastern rays and commanded a view of vast extent. Below him lay the little town, built on the cliffs above its landing-place; the hillsides on either hand were clad with vineyards, splendid in the purple of autumn, and with olives. Sky and sea shone to each other in perfect calm; the softly breathing air mingled its morning freshness with a scent of fallen flower and leaf. A rosy vapour from Vesuvius floated gently inland; and this the eye of Maximus marked with contentment, as it signified a favourable wind for a boat crossing hither from the far side of the bay. For the loveliness of the scene before him, its noble lines, its jewelled colouring, he had little care; but the infinite sadness of its suggestion, the decay and the desolation uttered by all he saw, sank deep into his heart. If his look turned to the gleaming spot which was the city of Neapolis, there came into his mind the sack and massacre of a few years ago, when Belisarius so terribly avenged upon the Neapolitans their stubborn resistance to his siege. Faithful to the traditions of his house, of his order, Maximus had welcomed the invasion which promised to restore Italy to the Empire; now that the restoration was effected, he saw with bitterness the evils resulting from it, and all but hoped that this new king of the Goths, this fortune-favoured Totila, might sweep the land of its Greek oppressors. He looked back upon his own life, on the placid dignity of his career under the rule of Theodoric, the offices by which he had risen, until he sat in the chair of the Consul. Yet in that time, which now seemed so full of peaceful glories, he had never at heart been loyal to the great king; in his view, as in that of the nobles generally, Theodoric was but a usurper, who had abused the mandate intrusted to him by the Emperor Zeno, to deliver Italy from the barbarians. When his own kinsmen, Boethius and Symmachus, were put to death on a charge of treachery, Maximus burned with hatred of the Goth. He regarded with disdain the principles of Cassiodorus, who devoted his life to the Gothic cause, and who held that only as an independent kingdom could there be hope for Italy. Having for a moment the ear of Theodoric's daughter, Amalasuntha, when she ruled for her son, Maximus urged her to yield her kingdom to the Emperor, and all but saw his counsel acted upon. After all, was not Cassiodorus right? Were not the senators who had ceaselessly intrigued with Byzantium in truth traitors to Rome? It was a bitter thought for the dying man that all his life he had not only failed in service to his country, but had obstinately wrought for her ruin.

Attendants placed food beside him. He mingled wine with water and soothed a feverish thirst. His physician, an elderly man of Oriental visage, moved respectfully to his side, greeted him as Illustrious, inquired how his Magnificence had passed the latter part of the night. Whilst replying, as ever courteously—for in the look and bearing of Maximus there was that *senatorius decor* which Pliny noted in a great Roman of another time—his straining eyes seemed to descry a sail in the quarter he continually watched. Was it only a fishing boat? Raised upon the couch, he gazed long and fixedly. Impossible as yet to be sure whether he saw the expected bark; but the sail seemed to draw nearer, and he watched.

The voice of a servant, who stood at a respectful distance, announced: 'The gracious Lady'; and there appeared a little procession. Ushered by her eunuch, and attended by half a dozen maidens, one of whom held over her a silk sunshade with a handle of gold, the sister of Maximus approached at a stately pace. She was tall, and of features severely regular; her dark hair—richer in tone and more abundant than her years could warrant—rose in elaborate braiding intermingled with golden threads; her waistless robe was of white silk adorned with narrow stripes of purple, which descended, two on each side, from the shoulders to the hem, and about her neck lay a shawl of delicate tissue. In her hand, which glistened with many gems, she carried a small volume, richly bound, the Psalter. Courtesies of the gravest passed between her and Maximus, who, though he could not rise from his couch, assumed an attitude of graceful deference, and Petronilla seated herself in a chair which a slave had placed for her. After many inquiries as to her brother's health, the lady allowed her eyes to wander for a moment, then spoke with the smile of one who imparts rare tidings.

'Late last night—too late to trouble you with the news—there came a post from the reverend deacon Leander. He disembarked yesterday at Salernum, and, after brief repose, hopes to visit us. Your Amiability will, I am sure, welcome his coming.'

'Assuredly,' answered Maximus, bending his head, whilst his eyes watched the distant sail. 'Whence comes he?'

'From Sicily. We shall learn, I dare say, the business which took him there,' added Petronilla, with a self-satisfied softening of her lips. 'The deacon is wont to talk freely with me of whatever concerns the interests of our holy Church, even as I think you remember, has now and then deigned—though I know not how I have deserved such honour—to ask, I dare not say my counsel, but my humble thoughts on this or that. I think we may expect him before morning. The day will not be too warm for travel.'

Maximus wore an anxious look, and spoke after hesitation.

'Will his reverend leisure permit him to pass more than one day with us?'

'Earnestly I hope so. You, beyond doubt, dear lord, my brother, will desire long privacy with the holy man. His coming at this time is plainly of Heaven's direction.'

'Lady sister,' answered Maximus, with the faintest smile on his sad features, 'I would not willingly rob you of a moment's conference with the good deacon. My own business with him is soon despatched. I would fain be assured of burial in the Temple of Probus where sleep our ancestors.'

'Of that,' replied Petronilla, solemnly and not unkindly, 'doubt not for a moment. Your body shall lie there, by the blessed Peter's sanctuary, and your tomb be honoured among those of the greatest of our blood. But there is another honour that I covet for you, an honour above all that the world can bestow. In these sad times, Maximus, the Church has need of strengthening. You have no children—'

A glance from the listener checked her, and, before she could resume, Maximus interposed in a low voice:

'I have yet a daughter.'

'A daughter?' exclaimed Petronilla, troubled, confused, scarce subduing indignation.

'It is better I should tell you,' continued her brother, with some sternness, resulting from the efforts to command himself, 'that Basil is gone to Cumae to see Aurelia, and, if it may be, to lead her to me. Perhaps even now'—he pointed to the sea—'they are on the way hither. Let us not speak of it, Petronilla,' he added in a firmer tone. 'It is my will; that must suffice. Of you I ask nothing save silence.'

The lady arose. Her countenance expressed angry and bitter feeling, but there was no danger of her uttering what she thought. Gravely, somewhat coldly, she spoke good wishes for her brother's ease during the day, and so retired with her retinue. Alone, Maximus sighed, and looked again across the waters.

In a few minutes the servant who guarded his privacy was again heard announcing the lord Decius. The Senator turned his eyes with a look of good-humoured greeting.

'Abroad so early, good cousin? Did the oil fail you last night and send you too soon to bed?'

'You have not chanced to remember, dear my lord, what day it is?' returned Decius, when he had bestowed a kiss on his kinsman's cheek. 'Had I but vigour enough, this morning would have seen me on a pilgrimage to the tomb.' He put out a hand towards Neapolis. 'I rose at daybreak to meditate the Fourth Eclogue.'

'The ides of October—true. I take shame to myself for having lost the memory of Virgil in my own distresses.'

Decius, whose years were scarce thirty, had the aspect and the gait of an elderly man; his thin hair streaked with grey, his cheeks hollow, his eyes heavy, he stooped in walking and breathed with difficulty; the tunic and the light cloak, which were all his attire, manifested an infinite carelessness in matters of costume, being worn and soiled. Than he, no Roman was poorer;

he owned nothing but his clothing and a few books. Akin to the greatest, and bearing a name of which he was inordinately proud—as a schoolboy he had once burst into tears when reciting with passion the Lay of the Decii—felt content to owe his sustenance to the delicate and respectful kindness of Maximus, who sympathised with the great wrong he had suffered early in life. This was no less than wilful impoverishment by his father, who, seeking to atone for sins by fanaticism, had sold the little he possessed to found a pilgrims' hospice at Portus, whither, accompanied by the twelve-year-old boy, he went to live as monk-servitor In a year or two the penitent died; Decius, in revolt against the tasks to which he was subjected, managed to escape, made his way to Rome, and appealed to Maximus. Nominally he still held the post of secretary to his benefactor, but for many years he had enjoyed entire leisure, all of it devoted to study. Several times illness had brought him to the threshold of death, yet it had never conquered his love of letters, his enthusiasm for his country's past. Few liked him only one or two understood him: Decius was content that it should be so.

'Let us speak of it,' he continued, unrolling a manuscript of Virgil some two hundred years old, a gift to him from Maximus. 'Tell me, dear lord, your true thought: is it indeed a prophecy of the Divine Birth? To you'—he smiled his gentle, beautiful smile—'may I not confess that I have doubted this interpretation? Yet'—he cast his eyes down—'the doubt is perhaps a prompting of the spirit of evil.'

'I know not, Decius, I know not,' replied the sick man with thoughtful melancholy. 'My father held it a prophecy his father before him.—But forgive me, I am expecting anxiously the return of Basil; yonder sail—is it his? Your eyes see further than mine.'

Decius at once put aside his own reflections, and watched the oncoming bark. Before long there was an end of doubt. Rising in agitation to his feet, Maximus gave orders that the litter, which since yesterday morning had been in readiness, should at once be borne with all speed down to the landing-place. Sail and oars soon brought the boat so near that Decius was able to descry certain female figures and that of a man, doubtless Basil, who stood up and waved his arms shoreward.

'She has come,' broke from Maximus; and, in reply to his kinsman's face of inquiry, he told of whom it was he spoke.

The landing-place was not visible from here. As soon as the boat disappeared beneath the buildings of the town, Maximus requested of his companion a service which asked some courage in the performance: it was, to wait forthwith upon the Lady Petronilla, to inform her that Aurelia had just disembarked, to require that three female slaves should be selected to attend upon the visitor. This mission Decius discharged, not without trembling; he then walked to the main entrance of the villa, and stood there, the roll of Virgil still in his hand, until the sound of a horse's hoofs on the upward road announced the arrival of the travellers. The horseman, who came some yards in advance of the slave-borne litter, was Basil. At sight of Decius, he dismounted, and asked in an undertone: 'You know?' The other replied with the instructions given by Maximus, that the litter, which was closed against curious eyes, should be straightway conveyed to the Senator's presence, Basil himself to hold apart until summoned.

And so it was done. Having deposited their burden between two columns of the portico, the bearers withdrew. The father's voice uttered the name of Aurelia, and, putting aside the curtains that had concealed her, she stood before him. A woman still young, and of bearing which became her birth; a woman who would have had much grace, much charm, but for the passion which, turned to vehement self-will, had made her blood acrid. Her great dark eyes burned with quenchless resentment; her sunken and pallid face told of the sufferings of a tortured pride.

'Lord Maximus,' were her first words, as she stood holding by the litter, glancing distrustfully about her, 'you have sworn!'

'Hear me repeat my oath,' answered the father, strengthened by his emotion to move forward from the couch. 'By the blessed martyr Pancratius, I swear that no harm shall befall you, no constraint shall be put upon you, that you shall be free to come and to go as you will.'

It was the oath no perjurer durst make. Aurelia gazed into her father's face, which was wet with tears. She stepped nearer to him, took his thin, hot hand, and, as in her childhood, bent to kiss the back of the wrist. But Maximus folded her to his heart.

CHAPTER II
BASIL'S VISION

Basil and Decius paced together a garden alley, between a row of quince-trees and a hedge of Christ's-thorn; at one end was a fountain in a great basin of porphyry, at the other a little temple, very old and built for the worship of Isis, now an oratory under the invocation of the Blessed Mary. The two young men made a singular contrast, for Basil, who was in his twenty-third year, had all the traits of health and vigour: a straight back, lithe limbs, a face looking level on the world, a lustrous eye often touched to ardour, a cheek of the purest carnation, a mouth that told of fine instincts, delicate sensibilities, love of laughter. No less did his costume differ from the student's huddled garb; his tunic was finely embroidered in many hues, his silken cloak had a great buckle of gold on the shoulder; he wore ornate shoes, and by his waist hung a silver-handled dagger in a sheath of chased bronze. He stepped lightly, as one who asks but the occasion to run and leap. In their intimate talk, he threw an arm over his companion's neck, a movement graceful as it was affectionate; his voice had a note frank and cordial.

Yet Basil was not quite his familiar self to-day; he talked with less than his natural gaiety, wore a musing look, fell into silences. Now that Aurelia had come, there was no motive for reserve on that subject with Decius, and indeed they conversed of their kinswoman with perfect openness, pitying rather than condemning her, and wondering what would result from her presence under one roof with the rigid Petronilla. Not on Aurelia's account did Basil droop his head now and then, look about him vacantly, bite his lip, answer a question at hazard, play nervously with his dagger's hilt. All at once, with an abruptness which moved his companion's surprise, he made an inquiry, seemingly little relevant to their topic.

'Heard you ever of a Gothic princess—a lady of the lineage of Theodoric—still living in Italy?'

'Never,' responded Decius, with a puzzled smile. 'Is there such a one?'

'I am told so—I heard it by chance. Yet I know not who she can be. Did not the direct line of Theodoric end with Athalaric and his sister Matasuntha, who is now at the Emperor's court?'

'So I believed,' said Decius, 'though I have thought but little of the matter.'

'I too, trust me,' let fall Basil, with careful carelessness; no actor he. 'And the vile Theodahad—what descendants did he leave?'

'He was a scholar,' said the other musingly, 'deep read in Plato.'

'None the less a glutton and a murderer and a coward, who did well to give his throat to the butcher as he ran away from his enemies. Children he had, I think—but—'

Basil broke off on a wandering thought. He stood still, knitted his brows, and sniffed the air. At this moment there appeared in the alley a serving man, a young and active fellow of very honest visage, who stood at some yards' distance until Basil observed him.

'What is it, Felix?' inquired his master.

The attendant stepped forward, and made known that the lord Marcian had even now ridden up to the villa, with two followers, and desired to wait upon Basil. This news brought a joyful light to the eyes of the young noble; he hastened to welcome his friend, the dearest he had. Marcian, a year or two his elder, was less favoured by nature in face and form: tall and vigorous enough of carriage, he showed more bone and sinew than flesh; and his face might have been that of a man worn by much fasting, so deep sunk were the eyes, so jutting the cheek-bones, and so sharp the chin; its cast, too, was that of a fixed and native melancholy. But when he smiled, these features became much more pleasing, and revealed a kindliness of temper such as might win the love of one who knew him well. His dress was plain, and the dust of Campanian roads lay somewhat thick upon him.

'By Bacchus!' cried his friend, as they embraced each other, 'fortune is good to me to-day. Could I have had but one wish granted, it would have been to see Marcian. I thought you still in Rome. What makes you travel? Not in these days solely to visit a friend, I warrant. By Peter and Paul and as many more saints as you can remember, I am glad to hold your hand! What news do you bring?'

'Little enough,' answered Marcian, with a shrug of the shoulders. The natural tune of his voice harmonised with his visage, and he spoke as one who feels a scornful impatience with the affairs of men. 'At Rome, they wrangle about goats' wool, as is their wont. Anything else? Why, yes; the freedman Chrysanthus glories in an ex-consulate. It cost him the trifle of thirty pounds of gold.'

Basil laughed contemptuously, half angrily.

'We must look to our honours,' he exclaimed. 'If Chrysanthus be ex-consul, can you and I be satisfied with less than ex-Praetorian-Prefect? What will be the price, think you? Has Bessas hung out a tariff yet in the Forum?'

'He knows better than to fix a maximum, as long as a wealthy fool remains in the city—though that won't be much longer, I take it.'

'Why come you hither, dear my lord?' urged Basil, with more seriousness.

Regarding him with a grave eye, his friend replied in an undertone:

'To spy upon you.'

'Ha!—In very truth?'

'You could wish me a more honourable office,' Marcian went on, smiling sadly. 'Yet, if you think of it, in these days, it is some honour to be a traitor to both sides. There has been talk of you in Rome. Nay, who knows how or why! They have nothing to do but talk, and these victories of the Goth have set up such a Greek cackle as was never heard since Helen ran away to Troy,—and, talking of Greek, I bear a letter for you from Heliodora.'

Basil, who had been listening gravely, started at this name and uttered an idle laugh. From a wallet hanging at his girdle, Marcian drew forth the missive.

'That may wait,' said Basil, glancing indifferently at the folded and sealed paper before he hid it away. 'Having said so much, you must tell me more. Put off that sardonic mask—I know very well what hides beneath it—and look me in the eye. You have surprised some danger?'

'I heard you spoken of—by one who seldom opens his lips but to ill purpose. It was not difficult for me to wade through the shallows of the man's mind, and for my friend's sake to win his base confidence. Needing a spy, and being himself a born traitor, he readily believed me at his beck; in truth he had long marked me, so I found, for a cankered soul who waited but the occasion to advance by infamy. I held the creature in my hand; I turned him over and over, and he, the while, thinking me his greedy slave. And so, usurping the place of some other who would have ambushed you in real enmity, I came hither on his errand.'

'Marcian,' said the listener, 'I could make a guess at that man's name.'

'Nay, I doubt if you could, and indeed it matters nothing. Enough that I may do you some little service.'

'For which,' replied Basil, 'I cannot pay you, since all my love is already yours. And she—Heliodora,' he added, with a careless gesture, 'knows of your mission?'

'Of my mission, no; but of my proposed journey. Though indeed she may know more than I suppose. Who shall say what reaches the ear of Heliodora—?'

'You have not heard perhaps that her husband is dead?'

'The Prefect dead?' exclaimed Basil.

'Three weeks ago.—Rather suddenly—after supper. An indigestion, no doubt.'

Marcian spoke with peculiar dryness, averting his eyes from the listener. Upon Basil's face came a deep flush; he took out the folded paper again, and held it at arm's length.

'You mean—? You think—?' he stammered.

'About women I think not at all,' said the other, 'as you well know. There is talk, talk—what care I?'

Basil tore the letter open. It contained a lock of raven-black hair, tied with gold thread, and on the paper was written, in Greek, 'I am free.' Again his cheek flushed; he crushed paper and hair together in his hand.

'Let us never again speak of her,' he exclaimed, moving away from the spot. 'Before I left Rome, I told you that I would gladly see her no more, and you smiled dubiously. Believe me now. I abhor the thought of her. If she ask you for my reply, repeat those words.'

'Nay, dear my lord, in that I will beg to be excused,' replied Marcian with his melancholy smile.

They were walking silently, side by side, when the servant Felix again presented himself before them. Maximus, having heard of the arrival of Marcian from Rome, requested that he and Basil would grant him a moment of their leisure. At once the young men turned to obey this summons. On the way, Basil communicated to his friend in a whisper the event of the day. A couple of hours having passed since Aurelia's coming, the Senator had in some degree recovered from his agitation; he lay now in a room which opened upon the central court of the villa, a room adorned with rich marbles and with wall-paintings which were fading under the hand of time. Deathly pale, scarce able to raise his head from the cushion of the couch, he none the less showed a countenance bright with joyous emotion. His quivering voice strove to welcome the visitor cheerily.

'What news from the city, dear lord Marcian? How are all our friends? Do they begin to forget us?'

'Not so, Illustrious,' answered the young man, with head bent. 'You are much desired in the Senate, where grave counsel is just now greatly in demand.'

'The Senate, the Senate,' murmured Maximus, as if reminded of something he had long forgotten. 'They must needs lack my voice, I fear. What do men say of the Gothic king?'

Marcian threw a glance at Basil, then towards the curtained portals of the room; lastly, his eyes turned upon the sick man, whom he regarded steadily.

'They say much—or little,' fell from his lips.

'I understand you,' replied the Senator, with a friendly movement of the head. 'Here we may speak freely. Does Totila draw near to Rome?'

'He is still in Tuscany, and rumours come from his army that he will pass into Samnium. All the strongholds of Umbria are his; all the conquests of Belisarius from Ariminum to Spoletium.'

'Where are the Roman captains?'

'Each in his city of the far north, holding the plunder he has got, and looking for the chance of more. In Rome—'

Marcian paused significantly, and the Senator took up his words.

'In Rome rules Bessas.'

'The Thracian,' remarked Basil bitterly.

'And in Ravenna,' added the sick man, 'Alexandros—the coin-clipper.'

The eyes of Basil and of Marcian encountered. Between them came no shadow of distrust, the smile they exchanged told of loyal affection.

'This Totila,' pursued Marcian, 'seems to be not only a brave and capable commander, but a shrewd politician. Everywhere he spares the people; he takes nothing by force; his soldiers buy at market; he protects the farmer against the taxing Greek. As a result, his army grows; where he passes, he leaves a good report, and before him goes a welcome. At this rate he will soon make all Italy his own. And unless the Patricius returns—'

By this title men were wont to speak of Belisarius. Hearing it, Basil threw up an arm, his eyes flashing.

'The Patricius!' he exclaimed fervently. 'There is the man who might have saved us!'

'By the holy Laurentius!' murmured Maximus, looking sadly at his nephew, 'I have all but come to think as you do.'

'Who that knew him,' cried Basil, 'but must have seen him, in thought—not King, for only the barbarians have kings—but Emperor—Emperor of the West, ruling at Rome as in the days gone by! There lives no man more royal. I have seen him day by day commanding and taking counsel; I have talked with him in his privacy. In the camp before Ravenna there was but one voice, one hope, as to what should follow when the city opened its gates, and the Goths themselves only surrendered because they thought to be ruled by him. But for the scruple of his conscience—and should not that have yielded to the general good?'

'Is breach of faith so light a thing?' fell from Marcian, under his breath.

'Nay,' answered the other, with drooping head, 'but he did break faith with *us*. We had his promise; we saw him Emperor—'

'You should have won Antonina,' said Marcian, with a return to his sarcastic humour. 'She must have mused long and anxiously, weighing the purple against Theodora's fury. The Patrician's fidelity stood by his wife's prudence.'

'The one blot upon his noble nature,' uttered Basil, with a sigh. 'His one weakness. How,' he cried scornfully, 'can the conqueror of half the world bend before such a woman?'

Fatigued already by the conversation, Maximus had lain back and closed his eyes. Very soon the two young men received his permission to withdraw, and, as they left the room, the physician entered. Obedient to this counsellor the invalid gave several hours to repose, but midway in the afternoon he again summoned his daughter, with whom he had a long and agitating conversation. He besought Aurelia to cast off her heretical religion, putting before her all the perils to which she exposed herself, by abandonment of the true faith, in this world and the next. His life was hurrying to its end; hour by hour he felt the fever wasting what little strength remained to him; and when he was gone who would protect her against the enmities to which religion and avarice would expose her? Aurelia's resistance was sullen rather than resolute; her countenance, her words, suggested that she was thinking more of what it would cost her pride to become a penitent than of any obstacle in conscience. At length she declared plainly that never would she humiliate herself before her aunt Petronilla, who had offered her no greeting and held scornfully apart. Here, as Maximus too well knew, lay the great difficulty of the situation; these women hated each other, and their hate would only be exasperated by Aurelia's conversion. He spoke of the deacon Leander, now on his way hither—begged Aurelia to listen to the reverend man, and gave solemn assurance that, the moment she abjured her errors, he would place her in a position of wealth and authority far above that of Petronilla. So utterly did he exhaust himself in entreaty and argument that he fell into a fainting fit. The physician was called for, and Aurelia, she too overcome with violent emotions, again retired to the part of the villa which had been assigned to her.

The Anicii of a bygone time, who took their solace here when marbles and mosaics, paintings and tapestries, were yet new, would have looked with consternation on halls so crumbling and bare, chambers so ill-appointed, as these in which the guests of the Senator Maximus had their dwelling. Space there was in abundance, but of comfort in the guest-rooms little enough; and despite her brother's commands, Petronilla had seen to it that Aurelia was not luxuriously lodged. Better accommodation awaited the deacon Leander, whose arrival was announced an hour before sunset by a trotting courier. His journey from Salernum had so wearied the ecclesiastic that he could but give a hand to be kissed by his hostess, and straightway retire into privacy; the repast that was ready for him had to be served beside his couch, and soon after night had fallen, Leander slumbered peacefully. Meanwhile Basil and Decius and their friend from Rome had supped together, making what cheer they might under the circumstances; the Surrentine wine was a little acrid, falling short of its due age, but it sufficed to animate the talk. Presently Decius withdrew, to study or to meditate through some hours of the night, for he slept ill; the others, going apart to a gallery lighted by the full moon, sat wrapped in thick, hooded cloaks, to converse awhile before they slept. With their voices mingled the soft splash of a fountain.

Basil was telling of his journey to Cumae, and of the difficulty he had had in persuading Aurelia to visit her father.

'Does she live alone there?' inquired Marcian.

There was a pause before the reply, and when Basil spoke his voice fell to a note of half-hesitating confidence.

'Alone? yes,' he said, 'in the sense that no relative abode with her; but she had a companion—a lady—very young.' And here he again paused, as if in some embarrassment.

'A Roman?' was Marcian's next question, carelessly thrown out for he had little interest in Aurelia, and was half occupied with other thoughts.

'No,' answered Basil, his voice subdued. 'A Goth; and, she says, of the royal blood, of the line of Theodoric.'

His friend became attentive. 'A Gothic princess? Whose daughter, then?' asked Marcian. And Basil, who desired nothing more than to speak on this subject, little by little threw off his hesitancy, grew rapid and eager in narration. He told how, on his first introduction to Aurelia's presence, he had found sitting with her a young girl, whose aspect proclaimed her of the Gothic race. In a second interview with his cousin, alone, Aurelia had spoken of this companion, bestowing much praise upon her, and declaring that they were united by an affection which nothing could diminish. She was of Amal blood; more than that Aurelia seemed unwilling to reveal.

'Did you not learn her name?' asked the listener.

'Veranilda.'

Marcian echoed the melodious syllables, but they told him nothing.

'And did you make no inquiry of those with whom you spoke?'

'I conversed as little as might be with strangers, and purposely held apart from our acquaintances in the town; this was my uncle's express command.'

'You had no second sight of her?'

'Indeed I had; and talked with her moreover. Marcian, how can I describe her to you? The words which suffice for common beauty sound meaningless when I would use them to depict Veranilda. Shall I tell you that she has hair of the purest gold, eyes brighter than the sky at noon, lips like the flower of the pomegranate, a cheek so fair, so soft—nay, you may well laugh at these idle phrases—'

'Not your phrases,' said Marcian, 'but your voice as it utters them sets me smiling. Talk on. The chaste goddess who beams above us inspire you with worthy terms!'

'There you speak to the point,' pursued Basil ardently. 'For Veranilda is chaste as she is beautiful. Blessed saints! how my heart shrank in abhorrence when I saw that letter this morning; and how fain I would blot from my memory that baseness of the past! O Marcian, truest of friends, I slighted your counsel, scoffed at your warnings, but now I know how wisely and how honestly you spoke.'

'Be that as it may,' said the other. 'But is it possible that, on a mere glimpse, this Gothic maiden should so have vanquished you?'

'It had been more prudent to hold my peace. But you know me of old. When I am moved, I must needs unbosom myself; happy that I have one whom I can trust. Her voice, Marcian! This whisper of the night breeze in the laurels falls rudely upon the ear after Veranilda's speech. Never have I heard a tone so soft, so gentle. The first word she spoke thrilled through me, as never did voice before; and I listened, listened, hoping she would speak again.'

'Who may she be? Has not the lady Aurelia adorned her origin? Golden hair and blue eyes are no rarity among daughters of the Goths.'

'Had you seen her!' exclaimed Basil, and grew rapturous again. Whilst he exhausted language in the effort to prove how remote was Veranilda from any shape of loveliness easily presented by memory or imagination, Marcian pondered.

'I can think of but one likelihood,' was his quiet remark, when his friend had become silent. 'King Theodahad had a daughter, who married the Gothic captain, Ebrimut.'

'The traitor,' murmured Basil uneasily.

'Or friend of the Romans, as you will. He delivered Rhegium to Belisarius, and enjoys his reward at Byzantium. What if he left a child behind him?'

Basil repulsed the suggestion vehemently.

'Not that! I had half thought of it myself; but no. Aurelia said of the house of Theodoric.'

'Why so would be a daughter of Ebrimut, through her mother—who was the daughter of Theodahad, who was the son of Amalafrida, who was the sister of Theodoric himself.'

'She could not have meant that,' protested Basil. 'Child of a mercenary traitor, who opened Italy to his people's foe! Not that! Had you seen her, you would not believe it.'

'Oh, my good Basil,' laughed the other, 'do you think I should see her with your eyes? But perhaps we conjecture idly quite missing the mark. What does it matter? You have no intention, I hope, of returning to Cumae?'

Basil opened his lips to reply, but thought better of it, and said nothing. Then his friend turned to speak of the ecclesiastical visitor who had that evening arrived, and, the subject not proving very fruitful, each presently betook himself to his night's repose.

CHAPTER III
THE DEACON LEANDER

The deacon Leander was some forty years of age, stoutish, a trifle asthmatic, with a long visage expressive of much shrewdness, and bushy eyebrows, which lent themselves at will to a look of genial condescension, of pious austerity, or of stern command. His dark hair and reddish beard were carefully trimmed; so were the nails of his shapely, delicate hands. His voice, now subject to huskiness, had until a few years ago been remarkably powerful and melodious; no deacon in Rome was wont to excite more admiration by his chanting of the Gradual; but that glory had passed away, and at the present time Leander's spiritual activity was less prominent than his services as a most capable steward of the patrimony of St. Peter. He travelled much, had an extensive correspondence, and was probably rather respected than reverenced by most lay folk with whom he came in contact.

But in the eyes of the lady Petronilla, Leander was an ideal churchman. No one treated her judgment with so much respect; no one confided to her curious ear so many confidential matters, ranging from the secret scandals of aristocratic Rome to high debates of ecclesiastical polity—or what Petronilla regarded as such. Their closer acquaintance began with the lady's presentation of certain columns of tawny Numidian marble, from a ruined temple she had inherited, to the deacon's basilica, St. Laurentius; and many were the donations which Leander had since accepted from her on behalf of the Church. In return, he had once or twice rejoiced her with the gift of a precious relic, such as came into the hands of few below royal rank; thus had Petronilla obtained the filings of the chain of St. Peter, which, enclosed in a golden key, hung upon her bosom. Some day, as the deacon well knew, this pious virgin would beg him to relieve her of all her earthly possessions, and enter into some holy retreat; but she awaited the death of her brother, by whose will she would doubtless benefit more or less substantially.

If in view of the illness of Maximus, Petronilla had regarded the deacon's visit as providential, the event of yesterday moved her to a more agitated thankfulness for the conference she was about to enjoy. After a night made sleepless by dread and wrath, she rose at daybreak and passed in a fever of impatience the time which elapsed before her reverend guest issued from his chamber. This being the fourth day of the week, Petronilla held rigid fast until the hour of nones; and of course no refreshment was offered to the churchman, who, with that smiling placidity, that graceful self-possession, which ever distinguished him in such society, at length entered the inner hall, and suavely, almost tenderly, greeted his noble hostess. Brimming over as she was with anxiety and indignation, Petronilla allowed nothing of this to appear in her reception of the revered friend. To his inquiries touching the health of the Senator, she replied with significant gravity that Maximus had suffered during the night, and was this morning, by the physician's report, much weaker; she added not a word on the momentous subject presently to be broached. Then Leander, after viewing with many compliments a piece of rich embroidery which occupied the lady's leisure, and or its completion would of course be put at his disposal, took a seat, set the tips of his fingers together, and began to chat pleasantly of his journey. Many were the pious offerings which had fallen to him upon his way: that of the Sicilian lady who gave her little all to be used to maintain the lamps in the basilica of the Chief Apostle; that of the merchant encountered on shipboard, who gave ten pounds of gold to purchase the freedom of slaves; that of the wealthy curial in Lucania, healed of disease by miracle on the feast of St. Cyprian, who bestowed upon the church in gratitude many acres of olive-bearing land, and promised an annual shipload of prime hogs to feed St. Peter's poor. By smooth transition he passed to higher themes: with absent eyes turned to the laurel-planted court on to which the hall opened, he spoke as if scarcely aware of a listener, of troubles at Rome occasioned by imprudences, indiscretions—what should he say—of the Holy Father. As Petronilla bent forward, all tremulous curiosity, he lowered his voice, grew frankly confidential. The Pope had been summoned to Byzantium, to discuss certain points of doctrine with the Emperor; his departure was delayed, but no doubt in his weakness he would obey. Verily, the lack of courage—not to use severer terms—so painfully evident in Pope Vigilius, was a grave menace to the Church—the Catholic Church, which, rightly claiming to rule Christendom, should hold no terms with the arrogance of Justinian. Could it be wondered that the Holy Father was disliked—not to say hated—by the people of Rome? By his ill management the papal granaries had of late been so ill stored that the poor had suffered famine, the Greeks having put an end to that gratuitous distribution of food to which the Roman populace had from of old been accustomed. On this account, chiefly, had Leander journeyed to Sicily, to look after the supplies of corn, and seek out those who were to blame for the recent negligence. His bushy eyebrows gave a hint of their sterner possibilities as he spoke of the measures he had taken, the reproofs and threats he had distributed.

'May I live,' breathed Petronilla, with modest emphasis, 'to see a great, a noble, a puissant Pontiff in the Apostolic Chair!'

Whereat the deacon smiled, well understanding whither the lady looked for her ideal Pope. She went on to speak of the part Vigilius had played in the deposition and miserable death of his predecessor Silverius, and that, as was too well known, at the bidding of haughty, unscrupulous women, the Empress Theodora and her friend Antonina, wife of Belisarius. Verily, the time had come for a great reform at the Lateran; the time had come, and perhaps the divine instrument was not far to seek. Whereupon Petronilla murmured ardently, and the deacon again smiled.

There was a pause. Having permitted Leander to muse a little, his hostess turned the conversation to the troublous topic of her thoughts; and began by saying how her brother would esteem the privilege of counsel and solace from one so qualified to impart them. But alas she must make known a distressful occurrence, whereby the office of a spiritual adviser by the bedside of Maximus must needs be complicated and made painful; and therewith Petronilla related the events of yesterday. As he listened, the deacon knitted his brows, but in thought rather than in affliction; and when the speaker was silent, he still mused awhile.

'Gracious madam,' he began at length solemnly, 'you of course hold no intercourse with this lady?'

'None! I have shrunk ever from the sight of her.'

'Such abhorrence of error witnesses to the purity and the illumination of your soul: I could have expected nothing less from Petronilla. You know not whether the misguided woman shows any disposition to return to the true faith?'

'I fear not,' replied Petronilla, looking rather as if the fear were a hope. 'Her nature is stubborn: she has the pride of the fallen angels.'

'And her father, I am afraid, has no longer the strength to treat her sin with due severity?'

'Earthly affection has subdued him,' replied the lady, shaking her head. 'Who knows,' she added, 'how far his weakness may lead my poor brother?'

She glanced about the hall, and Leander perfectly understood what was in her mind.

'Be not over anxious,' he replied soothingly. 'Leave this in my hands. Should it be necessary, I can dispose of some days before pursuing my journey. Take comfort, noble and pious lady! The truth will prevail.'

The deacon's first step was to obtain a private interview with the physician. He then made known his desire to wait upon Maximus, and with no great delay was admitted. Tactfully, sagaciously, he drew the sufferer to confide in him, to see in him, not so much a spiritual admonisher as a counsellor and a support in worldly difficulties. Leander was already well aware that the Senator had small religious zeal, but belonged to the class of men, numerous at this time, who, whilst professing the Christian and the orthodox faith, were in truth philosophers rather than devotees, and regarded dogmatic questions with a calm not easily distinguished from indifference. Maximus had scarcely spoken of his daughter, when the deacon understood it was Aurelia's temporal, much more than her eternal, interests which disturbed the peace of the dying man. Under Roman law, bequests to a heretic were null and void; though this enactment had for the most part been set aside in Italy under Gothic rule, it might be that the Imperial code would henceforth prevail. Maximus desired to bestow upon his daughter a great part of his possessions. Petronilla, having sufficient means of her own, might well be content with a moderate bequest; Basil, the relative next of kin, had a worthy claim upon his uncle's generous treatment, and Decius, who needed but little, must have that little assured. The father had hoped that his entreaties, together with a prospect of substantial reward, would prevail against Aurelia's pride-rooted heresy, but as yet he pleaded and tempted in vain. Could the deacon help him?

Leander seemed to meditate profoundly. The subject of his thought was what seemed to him a glaring omission in this testament of Maximus. He breathed an intimate inquiry: Was the sick man at peace with his own soul? Had he sought strength and solace from the reverend presbyter of Surrentum, his spiritual father in this district? Maximus replied that he had neglected no ordinary means of grace. Whilst speaking, he met the deacon's eye; its significance was not to be mistaken.

'I should have mentioned,' he said, averting his look, 'that the presbyter Andreas and his poor will not be forgotten. Moreover, many of my slaves will receive their freedom.'

Leander murmured approvingly. Again he reflected, and again he ventured an inquiry: Maximus would desire, no doubt, to rest with his glorious ancestors in the mortuary chapel known as the Temple of Probus, by St. Peter's? And seeing the emotion this excited in his listener he went on to speak at large of the Anician house—first among the great families of Rome to embrace Christianity, and distinguished, generation after generation, by their support of the church, which indeed numbered among its Supreme Pontiffs one of their line, the third Felix. Did not the illustrious father of Maximus lead the Christian senators in their attack upon that lingering shame, the heathen Lupercalia, since so happily supplanted by the Feast of the Purification of the Blessed Mary? He, dying—added Leander, with an ecstatic smile—made over to the Apostolic See an estate in Sicily which yielded every year two rich harvests to the widows, the orphans, the sick, and the destitute of Rome.

'Deacon,' broke from the hot lips of Maximus, who struggled to raise himself, 'if I do the like, will you swear to me to use your influence, your power, for the protection of my daughter?'

It was the voice of nature in its struggle with the universal doom; reason had little part in the hope with which those fading eyes fixed themselves upon the countenance of the self-possessed churchman.

'Heaven forbid,' was Leander's reply, 'that I should bind myself in such terms to perform an office of friendship, which under any circumstances would be my anxious care.'

'Even,' asked Maximus, 'if she persist in her heresy?'

'Even so, my dear lord, remembering from whom she springs. But,' he added, in a soothing voice, 'let me put your mind at rest. Trust me, the lady Aurelia will not long cling to her error. In poverty, in humiliation, she might be obstinate; but as the possessor of wealth—restored to her due rank—oh, my gracious lord, be assured that her conversion will soon follow.'

The same thought had occurred to Maximus. He sighed in profound relief, and regarded the deacon gratefully.

'In that hope I rest. Give me your promise to befriend her, and ask of me what you will.'

Save for the hours she passed at her father's side, Aurelia kept a strict retirement, guarded by the three female slaves whom Petronilla had reluctantly assigned to her. Of them she required no intimate service, having her own attendants, an elderly woman, the nurse of her childhood, who through all changes of fortune had never quitted her, and a younger, half-Goth, half-Italian, who discharged humbler duties. She occupied a small dwelling apart from the main structure of the villa, but connected with it by a portico: this was called the House of Proba, it having been constructed a hundred years ago for the lady Faltonia Proba, who wrote verses, and perhaps on that account desired a special privacy. Though much neglected, the building had beauty of form, and was full of fine work in mosaic. Here, in a little peristyle, where shrubs and creepers had come to wild growth, the sore-hearted lady sat brooding or paced backwards and forwards, her eyes ever on the ground. When yet a maiden she had several times spent summer at Surrentum; her memory revived that early day which seemed so long ago; she lived again with her brothers and sisters, all dead, with her mother whom griefs had aged so soon. Then came a loveless marriage, which soon involved her in the public troubles of the time; for her husband, whose estates lay in Tuscany, was robbed of all by Theodahad, and having vainly sought redress from the young King Athalaric, decided to leave Italy for Byzantium, to which end Aurelia sold a property in Campania, her dower. Before they could set forth upon their journey, her husband caught the plague and died. In second wedlock she would have known contentment but for the alienation of her kin and the scornful hostility of all her class. When widowhood again befell her she was saved from want by a small treasure of money which remained hidden in the dwelling at Cumae when the Gothic warrior, her lord, escaped from Belisarius. As this store diminished, Aurelia had looked forward with dread, for she hoped nothing from her father. And now that such fears seemed to be over, her long tortured pride clamoured for solace. It was not enough to regain her father's love and enjoy an inheritance; she wished to see her enemies at her feet, and to trample upon them—her enemies being not only Petronilla and certain other kinsfolk but all the nobility of Rome, nay, all the orthodox of the Christian church. Pacing, pacing alone, she brooded vast schemes of vengeance.

When it was announced to her that the Roman deacon besought an interview, she at first refused to receive him. Thereupon Leander sent her a few lines in writing, most ceremoniously worded, in which he declared that his purposes were those of a disinterested friend, that no word such as could pain or offend her would pass his lips, and that he had it in his power to communicate something which would greatly benefit her. Aurelia reflected disdainfully, but at length consented to the churchman's approach. Leander's bearing as he entered her presence was as elaborately courteous as the phrasing of his letter.

'Noble lady,' he began, standing with bowed head, 'let not your eyes take note of my garb. See in me only a devoted servant of your illustrious house. His Magnificence, your father, assured of the sincerity wherewith I place at his command such powers and opportunities as I owe to heaven's grace, has deigned to confide in me regarding the disposition of his worldly affairs whereto he is prompted by languishing health.'

He paused a moment, but Aurelia had no word of reply to this exordium. Seeing her keep the same haughty posture in her chair, with eyes scornfully averted as if she scarce listened, Leander proceeded to disclose his mind in less ornate terms By subtle grades of confidential speech, beginning with a declaration of the sympathy moved in him by the parent's love, the daughter's distress, he came with lowering voice, with insinuating tone, with blandly tolerant countenance, to the kernel of his discourse; it contained a suggestion which might—he only said *might*—aid her amid the manifold perplexities of her position. By this time Aurelia was more attentive; the churchman almost affectionate in his suavity, grew still more direct; and at length, in a voice which only reached the ear of the listener, he spoke thus:

'I understand why you stepped aside from the way of truth; I perceive the obstacles hindering your return. I know the tender impulses which urge you to soothe your father's last hours, and, no less, the motives, natural to a woman of your beauty, of your birth, which are at strife with that tenderness and threaten to overcome it. Could you discover a means of yielding to your filial affection, and at the same time safeguarding your noble pride, would you not gladly use it? Such a means I can point out to you.'

He became silent, watching Aurelia. She, won by the perspicacity which read her heart, had put aside all arrogance, and wore a look of grave intentness.

'Let me know it,' she murmured.

'It is this. Return to the true belief, but guard awhile the secret of your conversion. That it shall not be disclosed until you wish, I can give you firm assurance—if need be, on solemn oath. You will privately make known to your father that he has prevailed, thereby you put his flesh and spirit at rest,—he will die blessing you, and enriching you to the full extent of his desire. You will then also set your signature to a paper, which I shall write, making confession of the orthodox faith, and undertaking to be duly reconciled with the church, by the imposition of hands, at some convenient season. That is all that will be asked of you for the present. The lady Petronilla'—he all but smiled in uttering the name—'shall not even suspect what has happened.'

'Will this villa be mine?' asked the listener after brief reflection.

'This villa shall be yours.'

An exultant gleam shone in Aurelia's eyes.

'Deacon,' she said sternly, 'your promise is not enough. Swear to me that no one living, save my father and you, shall know.'

From his bosom Leander drew forth a little golden cross.

'This,' he said reverently, 'contains dust of iron from the bars on which the blessed Laurentius suffered martyrdom.'

'Swear also,' demanded Aurelia, 'by the Holy Pancratius.' In the name of both saints Leander took his oath of secrecy. Petronilla was of course aware that the deacon had been admitted to audience by her niece. When he descended, she awaited him at the end of the portico, and her look questioned him.

'Stubborn, stubborn!' murmured Leander, shaking his head, and passed on as though in troubled thought.

Later in the day, when she had seen her father, Aurelia made known to her cousin Basil, who had requested an interview, that he might come. His cousin received him smilingly, almost affectionately.

Marcian having this morning taken his leave, called away by some unexplained business to Neapolis, Basil had been on the point of taking Decius into his amorous confidence, when this summons rejoiced him.

'Is the letter written?' were Basil's first words.

'It is here. Can you despatch it at once?'

'I will take it myself,' he answered promptly.

Aurelia shook her head.

'You must not. My father's life is fast failing. No one can say which hour may be his last. If he asked for you, and you were absent—'

'Felix shall go,' said Basil. 'The wind is favourable. He may have to ride back to-morrow, but we can trust him to make all speed.'

'He took the letter, which was superscribed, 'To the most noble lady Veranilda.'

'Dear cousin, you have spoken of me?' he asked with a wistful look.

'I have said, good cousin,' Aurelia answered pleasantly, 'that you wished to be spoken of.'

'Only that?'

'What more should I say? Your Amiability is too hasty. Remember that you have scarce seen her.'

'Scarce seen Veranilda!' exclaimed Basil. 'Why, it seems to me as though I had known her for years! Have we not talked together?'

'Once. The first time does not count; you exchanged hardly a dozen words. When,' added Aurelia, smiling, 'were you so dashed in a maid's presence?'

'Nay, never! I am not accused of too much modesty; but when I entered and looked on Veranilda—oh, it was the strangest moment of my life! Noble cousin,' he added pleadingly, 'honoured Aurelia, do but tell me what is her parentage?'

'How does that concern your Excellence? I have told you all that it imports you to know—at all events for the present. Cousin Basil, you delay the letter; I should wish her to have it before nightfall, for she thinks anxiously of me.'

'I go. When may I again speak with you?'

'You shall hear when I am at leisure.'

Basil despatched his servant to Cumae not with one letter only, but with two. Greatly daring, he had himself written to Veranilda; in brief terms, but every word tremulous with his passion. And for half an hour he stood watching the sail which wafted his messenger over the gulf, ruffled to-day by a south-west wind, driver of clouds. Little thought had he to give to the dying Maximus, but at the ninth hour he turned his steps to the oratory, once a temple of Isis, and heard the office, and breathed a prayer for his kindly relative. Which duty discharged, he prayed more fervently, to whatever saint or deity has ear for such petitions, that he might be loved by the Gothic maid.

This evening Maximus seemed to suffer less. He lay with closed eyes, a look of calm on his worn countenance. Beside him sat Decius, reading in low tones from that treatise on the Consolation of Philosophy, which Boethius wrote in prison, a book wherein Maximus sought comfort, this last year or two more often than in the Evangel, or the Lives of Saints. Decius himself would have chosen a philosopher of older time, but in the words of his own kinsman, Maximus found an appeal more intimate, a closer sympathy, than in ancient teaching. He loved especially the passages of verse; and when the reader came to those lines—

'O felix hominum genus,
Si vestros animos amor
Quo coelum regitur, regat,'

he raised his hand, smiling with peculiar sweetness.

'Pause there, O Decius,' he said, in a weak but clear voice; 'let me muse awhile.' And he murmured the verses to himself.

CHAPTER IV
TO CUMAE

The Bishop of Surrentum, an elderly man and infirm, had for the past fortnight been unable to leave his house, but day by day he received news of what passed at the villa of Maximus, and held with the presbyter, Andreas, many colloquies on that weighty topic, the senator's testament. As it happened, neither bishop nor presbyter had much aptitude for worldly affairs; they were honest, simple-minded clerics, occupied with visions and marvels and the saving details of dogma; exultant whenever a piece of good fortune befell their church, but modest in urging a claim at the bedside of the sick. Being the son of a freedman who had served in the Anician house, the bishop could not approach Maximus without excessive reverence; before Petronilla he was even more unduly awed.

On Sunday morning the good prelate lay wakeful at the hour of matins, and with quavering voice chanted to himself the psalm of the office from which his weakness held him apart. Presently the door opened, and in the dim lamp-light appeared the presbyter Andreas, stepping softly. He made known that an urgent message had just summoned him to the villa; Maximus was near his end.

'I, too, will come,' exclaimed the bishop, rising in his bed and ringing loudly a little hand-bell.

'Venerable father! your health—'

'Hasten, hasten, Andreas! I follow.'

In less than an hour he descended from his litter, and, resting on the arms of two servants, was conducted to the chamber of the dying man. Andreas had just administered the last rites; whether the fixed eyes still saw was doubtful. At a murmur of 'the bishop' those by the doorway reverently drew aside. On one side of the bed were Aurelia and the deacon; on the other, Petronilla and Basil and Decius. Though kneeling, the senator's daughter held herself proudly. Though tears were on her face, she hardly disguised an air of triumph. Nor was the head of Petronilla bent; her countenance looked hard and cold as marble. Leander, a model of decorum, stepped with grave greeting towards the prelate, and whispered a word or two. In the stillness that followed there quivered a deep breath. Flavius Anicius Maximus had lived his life.

When the bishop, supported by Leander and Andreas, rose from prayer, he was led by the obsequious clerics to a hall illumined by several lamps, where two brasiers gave forth a grateful glow in the chill of the autumn morning. Round about the walls, in niches, stood busts carved or cast of the ancestors of him who lay dead. Here, whilst voices of lamentation sounded from without, Leander made known to the prelate and the presbyter the terms of the will. Basil was instituted 'heir'; that is to say, he became the legal representative of the dead man, and was charged with the distribution of those parts of the estate bequeathed to others. First of the legatees stood Aurelia. The listeners learnt with astonishment that the obstinate heretic was treated as though her father had had no cause of complaint against her; she was now mistress of the Surrentine estate, as well as of the great house in Rome, and of other property. A lamentable thing, the deacon admitted suavely; but, for his part, he was not without hope, and he fixed his eyes with a peculiar intensity on the troubled bishop.

Petronilla drew near. The will was already known to her in every detail, and she harboured a keen suspicion of the secret which lay behind it. Leander, she could not doubt, was behaving to her with duplicity, and this grieved her to the heart. It was to the bishop that she now addressed herself.

'Holy father, I am your suppliant. Not even for a day will I remain under this roof, even if—which is doubtful—I should be suffered to do so. I put myself under the protection of your Holiness, until such time as I can set forth on my sad journey to Rome. At Surrentum I must abide until the corpse of my brother can be conveyed to its final resting place—as I promised him.'

Much agitated, the prelate made answer that a fitting residence should be prepared for her before noon, and the presbyter Andreas added that he would instantly betake himself to the city on that business. Petronilla thanked him with the loftiest humility. For any lack of respect, or for common courtesy, to which they might be exposed ere they quitted the villa, she besought their Sanctities not to hold her responsible, she herself being now an unwilling intruder at this hearth, and liable at any moment to insult. Uttering which words in a resonant voice, she turned her eyes to where, a few yards away, stood Aurelia, with Basil and Decius behind her.

'Reverend bishop,' spoke a voice not less steady and sonorous than that of the elder lady, 'should you suffer any discourtesy in my house, it will come not from me, but from her who suggests its possibility, and whose mind is bent upon such things. Indeed, she has already scanted the respect she owes you in uttering these words. As for herself, remain she here for an hour or for a month, she is in no danger of insult—unless she deem it an insult to have her base falsehood flung back at her, and the enmity in her fierce eyes answered with the scorn it merits.'

Petronilla trembled with wrath.

'Falsehood!' she echoed, on a high, mocking note. 'A charge of falsehood upon *her* lips! Your Holiness will ere long, I do not doubt, be enlightened as to that woman's principles in the matter of truth and falsehood. Meanwhile, we shall consult our souls' welfare, as well as our dignity, in holding as little intercourse as may be with one who has renounced the faith in Christ.'

Aurelia bent her eyes upon the deacon, who met the look with austere fixedness. There was dead silence for a moment, then she turned to the young men behind her.

'My noble cousins, I desired your company because I foresaw this woman's violence, and knew not to what length it might carry her. She pretends to fear my tongue; for my part, I would not lightly trust myself within reach of her hands, of which I learnt the weight when I was a little child. Lord Decius, attend, I beg you, these reverend men whilst they honour my house and on their way homeward. My cousin Basil, I must needs ask you to be my guard, until I can command service here. Follow me, I pray.'

With another piercing glance at Leander she withdrew from the assembly.

It was a morning of wind and cloud; the day broke sadly. When the first gleam of yellow sunlight flitted over Surrentum towards the cliffs of Capreae, silence had fallen upon the villa. Wearied by their night of watching, the inhabitants slept, or at least reposed in privacy. But this quiet was of short duration. When the customary bell had given notice of the third hour, Aurelia called together the servants of the house—only those who belonged to Petronilla failing to answer her summons—and announced to them her new authority. At the same time the steward of the estate read out a list of those slaves who, under the will of Maximus, could claim their emancipation. The gathering having dispersed, there appeared an attendant of the deacon Leander; his reverend master would wait upon the lady Aurelia, as soon as her leisure permitted, for the purpose of taking leave. Forthwith the deacon was admitted. Alone in the great hall, Aurelia sat beside a brasier, at which she warmed her hands; she scarcely deigned to glance at the ecclesiastic.

'You pursue your journey, reverend?' were her first words.

'As far as Neapolis, gracious lady,' came the suave reply. 'There or in the neighbourhood I shall remain at least ten days. Should you desire to communicate with me—'

'I think I can save that trouble,' interrupted Aurelia, with quivering lips. 'All I have to say to your Sanctity, I will say at once. It is, that you have enlightened me as to the value of solemn oaths on the lips of the Roman clergy.'

'Your meaning, dear madam?' asked Leander, with a look of bland disdain.

'You have the face to ask it, deacon, after Petronilla's words this morning?'

'I feared they might mislead you. The lady Petronilla knows nothing of what has passed between us. She spoke in anger, and hazarded an accusation—as angry ladies are wont.'

'Of course you say so,' returned Aurelia. 'I will believe you if you give me back the paper I signed, and trust to my word for the fulfilment of what I promised.'

Leander smiled, almost as if he had heard some happy intelligence.

'You ask,' he said, 'for a trust you yourself refuse.'

'Then go your way, perjurer!' exclaimed Aurelia, her cheeks aflame with passion. 'I know henceforth on whom to rely.'

For a moment Leander stood as if reflecting on these last words; then he bowed, and with placid dignity retired.

Meanwhile Basil and Decius were conversing with Petronilla. Neither of them had ever stood on terms of more than courteous forbearance with this authoritative lady; at present they maintained their usual demeanour, and did not think it needful to apologise for friendly relations with Aurelia. The only subject on which Petronilla deigned to hold colloquy with them was that of her brother's burial at Rome. Should the transport be by land or by sea? This evening the corpse would be conveyed to the cathedral of Surrentum, where due rites would be performed early on the morrow; there it would remain in temporary interment until a coffin of lead could be prepared, and arrangements completed for the removal. Was the year too advanced, questioned Petronilla, to allow of the sea voyage? On the other hand, would the land journey be safe, having regard to the advance of the Gothic army? Basil pronounced for the sea, and undertook to seek for a vessel. Was he willing, asked Petronilla, to accompany the body to Rome? This question gave Basil pause; he reflected uneasily; he hesitated. Yet who could discharge this duty, if he did not? Suddenly ashamed of his hesitation, the true reason of which could not be avowed, he declared that he would make the voyage.

Hereupon entered the deacon, who, the matter being put before him, approved these arrangements. He himself would doubtless be in Rome before the arrival of the remains of Maximus, and all the details of the burial there might be left to him. So Petronilla thanked and dismissed the young men, on whose retirement she turned eagerly to Leander.

'Forgive me!' broke from her lips. 'I know how deeply I have offended your Sanctity. It was my fear that you would go away without a word. My haste, my vehemence, merited even that punishment.'

'Calm yourself, noble lady,' returned the deacon. 'I was indeed grieved, but I know your provocation. We may speak on this subject again; but not here.

For the present, I take my leave of you, all being ready for my departure. As you are quitting this house at once, you need no counsel as to immediate difficulties; I will only say, in all things be prudent, be self-controlled; before long, you may see reason for the discreet silence which I urge upon you.'

'When do you set forth to Rome?' asked Petronilla. 'If it might be my privilege to journey in your company—?'

'The day is uncertain,' replied Leander; 'but if it be possible for us to travel together, trust me to beg for the honour. You shall hear of my projects in a week's time from Neapolis.'

Petronilla fell to her knees, and again besought his forgiveness with his benediction. The deacon magnanimously granted both, and whilst bending over the devout lady, whispered one word:

'Patience!'

An hour after mid-day, Petronilla quitted the villa. Her great travelling chariot, drawn by four mules, wherein she and her most precious possessions were conveyed, descended at a stately pace the winding road to Surrentum. Before it rode Basil; behind came a laden wagon, two light vehicles carrying female slaves, and mounted men-servants, armed as though for a long and perilous journey. Since the encounter before sunrise, there had been no meeting between the hostile ladies. Aurelia signified her scorn by paying no heed to her aunt's departure.

Alone in her dominion, the inheritress entered the death-chamber, and there passed an hour upon her knees. Whilst she was thus secluded, a pealing storm traversed the sky. When Aurelia came forth again, her face was wan, tearstained. She summoned her nurse, and held much talk with her as to the significance of thunder whilst a corpse lay in the house. The good woman, though she durst not utter all her thoughts, babbled concern, and used the occasion to beseech Aurelia—as she had often done since the death of her Gothic lord—to be reconciled with the true church.

'True church!' exclaimed Aurelia, with sudden passion. 'How do you know which is the true church? Have not emperors, have not bishops and numberless holy men lived and died in the faith I confess—?'

She checked herself; grew silent, brooded. Meanwhile, the old nurse talked on, and presently began to relate how a handmaid of Petronilla, in going with her this morning, professed to know on the surest evidence that Aurelia, by her father's deathbed, had renounced Arianism. The sullen countenance of her mistress flashed again into wrath.

'Did I not forbid you,' cried Aurelia, 'to converse with those women? And you dare repeat to me their loose-lipped chatter. I am too familiar with you; go and talk with your kind; go!'

Mutteringly the woman went apart. The mistress, alone, fell into a long weeping. When she had sobbed herself into quiet once more, she sought a volume of the Gospels, inserted her forefinger between the pages at random, and anxiously regarded the passage thus chosen.

'While ye have the light, believe in the light, that ye may be the children of light.'

She brooded, but in the end seemed to find solace.

Basil was absent all day. On his return, just before sunset, Aurelia met him in the atrium, heard the report of what he had done, and at length asked whether, on the day after to-morrow, he could go to Cumae.

'To Cumae?' exclaimed Basil. 'Ay, that I can! You are returning thither?'

'For a day only. I go to seek that which no one but myself can find.'

The listener had no difficulty in understanding this; it meant, of course, treasure concealed in the house Aurelia had long inhabited.

'We must both go and return by sea,' said Aurelia, 'even though it cause us delay. I have no mind to pass through Neapolis.'

'Be it so. The sky will be calm when this storm has passed Shall you return,' said Basil, 'alone?'

'Alone? Do you purpose to forsake me?'

'Think better of my manners, cousin—and more shrewdly of my meaning.'

'You mean fairly, I trust?' she returned, looking him steadily in the face.

'Nay,' cried the young man vehemently, 'if I have any thought other than honest, may I perish before I ever again behold her!'

Aurelia's gaze softened.

'It is well,' she said; 'we will speak again to-morrow.'

That night Petronilla kept vigil in the church of Surrentum, Basil and Decius relieving her an hour before dawn. At the funeral service, which began soon after sunrise, the greater part of the townsfolk attended. All were eager to see whether the daughter of Maximus would be present, for many rumours were rife touching Aurelia, some declaring that she had returned to the true faith, some that she remained obstinate in heresy. Her failure to appear did not set the debate at rest. A servant of Petronilla whispered it about that only by a false pretence of conversion had Aurelia made sure her inheritance; and at the mere thought of such wickedness the hearers shuddered, foretelling a dread retribution. The clergy were mute on the subject, even with the most favoured of their flock. Meanwhile the piety and austerity of Petronilla made a safe topic of talk, and a long procession reverently escorted her to her temporary abode near the bishop's house.

To-day the clouds spent themselves in rain; before nightfall the heavens began to clear. The island peak of Inarime stood purple against a crimson sunset. After supper, Aurelia and Basil held conference. The wind would not be favourable for their voyage; none the less, they decided to start at the earliest possible hour. Dawn was but just streaking the sky, when they rode down the dark gorge which led to the shore, Basil attended by Felix, the lady by one maid. The bark awaited them, swaying gently against the harbour-side. Aurelia descended to the little cabin curtained off below a half-deck, and—sails as yet being useless—four great oars urged the craft on its way.

What little wind there was breathed from the north For an hour they made but slow progress, but when the first rays of sun gleamed above the mountains, the breeze shifted westward; sails were presently hoisted, and the rippling water hissed before the prow. Soon a golden day shone upon sea and land. Aurelia came forth on to the deck, and sat gazing towards Neapolis.

'You know that the deacon is yonder,' she said in a low voice to Basil, this the first mention of Leander that had fallen from her lips in speaking with him.

'Is he?' returned the other carelessly. 'Yes, I remember.'

But Basil's eyes were turned to the long promontory of Misenum. He was wondering anxiously how his letter had affected Veranilda, and whether, when she heard of it, Aurelia would be angered.

'Where is your friend Marcian?' were her next words.

Basil replied that he, too, was sojourning at Neapolis; and, when Aurelia inquired what business held him there, her cousin answered truly that he did not know.

'Do you trust him?' asked the lady, after a thoughtful pause.

'Marcian? As I trust myself!'

One of the boatmen coming within earshot, their conversation ceased.

The hour before noon saw them drawing near to land. They left on the right the little island of Nesis, and drew towards Puteoli. On the left lay Baiae, all but forsaken, its ancient temples and villas stretching along the shore from the Lucrine lake to the harbour shadowed by Cape Misenum; desolate magnificence, marble overgrown with ivy, gardens where the rose grew wild, and terraces crumbling into the sea. Basil and Aurelia looked upon these things with an eye made careless by familiarity; all their lives ruin had lain about them, deserted sanctuaries of a bygone creed, unpeopled homes of a vanished greatness.

As the boat advanced into the bay, it lost the wind, and rowing again became needful. Thus they entered the harbour of Puteoli, where the travellers disembarked.

Hard by the port was a tavern, which, owing to its position midway between Neapolis and Cumae, still retained something of its character as a *mansio* of the posting service; but the vehicles and quadrupeds of which it boasted were no longer held in strict reserve for state officials and persons privileged. Gladly the innkeeper put at Basil's disposal his one covered carriage, a trifle cleaner inside than it was without, and a couple of saddle horses, declared to be Sicilian, but advanced in age. Thus, with slight delay, the party pursued their journey, Basil and his man riding before the carriage. The road ran coastwise as far as the Julian haven, once thronged with the shipping of the Roman world, now all but abandoned to a few fishermen; there it turned inland, skirted the Lucrine water, and presently reached the shore of Lake Avernus, where was the entrance to the long tunnel piercing the hill between the lake and Cumae. On an ill-kept way, under a low vault of rock dripping moisture, the carriage with difficulty tossed and rumbled through the gloom. Basil impatiently trotted on, and, as he issued into sunlight, there before him stood the walls of the ancient city, round about that little hill by the sea which, in an age remote, had been chosen for their abode by the first Hellenes tempted to the land of Italy. High above rose the acropolis, a frowning stronghold. Through Basil's mind passed the thought that ere long Cumae might again belong to the Goths, and this caused him no uneasiness; half, perchance, he hoped it.

A guard at the city gate inspected the carriage, and let it pass on. In a few minutes, guided by Basil, it drew up before a house in a narrow, climbing street, a small house, brick fronted, with stucco pilasters painted red at the door, and two windows, closed with wooden shutters, in the upper storey. On one side of the entrance stood a shop for the sale of earthenware; on the other, a vintner's with a projecting marble table, the jars of wine thereon exhibited being attached by chains to rings in the wall. Odours of cookery, and of worse things, oppressed the air, and down the street ran a noisome gutter. When Basil's servant had knocked, a little wicket slipped aside for observation; then, after a grinding of heavy locks and bars, the double doors were opened, and a grey-headed slave stepped forward to receive his mistress. Basil had jumped down from his horse, and would fain have entered, but, by an arrangement already made, this was forbidden. Saying that she would expect him at the second hour on the morrow, Aurelia disappeared. Her cousin after a longing look at the blind and mute house, rode away to another quarter of the city, near the harbour, where was an inn at which he had lodged during his previous visit. In a poor and dirty room, he made shift to dine on such food as could be offered him; then lay down on the truckle bed, and slept for an hour or two.

A knock at the door awoke him. It was Felix, who brought the news that Marcian was at Cumae.

'You have seen him?' cried Basil, astonished and eager.

'His servant Sagaris,' Felix replied. 'I met him but now in the forum, and learnt that his lord lodges at the house of the curial Venustus; hard by the Temple of Diana.'

'Go thither at once, and beg him, if his leisure serve, to come to me. I would go myself; but, if he have seen Sagaris, he may be already on the way here.'

And so it proved, for in a very few minutes Marcian himself entered the room.

'Your uncle is dead,' were his first words. 'I heard it in Neapolis yesterday. What brings you here?'

'Nay, best Marcian,' returned the other, with hands on his friend's shoulders, and peering him in the face, 'let me once again put that question to *you*.'

'I cannot answer it, yet,' said Marcian gravely. 'Your business is more easily guessed.'

'But must not be talked of here,' interrupted Basil, glancing at the door. 'Let us find some more suitable place.'

They descended the dark, foul stairs, and went out together. Before the house stood the two serving-men, who, as their masters walked away, followed at a respectful distance. When safe from being overheard, Basil recounted to his friend the course of events at the Surrentine villa since Marcian's departure, made known his suspicion that Aurelia had secretly returned to the Catholic faith. He then told of to day's journey and its purpose, his hearer wearing a look of grave attention.

'Can it be,' asked Marcian, 'that you think of wedding this Gothic beauty?'

'Assuredly,' answered Basil, with a laugh, 'I have thought of it.'

'And it looks as though Aurelia favoured your desire.'

'It has indeed something of that appearance.'

'Pray you now, dear lord,' said Marcian, 'be sober awhile. Have you reflected that, with such a wife, you would not dare return to Rome?'

Basil had not regarded that aspect of the matter, but his friend's reasoning soon brought him to perceive the danger he would lightly have incurred. Dangers, not merely those that resulted from the war; could he suppose, asked Marcian, that Heliodora would meekly endure his disdain, and that the life of Veranilda would be safe in such a rival's proximity? Hereat, Basil gnashed his teeth and handled his dagger. Why return to Rome at all? he cried impatiently. He had no mind to go through the torments of a long siege such as again threatened. Why should he not live on in Campania—

'And tend your sheep or your goats?' interrupted Marcian, with his familiar note of sad irony. 'And pipe *sub tegmine fagi* to your blue-eyed Amaryllis? Why not, indeed? But what if, on learning the death of Maximus, the Thracian who rules yonder see fit to command your instant return, and to exact from you an account of what you have inherited? Bessas loses no time—suspecting—perhaps—that his tenure of a fruitful office may not be long.'

'And if the suspicion be just?' said Basil, gazing hard at his friend.

'Well, if it be?' said the other, returning the look.

'Should we not do well to hold far from Rome, looking to King Totila, whom men praise, as a deliverer of our land from hateful tyranny?'

Marcian laid a hand on his friend's shoulder.

'O, brave Basil!' he murmured, with a smile. 'O, nobly confident in those you love! Never did man so merit love in return.—Do as you will. In a few days I shall again visit you at Surrentum, and perchance bring news that may give us matter for talk.'

From a portico hard by there approached a beggar, a filthy and hideous cripple, who, with whining prayer, besought alms. Marcian from his wallet took a copper coin, and, having glanced at it, drew Basil's attention.

'Look,' said he, smiling oddly, 'at the image and the superscription.'

It was a coin of Vitiges, showing a helmeted bust of the goddess of the city, with legend '*Invicta Roma*.'

'*Invicta Roma*,' muttered Basil sadly, with head bent.

Meanwhile, out of earshot of their masters, the two servants conversed with not less intimacy. At a glance these men were seen to be of different races. Felix, aged some five and thirty, could boast of free birth; he was the son of a curial—that is to say, municipal councillor—of Arpinum, who had been brought to ruin, like so many of his class in this age, by fiscal burdens, the curiales being responsible for the taxes payable by their colleagues, as well as for the dues on any estate in their district which might be abandoned, and, in brief, for whatsoever deficiencies of local revenue. Gravity and sincerity appeared in his countenance; he seldom smiled, spoke in a subdued voice, and often kept his eyes on the ground; but his service was performed with rare conscientiousness, and he had often given proof of affection for his master. Sagaris, a Syrian slave, less than thirty years old, had a comely visage which ever seemed to shine with contentment, and often twinkled with a sort of roguish mirth. Tall and of graceful bearing, the man's every movement betrayed personal vanity; his speech had the note of facile obsequiousness; he talked whenever occasion offered, and was fond of airing his views on political and other high matters. Therewithal, he was the most superstitious of mortals; wore amulets, phylacteries, charms of all sorts, and secretly prayed to many strange gods. When he had nothing else to do, and could find a genial companion, his delight was to play by the hour at *micare digitis*; but, in spite of his master's good opinion, not to Sagaris would have applied the proverb that you might play that game with him in the dark.

'Take my word for it,' he whispered to Felix, with his most important air, 'we shall see strange things ere long. Last night I counted seven shooting stars.'

'What does that argue?' asked the other soberly.

'More than I care to put into Latin. At Capua, three days ago, a woman gave birth to a serpent, a winged dragon, which flew away towards Rome. I talked at Neapolis with a man who saw it.'

'Strange, indeed,' murmured Felix, with raised eyebrows. 'I have often heard of such portents, but never had the luck to behold one of them. Yet,' he added gravely, 'I have received a sign. When my father died, I was far away from him, and at that very hour, as I prayed in the church of Holy Clement at Rome, I heard a voice that said in my ear, *Vale*! three times.'

'Oh, I have had signs far more wonderful than that,' exclaimed the Syrian. 'I was at sea, between Alexandria and Berytus—for you must know that in my boyhood I passed three years at Berytus, and there obtained that knowledge of law which you may have remarked in talking with me—well, I was at sea—'

'Peace!' interposed Felix. 'We are summoned.'

Sagaris sighed, and became the obsequious attendant.

CHAPTER V
BASIL AND VERANILDA

At the appointed hour next morning, when yet no ray of sunshine had touched the gloomy little street, though a limpid sky shone over it, Basil stood at Aurelia's door. The grey-headed porter silently admitted him, and he passed by a narrow corridor into a hall lighted as usual from above, paved with red tiles, here and there trodden away, the walls coloured a dusky yellow, and showing an imaginary line of pillars painted in blue. A tripod table, a couch, and a few chairs were the only furniture. When the visitor had waited for a few moments a curtain concealing the entrance to the inner part of the house moved aside, and Aurelia's voice bade her cousin come forward. He entered a smaller room opening upon a diminutive court where a few shrubs grew; around the walls hung old and faded tapestry; the floor was of crude mosaic; the furniture resembled that of the atrium, with the addition of a brasier.

'I have been anxious for your coming,' were Aurelia's first words. 'Do you think they will let us depart without hindrance? Yesterday I saw the owner of this house to transact my business with him. It is Venustus, a curial, a man who has always been well disposed to me. He said that he must perforce make known to the governor my intention of leaving the city, and hoped no obstacle would be put in our way. This morning, before sunrise, a messenger from the citadel came and put questions to the porter.'

Basil knitted his brows.

'Venustus? It is with Venustus that Marcian lodges. Yes, Marcian is here; I know not on what business. It would have been wiser,' he added, 'to have said nothing, to have gone away as before. When shall you be ready?'

'I am ready now. Why delay? What matter though we reach Surrentum by night? The moon rises early.'

'What reply was given to the messenger from the citadel?'

'He learned, perforce, that we were preparing for a journey.'

A moment's reflection and Basil decided to risk immediate departure; delay and uncertainty were at all times hateful to him, and at the present juncture intolerable. At once he quitted the house (not having ventured to speak the name of Veranilda), and in an hour's time the covered carriage from Puteoli, and another vehicle, were in waiting. The baggage was brought out; then, as Basil stood in the hall, he saw Aurelia come forward, accompanied by a slight female figure, whose grace could not be disguised by the long hooded cloak which wrapped it from head to foot, allowing not a glimpse of face. The young man trembled, and followed. He saw the ladies step into the carriage, and was himself about to mount his horse, when a military officer, attended by three soldiers, stepped towards him, and, without phrase of courtesy, demanded his name. Pallid, shaken with all manner of emotions, Basil replied to this and several other inquiries, the result being that the two vehicles were ordered to be driven to the citadel, and he to go thither under guard.

At the entrance to the citadel the carriage drew up and remained there under guard. Basil was led in, and presently stood before the military governor of Cumae; this was a Hun named Chorsoman, formerly one of Belisarius's bodyguard. He spoke Latin barbarously; none the less was his language direct and perspicuous. The Roman lady wished to quit Cumae, where she had lived for some years; she purposed, moreover, to take away with her a maiden of Gothic race, who, though not treated as a captive, had been under observation since she was sent to dwell here by Belisarius. This could not pass as a matter of small moment. Plainly, permission to depart must be sought of the authorities, and such permission, under the circumstances, could only be granted in return for substantial payment—a payment in proportion to the lady's rank. It was known that the senator Maximus had died, and report said that his daughter inherited great wealth. The price of her passport would be one thousand gold pieces.

Basil knew that Aurelia had not, in the coffer she was taking away, a quarter of this sum of money. He foresaw endless delay, infinite peril to his hopes. Schooling a hot tongue to submissive utterance, he asked that Aurelia might be consulted.

'Speak with her yourself,' said the Hun, 'and bring her answer.'

So Basil went forth, and, under the eyes of the guard, held converse with his cousin. Aurelia was willing to give all the treasure she carried with her—money, a few ornaments of gold and silver, two or three vessels of precious metal—everything for immediate liberty; all together she thought it might be the equivalent of half the sum demanded. The rest she would swear to pay. This being reported to Chorsoman, his hideous, ashen-grey countenance assumed a fierce expression; he commanded that all the baggage on the vehicles should be brought and opened before him; this was done. Whilst Basil, boiling with secret rage, saw his cousin's possessions turned out on to the floor a thought flashed into his mind.

'I ought to inform your Sublimity,' he said, with all the indifference he could assume, 'that the lady Aurelia despatched two days ago a courier to Rome apprising the noble commandant Bessas of her father's death, and of her intention to arrive in the city as soon as possible, and to put her means at his disposal for the defence of Rome against King Totila.'

Chorsoman stared.

'Is not this lady the widow of a Goth and a heretic?'

'The widow of a Goth, yes, but no longer a heretic,' answered Basil boldly, half believing what he said.

He saw that he had spoken to some purpose. The Hun blinked his little eyes, gazed greedily at the money, and was about to speak when a soldier announced that a Roman named Marcian desired immediate audience, therewith handing to the governor a piece of metal which looked like a large coin. Chorsoman had no sooner glanced at this than he bade admit the Roman; but immediately changing his mind, he went out into another room. On his return, after a quarter of an hour, he gruffly announced that the travellers were free to depart.

'We humbly thank your Clemency,' said Basil, his heart leaping in joy. 'Does your Greatness permit me to order these trifles to be removed?'

'Except the money,' replied Chorsoman, growling next moment, 'and the vessels'; then snarling with a savage glance about him, 'and the jewels.'

Not till the gates of Cumae were behind them, and they had entered the cavern in the hill, did Basil venture to recount what had happened. He alighted from his horse, and walking through the gloom beside the carriage he briefly narrated all in a whisper to Aurelia—all except his own ingenious device for balking the Hun's cupidity. What means Marcian had employed for their release he could but vaguely conjecture; that would be learned a few days hence when his friend came again to Surrentum. Aurelia's companion in the carriage, still hooded and cloaked, neither moved nor uttered a word.

At a distance of some twenty yards from the end of the tunnel, Felix, riding in advance, checked his horse and shouted. There on the ground lay a dead man, a countryman, who it was easy to see had been stabbed to death, and perhaps not more than an hour ago. Quarrel or robbery, who could say? An incident not so uncommon as greatly to perturb the travellers; they passed on and came to Puteoli. Here the waiting boatmen were soon found; the party embarked; the vessel oared away in a dead calm.

The long voyage was tedious to Basil only because Veranilda remained unseen in the cabin; the thought of bearing her off, as though she were already his own, was an exultation, a rapture. When he reflected on the indignities he had suffered in the citadel rage burned his throat, and Aurelia, all bitterness at the loss of her treasure, found words to increase this wrath. A Hun! A Scythian savage! A descendant perchance of the fearful Attila! He to represent the Roman Empire! Fit instrument, forsooth, of such an Emperor as Justinian, whose boundless avarice, whose shameful subjection to the base-born Theodora, were known to every one. To this had Rome fallen; and not one of her sons who dared to rise against so foul a servitude!

'Have patience, cousin,' Basil whispered, bidding her with a glance beware of the nearest boatman. 'There are some who will not grieve if Totila—'

'No more than that? To stand, and look on, and play the courtier to whichever may triumph!'

Basil muttered with himself. He wished he had been bred a soldier instead of growing to manhood in an age when the nobles of Rome were held to inglorious peace, their sole career that of the jurist And Aurelia, brooding, saw him involved beyond recall in her schemes of vengeance.

The purple evening fell about them, an afterglow of sunset trembling upon the violet sea. Above the heights of Capreae a star began to glimmer; and lo, yonder from behind the mountains rose the great orb of the moon. They were in the harbour at last, but had to wait on board until a messenger could go to the village and a conveyance arrive. The litter came, with a horse for Basil; Felix, together with Aurelia's grey-headed porter and a female slave—these two the only servants that had remained in the house at Cumae—followed on foot, and the baggage was carried up on men's shoulders.

'Decius!' cried Basil, in a passionate undertone, when he encountered his kinsman in the vestibule. 'Decius! we are here—and one with us whom you know not. Hush! Stifle your curiosity till to-morrow. Let them pass.'

So had the day gone by, and not once had he looked upon the face of Veranilda.

He saw her early on the morrow. Aurelia, though the whole villa was now at her command, chose still to inhabit the house of Proba; and thither, when the day was yet young, she summoned Basil. The room in which she sat was hung with pictured tapestry, representing Christ and the Apostles; crude work, but such as had pleased Faltonia Proba, whose pious muse inspired her to utter the Gospel in a Virgilian canto. And at Aurelia's side, bending over a piece of delicate needlework, sat the Gothic maiden, clad in white, her flaxen hair, loosely held with silk, falling behind her shoulders, shadowing her forehead, and half hiding the little ears. At Basil's entrance she did not look up; at the first sound of his voice she bent her head yet lower, and only when he directly addressed her, asking, with all the gentleness his lips could command, whether the journey had left much fatigue, did she show for a moment her watchet eyes, answering few words with rare sweetness.

'Be seated, dear my lord,' said his cousin, in the soft, womanly voice once her habitual utterance. 'There has been so little opportunity of free conversation, that we have almost, one might say, to make each other's acquaintance yet.

But I hope we may now enjoy a little leisure, and live as becomes good kinsfolk.'

Basil made such suitable answer as his agitation allowed.

'And the noble Decius,' pursued Aurelia, 'will, I trust, bestow at times a little of his leisure upon us. Perhaps this afternoon you could persuade him to forget his books for half an hour? But let us speak, to begin with, of sad things which must needs occupy us. Is it possible, yet, to know when the ship will sail for Rome?'

Aurelia meant, of course, the vessel which would convey her father's corpse, and the words cast gloom upon Basil, who had all but forgotten the duty that lay before him. He answered that a week at least must pass before the sailing, and, as he spoke, kept his eyes upon Veranilda, whose countenance—or so it seemed to him—had become graver, perhaps a little sad.

'Is it your purpose to stay long in Rome?' was Aurelia's next question, toned with rather excessive simplicity.

'To stay long?' exclaimed Basil. 'How can you think it? Perchance I shall not even enter the city. At Portus, I may resign my duty into other hands, and so straightway return.'

There was a conflict in Aurelia's mind. Reverence for her father approved the thought of his remains being transported under the guardianship of Basil; none the less did she dread this journey, and feel tempted to hinder it. She rose from her chair.

'Let us walk into the sunshine,' she said. 'The morning is chilly.' And, as she passed out into the court, hand in hand with Veranilda, 'O, the pleasure of these large spaces, this free air, after the straight house at Cumae! Do you not breathe more lightly, sweetest? Come into Proba's garden, and I will show you where I sat with my broidery when I was no older than you.'

The garden was approached by a vaulted passage. A garden long reconquered by nature; for the paths were lost in herbage, the seats were overgrown with creeping plants, and the fountain had crumbled into ruin. A high wall formerly enclosed it, but, in a shock of earthquake some years ago, part of this had fallen, leaving a gap which framed a lovely picture of the inland hills. Basil pulled away the trailing leafage from a marble hemicycle, and, having spread his cloak upon it, begged tremorously that Veranilda would rest.

'That wall shall be rebuilt,' said Aurelia, and, as if to inspect the ruin, wandered away. When she was distant not many paces, Basil bent to his seated companion, and breathed in a passionate undertone:

'My letter reached your hands, O fairest?'

'I received it—I read it.'

As she spoke, Veranilda's cheeks flushed as if in shame.

'Will you reply, were it but one word?'

Her head drooped lower. Basil seated himself at her side.

'One word, O Veranilda! I worship you—my soul longs for you—say only that you will be mine, my beloved lady, my wife!'

Her blue eyes glistened with moisture as for an instant they met the dark glow in his.

'Do you know who I am?' she whispered.

'You are Veranilda! You are beauty and sweetness and divine purity—'

He sought her hand, but at this moment Aurelia turned towards them, and the maiden, quivering, stood up.

'Perhaps the sun is too powerful,' said Aurelia, with her tenderest smile. 'My lily has lived so long in the shade.'

They lingered a little on the shadowed side, Aurelia reviving memories of her early life, then passed again under the vaulted arch. Basil, whose eyes scarcely moved from Veranilda's face, could not bring himself to address her in common words, and dreaded that she would soon vanish. So indeed it befell. With a murmur of apology to her friend, and a timid movement of indescribable grace in Basil's direction, she escaped, like a fugitive wild thing, into solitude.

'Why has she gone?' exclaimed the lover, all impatience. 'I must follow her—I cannot live away from her! Let me find her again.'

His cousin checked him.

'I have to speak to you, Basil. Come where we can be private.'

They entered the room where they had sat before, and Aurelia, taking up the needlework left by Veranilda, showed it to her companion with admiration.

'She is wondrous at this art. In a contest with Minerva, would she not have fared better than Arachne? This mourning garment which I wear is of her making, and look at the delicate work; it was wrought four years ago, when I heard of my brother's death—wrought in a few days. She was then but thirteen. In all that it beseems a woman to know, she is no less skilled. Yonder lies her cithern; she learnt to touch it, I scarce know how, out of mere desire to soothe my melancholy, and I suspect—though she will not avow it—that the music she plays is often her own. In sickness she has tended me with skill as rare as her gentleness; her touch on the hot forehead is like that of a flower plucked before sunrise. Hearing me speak thus of her, what think you, O Basil, must be my trust in the man to whom I would give her for wife?'

'Can you doubt my love, O Aurelia?' cried the listener, clasping his hands before him.

'Your love? No. But your prudence, is that as little beyond doubt?'

'I have thought long and well,' said Basil.

Aurelia regarded him steadily.

'You spoke with her in the garden just now. Did she reply?'

'But few words. She asked me if I knew her origin, and blushed as she spoke.'

'It is her wish that I should tell you; and I will.'

Scarce had Aurelia begun her narrative, when Basil perceived that his own conjecture, and that of Marcian, had hit the truth. Veranilda was a great-grandchild of Amalafrida, the sister of King Theodoric, being born of the daughter of King Theodahad; and her father was that Ebrimut, whose treachery at the beginning of the great war delivered Rhegium into the hands of the Greeks. Her mother, Theodenantha, a woman of noble spirit, scorned the unworthy Goth, and besought the conqueror to let her remain in Italy, even as a slave, rather than share with such a husband the honours of the Byzantine court. She won this grace from Belisarius, and was permitted to keep with her the little maiden, just growing out of childhood. But shame and grief had broken her heart; after a few months of imprisonment at Cumae she died. And Veranilda passed into the care of the daughter of Maximus.

'For I too was a captive,' said Aurelia, 'and of the same religion as the orphan child. By happy hazard I had become a friend of her mother, in those days of sorrow; and with careless scorn our conquerors permitted me to take Veranilda into my house. As the years went by, she was all but forgotten; there came a new governor—this thievish Hun—who paid no heed to us. I looked forward to a day when we might quit Cumae and live in freedom where we would. Then something unforeseen befell. Half a year ago, just when the air of spring began to breathe into that dark, chill house, a distant kinsman of ours, who has long dwelt in Byzantium—do you know Olybrius, the son of Probinus?'

'I have heard his name.'

'He came to me, as if from my father; but I soon discovered that he had another mission, his main purpose being to seek for Veranilda. By whom sent, I could not learn; but he told me that Ebrimut was dead, and that his son, Veranilda's only brother, was winning glory in the war with the Persians.

For many days I lived in fear lest my pearl should be torn from me. Olybrius it was, no doubt, who bade the Hun keep watch upon us, and it can only have been by chance that I was allowed to go forth unmolested when you led me hither the first time. He returned to Byzantium, and I have heard no more. But a suspicion haunts my mind. What if Marcian were also watching Veranilda?'

'Marcian!' cried the listener incredulously. 'You do not know him. He is the staunchest and frankest of friends. He knows of my love; we have talked from heart to heart.'

'Yet it was at his intercession that the Hun allowed us to go; why, you cannot guess. What if he have power and motives which threaten Veranilda's peace?'

Basil exclaimed against this as the baseless fear of a woman. Had there been a previous command from some high source touching the Gothic maiden, Chorsoman would never have dared to sell her freedom. As to Marcian's power, that was derived from the authorities at Rome, and granted him for other ends; if he used it to release Veranilda, he acted merely out of love to his friend, as would soon be seen.

'I will hope so,' murmured Aurelia. 'Now you have heard what she herself desired that I should tell you, for she could not meet your look until you knew it. Her father's treachery is Veranilda's shame; she saw her noble mother die for it, and it has made her mourning keener than a common sorrow. I think she would never have dared to wed a Goth; all true Goths, she believes in her heart, must despise her. It is her dread lest you, learning who she is, should find your love chilled.'

'Call her,' cried Basil, starting to his feet. 'Or let me go to her. She shall not suffer that fear for another moment. Veranilda! Veranilda!'

His companion retained and quieted him. He should see Veranilda ere long. But there was yet something to be spoken of.

'Have you forgotten that she is not of your faith?'

'Do I love her, adore her, the less?' exclaimed Basil. 'Does she shrink from me on that account?'

'I know,' pursued his cousin, 'what the Apostle of the Gentiles has said: "For the husband who believes not is sanctified by the wife, and the wife who believes not is sanctified by the husband." None the less, Veranilda is under the menace of the Roman law; and you, if it be known that you have wedded her, will be in peril from all who serve the Emperor—at least in dark suspicion; and will be slightly esteemed by all of our house.'

The lover paced about, and all at once, with a wild gesture, uttered his inmost thought.

'What if I care naught for those of our house? And what if the Emperor of the East is of as little account to me? My country is not Byzantium, but Rome.'

Aurelia hushed his voice, but her eyes shone with stern gladness as she stood before him, and took him by the hand, and spoke what he alone could hear.

'Then unite yourself in faith with those who would make Rome free. Be one in religion with the brave Goths—with Veranilda.'

He cast down his eyes and drew a deep breath.

'I scarce know what that religion is, O Aurelia,' came from him stammeringly. 'I am no theologian; I never cared to puzzle my head about the mysteries which men much wiser than I declare to pass all human understanding. Ask Decius if he can defend the faith of Athanasius against that of the Arians; he will smile, and shake his head in that droll way he has. I believe,' he added after a brief hesitancy, 'in Christ and in the Saints. Does not Veranilda also?'

The temptress drew back a little, seated herself; yielded to troublous thought. It was long since she had joined in the worship of a congregation, for at Cumae there was no Arian church. Once only since her captivity had she received spiritual comfort from an Arian priest, who came to that city in disguise. What her religion truly was she could not have declared, for the memories of early life were sometimes as strong in her as rancour against the faith of her enemies. Basil's simple and honest utterance touched her conscience. She put an end to the conversation, promising to renew it before long; whilst Basil, for his part, went away to brood, then to hold converse with Decius.

Through all but the whole of Theodoric's reign, Italy had enjoyed a large toleration in religion: Catholics, Arians, and even Jews observed their worship under the protection of the wise king. Only in the last few years of his life did he commit certain acts of harshness against his Catholic subjects, due to the wrath that was moved in him by a general persecution of the Arians proclaimed at Byzantium. His Gothic successors adhered to Theodoric's better principle, and only after the subjugation of the land by Belisarius had Arianism in Italy been formally condemned. Of course it was protected by the warring Goths: Totila's victories had now once more extended religious tolerance over a great part of the country; the Arian priesthood re-entered their churches; and even in Rome the Greek garrison grew careless of the reviving heresy. Of these things did Decius speak, when the distressed lover sought his counsel. No one more liberal than Decius; but he bore a name which he could not forget, and in his eyes the Goth was a barbarian, the Gothic woman hardly above the level of a slave. That Basil should take a Gothic wife, even one born of a royal line, seemed to him an indignity. Withheld by the gentleness of his temper from saying all he thought, he spoke only of the difficulties which would result from such a marriage, and when, in reply, Basil disclosed his mind, though less vehemently than to Aurelia, Decius fell into meditation. He, too, had often reflected with bitterness on the results of that restoration of Rome to the Empire which throughout the Gothic dominion most of the Roman nobles had never ceased to desire; all but was he persuaded to approve the statesmanship of Cassiodorus. Nevertheless, he could not, without shrinking, see a kinsman pass over to the side of Totila.

'I must think,' he murmured. 'I must think.'

He had not yet seen Veranilda. When, in the afternoon, Basil led him into the ladies' presence, and his eyes fell upon that white-robed loveliness, censure grew faint in him. Though a Decius, he was a man of the sixth century after Christ; his mind conceived an ideal of human excellence which would have been unintelligible to the Decii of old; in his heart meekness and chastity had more reverence than perhaps he imagined. He glanced at Basil; he understood. Though the future still troubled him, opposition to the lover's will must, he knew, be idle.

Several hours before, Basil had scratched on a waxed tablet a few emphatic lines, which his cousin allowed to be transmitted to Veranilda. They assured her that what he had learned could only—if that were possible—increase his love, and entreated her to grant him were it but a moment's speech after the formal visit, later in the day. The smile with which she now met him seemed at once gratitude and promise; she was calmer, and less timid. Though she took little part in the conversation, her words fell very sweetly after the men's speech and the self-confident tones of Aurelia; her language was that of an Italian lady, but in the accent could be marked a slight foreignness, which to Basil's ear had the charm of rarest music, and even to Decius sounded not unpleasing. Under the circumstances, talk, confined to indifferent subjects, could not last very long; as soon as it began to flag, Decius found an excuse for begging permission to retire. As though wishing for a word with him in confidence, Aurelia at the same time passed out of the room into the colonnade. Basil and Veranilda were left alone.

CHAPTER VI
THE EMPEROR'S COMMAND

His voice made tremulous music, inaudible a few paces away; his breath was on her cheek; his eyes, as she gazed into them, seemed to envelop her in their glow.

'My fairest! Let me but touch your hand. Lay it for a moment in mine—a pledge for ever!'

'You do not fear to love me, O lord of my life?'

The whisper made him faint with joy.

'What has fear to do with love, O thou with heaven in thine eyes! what room is there for fear in the heart where thy beauty dwells? Speak again, speak again, my beloved, and bless me above all men that live!'

'Basil! Basil! Utter my name once more. I never knew how sweet it could sound.'

'Nor I, how soft could be the sound of mine. Forgive me, O Veranilda, that out of my love pain has come to you. You will not ever be sad again? You will not think ever again of those bygone sorrows?'

She bent her head low.

'Can you believe in my truth, O Basil? Can *you* forget?'

'All save the nobleness of her who bore you, sweet and fair one.'

'Let *that* be ever in your thought,' said Veranilda, with a radiant look. 'She sees me now; and my hope, your strength and goodness, bring new joy to her in the life eternal.'

'Say the word I wait for—whisper low—the word of all words.'

'Out of my soul, O Basil, I love you!'

As the sound trembled into silence, his lips touched hers. In the golden shadow of her hair, the lily face flushed warm; yet she did not veil her eyes, vouchers of a life's loyalty.

When Aurelia entered the room again, she walked as though absorbed in thought.

'Decius tells me he must soon go to Rome,' were her words, in drawing near to the lovers.

Basil had heard of no such purpose. His kinsman, under the will of Maximus, enjoyed a share in the annual revenue of this Surrentine estate; moreover, he became the possessor of many books, which lay in the Anician mansion of Rome, and it was his impatience, thought Aurelia, to lay hands upon so precious a legacy, which might at any time be put in danger by the events of the war, that prompted him to set forth.

'Might he not perform the duty you have undertaken?' she added in a lower voice, as she met Basil's look.

Veranilda did not speak, but an anxious hope dawned in her face. And Basil saw it.

'Have you spoken of it, cousin?' he asked.

'The thought has but just come to me.'

'Decius is not in good health. Thus late in the year, to travel by sea—Yet the weather may be fair, the sea still; and then it would be easier for him than the journey by land.'

Basil spoke in a halting tone. He could not without a certain shame think of revoking his promise to Petronilla, a very distinct promise, in which natural obligation had part. Yet the thought of the journey, of an absence from Veranilda, not without peril of many kinds, grew terrible to him. He looked at Veranilda again, and smiled encouragement.

The lady Petronilla had been wont to dine and sup in dignified publicity, seated on the *sigma*, in the room which had seen so many festivals, together with her male relatives and any guest who might be at the villa; in her presence, no man permitted himself the recumbent attitude, which indeed had been unusual save among the effeminate. But Aurelia and her companion took their meals apart. This evening, Basil and Decius supped almost in silence, each busy with his reflections. They lingered over the wine, their attendants having left them, until Decius, as if rousing himself from a dream, asked how long it was likely to be before the ship could sail. Basil answered that the leaden coffin would be ready within a few days (it was being made at Neapolis, out of water-pipes which had served a villa in ruins), and after that there would only be delay through wind and weather.

'Are you greatly bent on going to Rome just now?' was the student's next inquiry, a twinkle in his eyes as he spoke.

'By Bacchus!' answered the other, handling his goblet. 'If I saw my way to avoid it!'

'I guessed as much. The suspicion came to me at a certain moment this morning—a mere grain, which ever since has been growing *tanquam favus*. I am not wont to consider myself as of much use, but is it not just possible that, in this case, your humble kinsman might serve you?'

'My good, my excellent, my very dear Decius!' broke from the listener. 'But would it not be with risk to your health?'

'I would beg permission not to weigh anchor in a tempest, that's all. The sea in its gentler moods I have never feared, and *alcyoneum medicamen*, you know, in other words the sea-foam, has always been recommended for freckles.'

He touched his face, which was in deed much freckle-spotted, and Basil, whose spirits rose each moment, gave a good-natured laugh.

'One thing only,' added Decius seriously. 'Inasmuch as this charge is a grave one, I would not undertake it without the consent of the ladies Aurelia and Petronilla. Perchance, in respect for the honoured Maximus, they would feel reluctant to see me take your place.'

'O modest Decius!' exclaimed the other. 'Which, pray, carries the more dignity, your name or mine?—not to speak of your learning and my ignorance. As to Aurelia, I can ease your mind at once. She would not dream of objecting.'

'Then let us, to-morrow, beg audience of the pious lady at Surrentum, and request her permission.'

The proposal made Basil uncomfortable; but a visit of respect to Petronilla was certainly due, and perhaps it would pass without troublesome incident. He nodded assent.

Early on the morrow they carried out their purpose. To the surprise of both, Petronilla received them in her modest abode not ungraciously, though with marked condescension; she gave them to understand that her days, and much of her nights, passed in religious exercises, the names of her kinsfolk not being omitted from her prayers; of the good bishop she spoke almost tenderly, and with a humble pride related that she had been able to ease a persistent headache from which his Sanctity suffered. When Basil found an opportunity of reporting what had passed between him and Decius, the lady's austere smile was for a moment clouded; it looked as though storm might follow. But the smile returned, with perhaps a slightly changed significance. Did Basil think of remaining long at the villa? Ah, he could not say; to be sure, the times were so uncertain. For her own part, she would start on her journey as soon as the coffin was on board the ship. Indeed, she saw no objection to the arrangement her dear nephew proposed; she only trusted that the learned and amiable Decius, so justly esteemed by all, would have a care of his health. Did he still take the infusion of marjoram which she had prescribed for him? A holy man, newly returned from the East, had deigned to visit her only yesterday, and had given her a small phial of water from Rebekah's well; it was of priceless virtue, and one drop of it had last evening restored to health and strength a child that lay at the point of death.

In the afternoon Basil was again permitted to see Veranilda, though not alone. To her and to Aurelia he made known that Decius would willingly undertake the voyage. After lingering for an hour in the vain hope that Aurelia would withdraw, were it but for a moment, he went away and scratched ardent words on his tablet. 'I will be in your garden,' he concluded, 'just at sunrise to-morrow. Try, try to meet me there.'

Scarcely had he despatched a servant with this when Felix announced to him the arrival of Marcian. On fire with eagerness, Basil sped to greet his friend.

'Give me to drink,' were the traveller's first words. 'I have ridden since before dawn, and have a tongue like leather.'

Wine and grapes, with other refreshments, were set forth for him. Marcian took up an earthenware jug full of spring water, and drank deeply. His host then urged the wine, but it was refused; and as Basil knew that one of his friend's peculiarities was a rigorous abstinence at times from all liquor save the pure element, he said no more.

'I have been at Nuceria,' Marcian continued, throwing himself on a seat, 'with Venantius. What a man! He was in the saddle yesterday from sunrise to sunset; drank from sunset to the third hour of the night; rose before light this morning, gay and brisk, and made me ride with him, so that I was all but tired out before I started on the road hither. Venantius declares that he can only talk of serious things on horseback.'

'My uncle regarded him as a Roman turned barbarian,' said Basil.

'Something of that, but such men have their worth and their place.'

'We will talk about him at another time,' Basil interrupted. 'Remember how we parted at Cumae and what happened afterwards. We are private here; you can speak freely. How did you release us from the grip of the Hun?'

'I told you before, good Basil, that I was here to spy upon you; and be sure that I did not undertake that office without exacting a proof of the confidence of our lords at Rome. Something I carry with me which has power over such dogs as Chorsoman.'

'I saw that, best Marcian. But it did not avail to save my cousin Aurelia from robbery.'

'Nothing would, where Chorsoman was sure of a week's—nay, of an hour's—impunity. But did he steal aught belonging to the Gothic maiden?'

'To Veranilda? She has but a bracelet and a ring, and those she was wearing. They came from her mother, a woman of noblest heart, who, when her husband Ebrimut played the traitor, and she was left behind in Italy, would keep nothing but these two trinkets, which once were worn by Amalafrida.'

'You know all that now,' observed Marcian quietly.

'The story of the trinkets only since an hour or two ago. That of Veranilda's parentage I learned from Aurelia, Veranilda refusing to converse with me until I knew.'

'Since when you have conversed, I take it, freely enough.'

'Good my lord,' replied Basil, with a look of some earnestness, 'let us not jest on this matter.'

'I am little disposed to do so, O fiery lover!' said Marcian, with a return of his wonted melancholy. 'For I have that to tell you which makes the matter grave enough. We were right, you see, in our guess of Veranilda's origin; I could wish she had been any one else. Patience, patience! You know that I left you here to go to Neapolis. There I received letters from Rome, one of them from Bessas himself, and, by strange hazard, the subject of it was the daughter of Ebrimut.'

Basil made a gesture of repugnance. 'Nay, call her the daughter of Theodenantha.'

'As you will. In any case the granddaughter of a king, and not likely to be quite forgotten by the royal family of her own race. Another king's grandchild, Matasuntha, lives, as you know, at Byzantium, and enjoys no little esteem at the Emperor's court; it is rumoured, indeed, that her husband Vitiges, having died somewhere in battle, Matasuntha is to wed a nephew of Justinian. This lady, I am told, desires to know the daughter of Ebri—nay, then, of Theodenantha; of whom, it seems, a report has reached her. A command of the Emperor has come to Bessas that the maiden Veranilda, resident at Cumae, be sent to Constantinople with all convenient speed. And upon me, O Basil, lies the charge of seeking her in her dwelling, and of conveying her safely to Rome, where she will be guarded until—'

'Will be guarded!' echoed Basil fiercely. 'Nay, by the holy Peter and Paul, that will she not! You are my friend, Marcian, and I hold you dear, but if you attempt to obey this order—'

Hand on dagger, and eyes glaring, the young noble had sprung to his feet. Marcian did not stir; his head was slightly bent, and a sad smile hovered about his lips.

'O descendant of all the Anicii,' he replied, 'O son of many consuls, remember the ancestral dignity. Time enough to threaten when you detect me in an unfriendly act. Did I play the traitor to you at Cumae? With the Hun this command of Justinian served you in good stead; Veranilda would not otherwise have escaped so easily. Chorsoman, fat-witted as he is, willingly believed that Veranilda and Aurelia, and you yourself, were all in my net—

which means the net of Bessas, whom he fears. Do you also believe it, my good Basil?'

For answer Basil embraced his friend, and kissed him on either cheek.

'I know how this has come about,' he said; and thereupon related the story of the visit of Olybrius to Aurelia six months ago. It seemed probable that a report of Veranilda's beauty had reached Matasuntha, who wished to adorn her retinue with so fair a remnant of the Amal race. How, he went on to ask, would Marcian excuse himself at Rome for his failure to perform this office?

'Leave that to my ingenuity,' was the reply. 'Enough for you to dare defiance of the Emperor's will.'

Basil made a scornful gesture, which his friend noted with the same melancholy smile.

'You have no misgiving?' said Marcian. 'Think who it is you brave. Imperator Caesar Flavius Justinianus—Africanus, Gothicus, Germanicus, Vandalicus, and I know not what else—Pius, Felix, Inclytus, Victor ac Triumphator, Semper Augustus—'

The other laid a hand upon his shoulder.

'Marcian, no word of this to Aurelia, I charge you!'

'I have no desire to talk about it, be assured. But it is time that we understood each other. Be plain with me. If you wed Veranilda how do you purpose to secure your safety? Not, I imagine, by prostrating yourself before Bessas. Where will you be safe from pursuit?'

Basil reflected, then asked boldly:

'Has not the King Totila welcomed and honourably entertained Romans who have embraced his cause?'

'Come now,' exclaimed the other, his sad visage lighting up, 'that is to speak like a man! So, we *do* understand each other. Be it known unto you then, O Basil, that at this moment the Gothic king is aware of your love for Veranilda, and of your purpose to espouse her. You indeed are a stranger to him, even in name; but not so the Anician house; and an Anician, be assured, will meet with no cold reception in the camp of the Goths.'

'You enjoy the confidence of Totila?' asked Basil, wondering, and a little confused.

'Did I not tell you that I claimed the merit of playing traitor to both sides?'

Marcian spoke with a note of bitterness, looking his friend fixedly in the face.

'It is a noble treachery,' said Basil, seizing both his hands. 'I am with you, heart and soul! Tell me more. Where is the king? Will he march upon Rome?'

'Neapolis will see him before Rome does. He comes slowly through Samnium, making sure his conquest on the way. Let me now speak again of Venantius. He would fain know you.'

'He is one of ours?'

'One of those true Romans who abhor the Eastern tyranny and see in the Goth a worthy ally. Will you ride with me to-morrow to Nuceria?'

'I cannot,' replied Basil, 'for I dare not leave Veranilda without protection, after what you have told me.'

'Why, then, Venantius must come hither.'

Whilst the friends were thus conversing a courier rode forth from Surrentum towards Neapolis. He bore a letter whereof the contents were these:—

'To the holy and reverend deacon Leander, Petronilla's humble salutation.

'I am most punctually informed of all that passes at the villa. My nephew goes not to Rome; his place will be taken by Decius. The reason is that which I have already suggested to your Sanctity. Marcian has arrived this afternoon, coming I know not whence, but I shall learn. I suspect things of the darkest moment. Let your Sanctity pursue the project with which heaven has inspired you. You shall receive, if necessary, two missives every day. Humbly I entreat your prayers.'

CHAPTER VII
HERESY

The Roman Empire, by confining privileges and honours to the senatorial order, created a noble caste, and this caste, as Imperial authority declined, became a power independent of the state, and a menace to its existence. In Italy, by the end of the fifth century, the great system of citizenship, with its principle of infinite devotion to the good of the commonwealth, was all but forgotten. In matters of justice and of finance the nobles were beginning to live by their own law, which was that of the right of the strongest. Having ceased to hold office and perform public services in the municipia, they became, in fact, rulers of the towns situated on or near their great estates. Theodoric, striving to uphold the ancient civility, made strenuous efforts to combat this aristocratic predominance; yet on some points he was obliged to yield to the tendency of the times, as when he forbade the freedmen, serfs, and slaves on any estate to plead against their lord, and so delivered the mass of the rural inhabitants of Italy to private jurisdiction. The Gothic war of course hastened the downfall of political and social order. The manners of the nobles grew violent in lawlessness; men calling themselves senators, but having in fact renounced that rank by permanent absence from Rome, and others who merely belonged to senatorial houses, turned to fortifying their villas, and to building castles on heights, whilst they gathered about them a body of retainers, armed for defence or for aggression.

Such a personage was Venantius, son of a senator of the same name, who, under Theodoric, had attained the dignity of Patrician and what other titular glories the time afforded. Venantius, the younger, coming into possession of an estate between Neapolis and Salernum, here took up his abode after the siege of Rome, and lived as seemed good to him, lord over the little town of Nuceria, and of a considerable tract of country, with a villa converted into a stronghold up on the mountain side. Having suffered wrongs at the hands of the Imperial conquerors—property of his in Rome had been seized—he heard with satisfaction of the rise of Totila, and, as soon as the king's progress southward justified such a step, entered into friendly communication with the Goth, whom he invited to come with all speed into Campania, where Salernum, Neapolis, Cumae, would readily fall into his hands. Marcian, on his double mission of spy in the Greek service and friend of the Goths, had naturally sought out Venantius; and the description he gave to Basil of the fortress above Nuceria filled the listener with enthusiasm.

'I would I could live in the same way,' Basil exclaimed. 'And why not? My own villa in Picenum might be strengthened with walls and towers. We have stone enough, and no lack of men to build.'

Yet as he spoke a misgiving betrayed itself on his countenance. Consciously or not, he had always had before him a life at Rome, the life which became a Roman, as distinguished from a barbarian. But the need to seek security for Veranilda again became vivid to his mind. At Rome, clearly, he could not live with his wife until the Goths had reconquered the city, which was not likely to happen soon. His means were represented chiefly by the Arpinum estate, which he had inherited from his father; in Rome he had nothing but his mansion on the Caelian. The treasure at his command, a considerable sum, he had brought away in a strong box, and it was now more than doubled in value by what fell to him under the will of Maximus—money to be paid out of the great coffer which the senator had conveyed hither. As they talked, Marcian urged upon him a close friendship with Venantius, in whose castle he would be welcomed. Here at Surrentum he could not long rest in safety, for Chorsoman might at any time have his suspicions awakened by learning the delay of Veranilda's journey to Rome, and the news of her marriage could not be prevented from spreading.

So Basil lay through an anxious hour or two before sleep fell upon him to-night. He resolved to change the habits of his life, to shake off indolence and the love of ease, to fortify himself with vigorous exercises, and become ready for warfare. It was all very well for an invalid, like Decius, to nurse a tranquil existence, unheeding the temper of the times. A strong and healthy man had no right to lurk away from the streaming flood of things; it behoved him to take his part in strife and tumult, to aid in re-establishing a civic state. This determination firmly grasped, he turned to think of the hoped-for meeting with Veranilda in the morning, and gentler emotions lulled him into dreams.

At dawn he bestirred himself. The gallery outside his chamber was lighted with a hanging lamp, and at a little distance sounded the footstep of the watchman, who told him that the morning was fair, and, at his bidding, opened a door which admitted to the open terrace overlooking the sea. Having stepped forth, Basil stood for a moment sniffing the cool air with its scent from the vineyards, and looking at the yellow rift in the eastern sky; then he followed a path which skirted the villa's outward wall and led towards the dwelling of Aurelia. Presently he reached the ruined wall of the little garden, and here a voice challenged him, that of a servant on watch until sunrise.

'It is well,' he replied. 'I will relieve you for this last half hour; go to your rest.'

But the slave hesitated. He had strictest orders, and feared to disobey them even at this bidding.

'You are an honest fellow,' said Basil, 'and the lady Aurelia shall know of your steadfastness. But get you gone; there is no danger whilst I am here.'

Impatiently he watched the man retire, then stood just within the gap of the wall, and waited with as much fear as hope. It might be that Veranilda would not venture forth without speaking to Aurelia, who might forbid the meeting; or, if she tried to steal out, she might be detected and hindered; perhaps she would fear to pass under the eyes of a watchman or other servant who might be in her way. He stamped nervously, and turned to look for a moment in the outward direction. This little villa stood on the edge of a declivity falling towards the sea; a thicket of myrtles grew below. At the distance of half a mile along the coast, beyond a hollow wooded with ilex, rose a temple, which time and the hand of man had yet spared; its whiteness glimmered against a sky whose cloudless dusk was warming with a reflection of the daybreak. An influence in the scene before him, something he neither understood nor tried to understand, held him gazing longer than he supposed, and with a start he heard his name spoken by the beloved voice. Close to him stood Veranilda. She was cloaked and hooded, so that he could hardly see her face; but her white hands were held out for his.

Heart to heart, mouth to mouth, they whispered. To be more private, Basil drew her without the garden. Veranilda's eyes fixed themselves upon the spreading glory of the east; and it moved her to utterance.

'When I was a child,' she said, 'at Ravenna, I gazed once at the sunrise, and behold, in the rays which shot upwards stood an angel, a great, beautiful angel, with wings of blue, and a garment which shone like gold, and on his head was a wreath of I know not what flowers. I ran to tell my mother, but when she came, alas! the angel had vanished. No one could tell me certainly what the vision meant. Often I have looked and hoped to see the angel again, but he has never come.'

Basil listened without a doubt, and murmured soft words. Then he asked whether Aurelia knew of this meeting; but Veranilda shook her head.

'I durst not speak. I so feared to disappoint you. This night I have hardly slept, lest I should miss the moment. Should I not return very soon, O Basil?'

'You shall; though your going will make the sky black as when Auster blows. But it is not for long. A few days—'

He broke off with the little laugh of a triumphing lover.

'A few days?' responded Veranilda, timidly questioning.

'We wait only until that dark ship has sailed for Rome.' 'Does Aurelia know that you purpose it so soon?' asked Veranilda.

'Why? Has she seemed to you to wish otherwise?'

'She has never spoken of it.—And afterwards? Shall we remain here, Basil?'

'For no long time. Here I am but a guest. We must dwell where I am lord and you lady of all about us.'

He told her of his possessions, of the great house in Rome with the villa at Arpinum. Then he asked her, playfully, but with a serious purpose in his mind, which of the two she would prefer for an abode.

'I have no choice but yours,' she replied. 'Where it seems good to my dear lord to dwell, there shall I be at rest.'

'We must be safe against our enemies,' said Basil, with graver countenance.

'Our enemies?'

'Has not Aurelia talked to you of the war? You know that the Gothic king is conquering all before him, coming from the north?'

Veranilda looked into her lover's face with a tender anxiety.

'And you fear him, O Basil? It is he that is our enemy?'

'Not so, sweetest. No foe of mine is he who wears the crown of Theodoric. They whom I fear and abhor are the slaves of Justinian, the robber captains who rule at Ravenna and in Rome.'

As she heard him, Veranilda trembled with joy. She caught his hand, and bent over it, and kissed it.

'Had I been the enemy of Totila,' said Basil, 'could you still have loved me as a wife should love?'

'I had not asked myself,' she answered, 'for it was needless. When I look on you, I think neither of Roman nor of Goth.'

Basil spoke of his hope that Rome might be restored to the same freedom it had enjoyed under the great king. Then they would dwell together in the sacred city. That, too, was Veranilda's desire; for on her ear the name of Rome fell with a magic sound; all her life she had heard it spoken reverentially, with awe, yet the city itself she had never seen. Rome, she knew, was vast; there, it seemed to her, she would live unobserved, unthought of save by him she loved. Seclusion from all strangers, from all who, learning her origin, would regard her slightingly, was what her soul desired.

Day had broken; behind the mountains there was light of the sun. Once more they held each other heart to heart, and Veranilda hastened through the garden to regain her chamber. Basil stood for some minutes lost in a delicious dream; the rising day made his face beautiful, his eyes gleamed with an unutterable rapture. At length he sighed and awoke and looked about him. At no great distance, as though just issued from the ilex wood, moved a man's figure. It approached very slowly, and Basil watched until he saw that the man was bent as if with age, and had black garments such as were worn by wandering mendicant monks. Carelessly he turned, and went his way back to the villa.

An hour later, Aurelia learnt that a 'holy man,' a pilgrim much travel worn, was begging to be admitted to her. She refused to see him. Still he urged his entreaty, declaring that he had a precious gift for her acceptance, and an important message for her ear. At length he was allowed to enter the atrium, and Aurelia saw before her a man in black monkish habit, his body bent and tremulous, but evidently not with age, for his aspect otherwise was that of middle life. What, she asked briefly and coldly, was his business with her? Thereupon the monk drew from his bosom a small wrappage of tissues, which when unfolded disclosed a scrap of something hairy.

'This, noble lady,' said the monk, in a voice reverently subdued, 'is from the camel-hair garment of Holy John the Baptist. I had it of a hermit in the Egyptian desert, who not many days after I quitted him was for his sanctity borne up to heaven by angels, and knew not death.'

Aurelia viewed the relic with emotion.

'Why,' she asked, 'do you offer it to me?'

The monk drew a step nearer and whispered:

'Because I know that you, like him from whom I received it, are of the true faith.'

Aurelia observed him closely. His robe was ragged and filthy; his bare feet were thick with the dust of the road; his visage, much begrimed, wore an expression of habitual suffering, and sighs as of pain frequently broke from him. The hand by which he supported himself on a staff trembled as with weakness.

'You are not a presbyter?' she said in an undertone, after a glance at his untonsured head.

'I am unworthy of the meanest order in the Church. In pilgrimings and fastings I do penance for a sin of youth. You see how wasted is my flesh.'

'What, then,' asked Aurelia, 'was the message you said you bore for me?'

'This. Though I myself have no power to perform the sacraments of our faith, I tend upon one who has. He lies not far from here, like myself sick and weary, and, because of a vow, may not come within the precincts of any dwelling. In Macedonia, oppressed by our persecutors, he was long imprisoned, and so sorely tormented that, in a moment when the Evil One prevailed over his flesh, he denied the truth. This sin gave him liberty, but scarce had he come forth when a torment of the soul, far worse than that of his body, fell upon him. He was delivered over to the Demon, and, being yet alive, saw about him the fires of Gehenna. Thus, for a season, did he suffer things unspeakable, wandering in desert places, ahungered, athirst, faint unto death, yet not permitted to die. One night of storm, he crept for shelter into the ruins of a heathen temple. Of a sudden, a dreadful light shone about him, and he beheld the Demon in the guise of that false god, who fell upon him and seemed like to slay him. But Sisinnius—so is the holy man named—strove in prayer and in conjuration, yea, strove hours until the crowing of the cock, and thus sank into slumber. And while he slept, an angel of the Most High appeared before him, and spoke words which I know not. Since then, Sisinnius wanders from land to land, seeking out the temples of the heathen which have not been purified, and passing the night in strife with the Powers of Darkness, wherein he is ever victorious.'

With intent look did Aurelia listen to this narrative. At its close, she asked eagerly:

'This man of God has sent you to me?'

'Moved by a vision—for in the sleep which follows upon his struggle it is often granted him to see beyond this world. He bids you resist temptation, and be of good courage.'

'Know you what this bidding means?' inquired the awed woman, gazing into the monk's eyes till they fell.

'I know nothing. I am but a follower of the holy Sisinnius—an unworthy follower.'

'May I not speak with him?'

The monk had a troubled look.

'I have told you, lady, that he must not, by reason of his vow, enter a human dwelling.'

'But may I not go to him?' she urged. 'May I not seek him in his solitude, guided by you?'

To this, said the monk, he could give no reply until he had spoken with Sisinnius. He promised to do so, and to return, though he knew not at what hour, nor even whether it would be this day. And, after demanding many assurances that he would come again as speedily as might be, Aurelia allowed the messenger to depart.

Meanwhile Basil and Marcian have spent an hour in talk, the result of which was a decision that Marcian should again repair to the stronghold of Venantius, and persuade him to come over to Surrentum. When his friend had ridden forth Basil sought conversation with Aurelia, whom he found in a mood unlike any she had yet shown to him, a mood of dreamy trouble, some suppressed emotion appearing in her look and in her speech. He began by telling her of Venantius, but this seemed to interest her less than he had expected.

'Cousin,' he resumed, 'I have a double thought in desiring that Venantius should come hither. It is not only that I may talk with him of the war, and learn his hopes, but that I may secure a safe retreat for Veranilda when she is my wife, and for you, dear cousin, if you desire it.'

He spoke as strongly as he could without revealing the secret danger, of the risks to which they would all be exposed when rumours of his marriage reached the governor of Cumae, or the Greeks in Neapolis. Until the Goths reached Campania, a Roman here who fell under suspicion of favouring them must be prepared either to flee or to defend himself. Defence of this villa was impossible even against the smallest body of soldiers, but within the walls, raised and fortified by Venantius, a long siege might be safely sustained.

'It is true,' said Aurelia at length, as if rousing herself from her abstraction, 'that we must think of safety. But you are not yet wedded.'

'A few days hence I shall be.'

'Have you forgotten,' she resumed, meeting his resolute smile, 'what still divides you from Veranilda?'

'You mean the difference of religion. Tell me, did that stand in the way of your marriage with a Goth?'

She cast down her eyes and was silent.

'Was your marriage,' Basil went on, 'blessed by a Catholic or by an Arian presbyter?'

'By neither,' replied Aurelia gently.

'Then why may it not be so with me and Veranilda? And so it shall be, lady cousin,' he added cheerily. 'Our good Decius will be gone; we await the sailing of the ship; but you and Marcian, and perhaps Venantius, will be our witnesses.'

For the validity of Christian wedlock no religious rite was necessary: the sufficient, the one indispensable, condition was mutual consent. The Church favoured a union which had been sanctified by the oblation and the blessing, but no ecclesiastical law imposed this ceremony. As in the days of the old religion, a man wedded his bride by putting the ring upon her finger and delivering her dowry in a written document, before chosen witnesses. Aurelia knew that even as this marriage had satisfied her, so would it suffice to Veranilda, whom a rapturous love made careless of doctrinal differences: She perceived, moreover, that Basil was in no mood for religious discussion; there was little hope that he would consent to postpone his marriage on such an account; yet to convert Basil to 'heresy' was a fine revenge she would not willingly forego, her own bias to Arianism being stronger than ever since the wrong she believed herself to have suffered at the hands of the deacon, and the insult cast at her by her long-hated aunt. After years of bitterness, her triumph seemed assured. It was much to have inherited from her father, to have expelled Petronilla; but the marriage of Basil with a Goth, his renunciation of Catholicism, and with it the Imperial cause, were greater things, and together with their attainment she foredreamt the greatest of all, Totila's complete conquest of Italy. She saw herself mistress in the Anician palace at Rome, commanding vast wealth, her enemies mute, powerless, submissive before her. Then, if it seemed good to her, she would again wed, and her excited imagination deigned to think of no spouse save him whose alliance would make her royal.

Providential was the coming of the holy Sisinnius. Beyond doubt he had the gift of prophecy. From him she would not only receive the consolations of religion, but might learn what awaited her. Very slowly passed the hours until the reappearance of the black monk. He came when day was declining, and joyfully she learnt that Sisinnius permitted her to visit him; it must be on the morrow at the second hour, the place a spot in the ilex wood, not far away, whither the monk would guide her. But she must come alone; were she accompanied, even at a distance, by any attendant, Sisinnius would refuse to see her. To all the conditions Aurelia readily consented, and bade the monk meet her at the appointed hour by the breach in her garden wall.

On the morrow there was no glory of sunrise; clouds hung heavy, and a sobbing wind shook the dry leaves of the vine. But at the second hour, after pretence of idling about the garden, Aurelia saw approach the black, bowed figure, with a gesture bade him go before, and followed. She was absent not long enough to excite the remark of her household. In going forth she had been pale with agitation; at her return she had a fire in her cheeks, a lustre in her eyes, which told of hopes abundantly fulfilled. At once she sought Veranilda, to whom she had not yet spoken of the monk's visit. At this juncture the coming even of an ordinary priest of the Arian faith would have been more than welcome to them, living as they perforce did without office or sacrament; but Sisinnius, declared Aurelia, was a veritable man of God, one who had visions and saw into the future, one whom merely to behold was a sacred privilege. She had begged his permission to visit him again, with Veranilda, and he had consented; but a few days must pass before that, as the holy man was called away she knew not whither. When he summoned them they must go forth in early morning, to a certain cave near at hand, where Sisinnius would say mass and administer to them the communion. Hearing such news, Veranilda gladdened.

'Will the holy man reveal our fate to us?' she asked, with a child's simplicity.

'To me he has already uttered a prophetic word,' answered Aurelia, 'but I may not repeat it, no, not even to you. Enough that it has filled my soul with wonder and joy.'

'May that joy also be mine!' said Veranilda, pressing her hands together.

This afternoon, when Basil sat with her and Aurelia, she took her cithern, and in a low voice sang songs she had heard her mother sing, in the days before shame and sorrow fell upon Theodenantha. There were old ballads of the Goths, oftener stern than tender, but to the listeners, ignorant of her tongue, Veranilda's singing made them sweet as lover's praise. One little song was Greek; it was all she knew of that language, and the sole inheritance that had come to her from her Greek-loving grandparent, the King Theodahad.

Auster was blowing; great lurid clouds rolled above the dark green waters, and at evening rain began to fall. Through the next day, and the day after that, the sky still lowered; there was thunder of waves upon the shore; at times a mist swept down from the mountains, which enveloped all in gloom. To Basil and Veranilda it mattered nothing. Where they sat together there was sunshine, and before them gleamed an eternity of cloudless azure.

CHAPTER VIII
THE SNARE

Meanwhile all was made ready for the sailing of the ship. Coffined in lead, the body of Maximus awaited only a return of fine weather for its conveyance to the vessel. When at length calm fell upon the sea, and after a still night of gentle rain the day broke radiantly, all Surrentum was in movement between church and harbour. Mass having been said, the bishop himself led the procession down the hollow way and through the chasm in the cliffs seaward, whilst psalms were chanted and incense burnt. Carried in her litter, Petronilla followed the bier; beside her walked Basil and Decius. Only by conscious effort could these two subdue their visages to a becoming sadness; for Basil thought of his marriage, Decius of Rome and his library. Nor did Petronilla wear an aspect of very profound gloom; at moments she forgot herself, and a singular animation appeared on her proud features; it was as though some exultancy took hold of her mind.

That Aurelia held apart, that the daughter gave no testimony of reverence for a father's remains, caused such murmuring in the crowd of Surrentines: her heresy seemed to be made more notorious, more abominable, by this neglect. At Surrentum, Arianism had never been known; no Goth had ever dwelt here; and since Aurelia's arrival public opinion had had time to gather force against her. It was believed that she had driven forth with insults the most noble Petronilla, that exemplar of charity and of a saintly life. Worse still was the rumour, now generally believed, that the Senator's daughter had obtained her inheritance by wicked hypocrisy, by a false show of return to the true faith. Being herself so evil, it was not to be wondered that she corrupted those who fell under her influence; the young lord Basil, for instance, who, incredible as it sounded, was said to be on the point of espousing a Gothic damsel, a mysterious attendant upon Aurelia, of whom strange stories were rife. Talk of these things made no little agitation in the town when ceremonies were over and the coffin had been embarked. The generality threw up their hands, and cried shame, and asked why the bishop did not take some action in so grave a scandal. But here and there folk whispered together in a different tone, with winkings and lips compressed, and nods significant of menace. Patience! Wait a day or two, and they would see what they would see. Heaven was not regardless of iniquity.

Scarce had the ship weighed anchor, to be wafted across the bay by a gentle wind, when Petronilla started on her land journey for Rome. The great chariot, the baggage, the servants riding, made fresh commotion in Surrentum; many accompanied the great lady along the winding road until they were weary and their curiosity satisfied. To this obsequious escort Petronilla uttered certain words which before evening were repeated throughout the town. 'Let us forgive our enemies,' she said, with that air of hers, at once so grand and so devout—'let us forgive our enemies, but let us omit no means, however rigorous, of saving their souls'; and of those who reported the saying, some winked and nodded more significantly than ever.

Just before sunset on this same day there was trampling of hoofs along the road ascending to the villa, as two horsemen, with a dozen followers, some on horses, some on mules, rode up. Summoned to the atrium, Basil greeted the return of Marcian, and looked with curiosity at the man standing beside him, who could be no other than Venantius. A tall and comely man, wearing a casque and a light breastplate, his years not more than thirty, rather slim, yet evidently muscular and vigorous, he had a look of good-humoured determination, and the tones in which he replied to Basil's welcome were those of a born commander. In contrast with his host's elaborate courtesy, the manners of Venantius might have been judged a trifle barbarous, but this bluntness was no result of defective breeding; had he chosen, he could have exchanged lofty titles and superlatives of compliment with any expert in such fashionable extravagances, but he chose a plainer speech, in keeping with his martial aspect. First of all he excused himself for having arrived with so many followers.

'But our good Marcian,' he added, clapping a hand on his companion's shoulder, 'had a story to tell me of a fair lady and fairer maiden—though not long to bear the name, she—who may belike need protection as well as honourable attendance; whereas you, noble Basil, have thought little of the use of arms, and probably keep no very warlike retinue at command. So I mounted half a dozen bowmen, who will ride and shoot with any Hun, and as many stout fellows who can wield lance or throw javelin, and here they are at your gates. Have no fear for the girls within doors; my men are both sober and chaste by prudence, if not by nature. There was a time when I had to make an example here and there'—he scowled a smile—'but now they know me.'

Basil replied as became him, not without some slight imitation of his guest's bluff manliness. Admiring, as he did, above all things, that which savoured of heroism, he was strongly impressed by Venantius, whose like, among natives of Rome, he had not yet beheld, who shone before him, indeed, in a nobler light than any man he had seen since the days when he worshipped Belisarius. Arrangements were speedily made for the entertainment of the little armed troop, and as dusk gathered the host and his two guests sat down to supper. Whilst the meal was being made ready, Basil had found opportunity of speech with Aurelia, who heard with great satisfaction of the coming of Venantius, and promised to receive him early on the morrow.

'The lady Aurelia's name is not unknown to me,' said Venantius, when Basil spoke of her at table. He would have added a remark, but paused with a look at the attendant slaves. 'Her illustrious father,' he went on, 'I spoke with when I was young. But for the illness of Maximus I should have ventured hither during this year gone by, notwithstanding some difference in our view of things; or rather, to make sure whether there really was as much difference as I supposed.'

'Perchance you would have found that there was not,' said Basil. 'Certainly not towards the end.'

'May his soul repose! He had the bearing which suited with his noble name—a true Anicius to look upon. If Rome have need in these times of another breed of citizens—and who can gainsay that?—she will not forget such men as he, who lived with dignity when they could do no more. You, my dear lord'—he turned towards Basil—'Anicius though you are, see another way before you, what?'

They talked far into the night. When he spoke of the Imperial conquerors—'Greeklings' he called them—Venantius gave vent to his wrath and scorn. The Goths were right when they asked what had ever come out of Greece save mimes and pirates; land-thieves they might have added, for what else were the generals of Justinian with their pillaging hordes? They dared to speak of the Goths as barbarians—these Herules, Isaurians, Huns, Armenians, and Teutons!—of the Goths, whose pride it had so long been to defend Roman civilisation, and even to restore the Roman edifices. What commander among them could compare with Totila, brave, just, generous?

'By the Holy Mother!' he cried, with a great gesture, 'if I were not wedded to a wife I love, who has borne me already three boys as healthy as wolf cubs, I would follow your example, O Basil, and take to myself a blue-eyed daughter of that noble race. They are heretics, why yes, but as far as I can make out they pray much as I do, and by heaven's grace may yet be brought to hold the truth as to the Three-in-One. When they had the power, did they meddle with our worship? Let every man believe as he list, say I, so that he believe sincerely, and trust God against the devil.'

In the stillness of their secluded abode, Aurelia and Veranilda went to rest earlier than usual this evening, for they were to arise before the dawn. This afternoon they had been visited by the black monk, who announced the return of Sisinnius, and invited them to the promised mass on the morrow; and such was their agitation in the foretaste of this religious ecstasy, as well as in the hope of having their future revealed to them, that neither slept much during the night. Not long after the crowing of the first cock, when all was silent and dark, Aurelia stepped, with a lamp in her hand, into the maiden's chamber.

'Is it the hour?' whispered Veranilda, raising herself.

'Not yet. I have had a troubled dream. I dreamt that this night the holy Sisinnius had fought with the demon, and had been worsted. O Veranilda!'—the speaker's voice trembled—'what may this mean?'

'Dearest lady,' answered the other reassuringly, 'may it not be a temptation of the demon himself; who at times is permitted to tempt even the holiest?'

'And you, sweet? You have not dreamt?'

'Only of Basil,' answered Veranilda, with a smile that asked pardon for her happiness.

They talked over the disquieting vision, whilst the little lamp-flame, wavering in breaths of air, cast strange shadows about the room. On the walls were faded frescoes, one of which represented the poetess Proba on her knees before St. Agnes. Impelled by her fears, Aurelia of a sudden knelt before this picture, and prayed silently to the virgin martyr. Then Veranilda rose from the couch, and knelt beside her. Having solaced their souls, they kissed each other tenderly.

'You are not afraid,' whispered Veranilda, 'that Basil may be in the garden when we go forth?'

'Basil? Ah, little rogue, have you betrayed yourself?'

'Of a truth, dearest lady, he has been there more than once, but not, oh not so early!'

'Nay, I hope not,' said Aurelia. 'It were scarce maidenly—'

'Never, never before the east had broken for the dayspring! Never, I swear to you, O my heart's friend!'

'Then there is small fear of his interrupting us this morning; all the more that he must have sat late with his friends, talking of many things. I am glad of the coming of this brave Venantius; it puts an end to every peril.'

They conversed on this encouraging theme until Aurelia's ear caught the sound of a footfall in the gallery. She stepped forth and encountered a female slave, who told her that there wanted two hours to dawn; it was time, then, to set forth and a few minutes saw them ready. In the garden they were met by the watchman, who carried a lantern. He, having merely been ordered to stand in readiness at this hour and being ignorant of his mistress's intention, showed astonishment when he saw Aurelia and her companion bent on going out. He took it for granted that he was to accompany them. But at this moment there appeared in the rays of the lantern a black figure, which had entered by the breach in the wall. Aurelia whispered a few words to her watchman, whose religion was the same as hers, and at once he dropped to his knees.

'Peace be with you, good brother,' said the monk, in his feeble voice, as he drew a lantern from beneath his cloak. 'You may not accompany us; but have no fear. The way is short.'

Forthwith he turned, and Aurelia, holding Veranilda's hand, followed where he lighted the way. For a few minutes they pursued a level path, then, passing between myrtles, began to descend the seaward slope. The ground was rough, but the monk, going before, marked the places for their footing. A few minutes thus, and they reached trees, black against a sky sown with stars and overshimmered by a wasted moon. Veranilda, who was trembling, clung to her companion's arm.

'How much further?' asked Aurelia, striving to make her voice firm. 'This is not the way by which I came before.'

'Scarce fifty steps. See you not the light yonder?'

Among the trees was perceptible a faint shining. Hand tight clasped in hand, the two moved forward over thick herbage, and still descended. They drew near to the light, and saw that it issued from a little cave. Within stood a man, bent as if with age and infirmities, his face half-hidden under a cowl. When the visitors were near, he stretched forth his arms, murmuring words of welcome, and the two knelt devoutly before him.

There was a moment of silence, then the cowled man again spoke, in a voice firmer and less senile.

'My daughters, you have come hither through the gloom of night and over rough places, led by a faithful guide, whom you followed without doubt or fear. You will have your reward. The darkness, the stones that made your feet to stumble, what are these but symbols of your spiritual state? In your blindness, you sought one blind as yourselves, to follow whom was to walk in darkness eternal. But a beneficent Power has watched over you, guiding your steps in the better way, whereof you recked not.'

Aurelia and Veranilda had raised their heads, and were gazing at him, in fearful astonishment.

'Be not troubled,' he went on, taking a step forward and speaking in a voice strong and clear. 'Though unworthy, I am a priest of the faith in which you, Aurelia, were baptized. In my hands you will suffer no harm, no indignity. Be still, be silent. Behind you stand those who will not permit you to flee, but who will conduct you hence as if they were your own attendants if you do but follow me, as you needs must, without cry or resistance.'

Aurelia turned and saw a number of figures whom the dim light showed to be men with weapons. A moan of anguish escaped her lips. Clinging to her in terrified silence, Veranilda seemed about to sink to the ground.

'Our way,' pursued the priest, who was now revealed as neither old nor infirm, 'is down to the harbour. Not far from here a litter awaits you; summon your strength for the short effort over rugged ground. Speak words of comfort to this maiden; she also will ere long walk in the light, and will be grateful to those who rescued her from the path of destruction. Think not to escape us when we pass through the city; it were vain to cry aloud; not a man in Surrentum would raise his hand to release you, knowing, as all do, that we confine your body only to free your soul from the bonds of the Enemy.'

'Whither are you taking us?' asked Aurelia, suddenly commanding herself, and speaking with cold scorn.

'That you will know before the evening. Enough for the present that you will travel without fatigue and without danger. Follow now whither I lead.'

He moved forward, and the armed men, half a dozen in number, among whom stood the black monk, closed about the prisoners. Seeing the futility of any resistance, Aurelia whispered to her companion such words of encouragement as she could find, and supported her with her arms. But Veranilda had overcome the first terror which made her droop.

'Basil will find and release us,' she whispered back. 'While he has life, Basil will not forsake us.'

And with unfaltering steps she moved onward, holding Aurelia's hand.

Their path, illumined by lanterns, the guards presently issued from the wood, and came to the place where the litter was waiting. Hence the captives were borne rapidly towards the haven. As they entered the city gates, Aurelia raised the curtain which concealed her, and looked out at the men on watch; words exchanged between them and her conductors only confirmed what the priest had said, and made her understand that she was powerless amid enemies.

'Are we not to have a look at the Gothic beauty?' cried one fellow, when the litter was passing.

'Peace!' answered the priest sternly; and nothing more was said.

Through the streets they were followed by a few persons. These, calling to each other, collected at length a small crowd, which hung about the litter when it reached the place of embarkation. Here torches were burning; their red glare fell upon angry or mocking faces, and every moment the crowd increased. With utmost speed the prisoners were passed into a little boat, then rowed to a vessel lying at the harbour mouth. As the ship hoisted sail, dawn began to glimmer over the flank of Vesuvius.

CHAPTER IX
CHORSOMAN

Fearful of sleeping till after sunrise, Basil had bidden Felix arouse him this morning; and, as he had much to talk of with Veranilda, he betook himself to the garden very early.

Aurelia's watchman was standing without, gazing anxiously now this way, now that, surprised by his mistress's failure to return; on the appearance of Basil he withdrew, but only to a spot whence he could survey the garden. All impatience, the lover waited, as minute after minute slowly passed. Dawn was broadening to day, but Veranilda came not. An agony of disappointment seized upon him, and he stood at length in the attitude of one sickening with despair. Then a footstep approached, and he saw the slave whose watch he had relieved come forward with so strange a look that Basil could only stare at him.

'My lord,' said the man, 'there is one at the gate of the villa who brings I know not what news for you.'

'One at the gate? News?' echoed Basil, his heart sinking with dread anticipation. 'What mean you, fellow?'

'Most noble, I know nothing,' stammered the frightened slave 'I beseech your greatness to inquire. They say—I know not what—'

Basil sped across the garden and into Aurelia's dwelling. Here he found a group of servants talking excitedly together; at view of him, they fell back as if fear-stricken. From one, Aurelia's old nurse, rose a wail of distress; upon her Basil rushed, grasped her by the arm, and sternly demanded what had happened. Dropping to her knees with a shrill cry, the woman declared that Aurelia had vanished, that some one from the city had seen her carried away before dawn.

'Alone?' asked Basil in a terrible voice.

'Lord, I know not,' wailed the woman, grovelling at his feet.

'Is Veranilda in her chamber?' he asked violently.

'Gone!' replied a faint voice from amid the group of servants.

'Where is this messenger?'

Without waiting for a reply, he sprang forward. In the portico which led to the villa he heard his name shouted, and he knew the voice for Marcian's; another moment and Marcian himself appeared, pale, agitated.

'Why do you seek me?' cried Basil.

'You come from yonder? Have you seen Aurelia? Then it is true.'

Marcian told the news brought up from Surrentum by some person unknown, who, having uttered it in the porter's ear, had at once fled.

'Go call Venantius,' said Basil, when he had heard the brief story, 'and bring him straight to Aurelia's house. They are gone; that slinking slave shall tell me how, or I will tear it out of him with his soul.'

Back he rushed, and found the nurse still crouching on the floor, wailing. He made her lead him to her lady's chamber, and to that of Veranilda, where nothing unusual met their eyes. The watchman was then summoned; he came like one half dead, and smote the ground with his forehead before the young noble, who stood hand on dagger. A fierce interrogatory elicited clear and truthful answers; when Basil learned what Aurelia had whispered to her servant as she went forth, he uttered a groan.

'Marcian! Venantius!' he cried, for at that moment the two entered the atrium. 'I understand it all. Why had I no fear of this?'

That Aurelia had been deceived and inveigled by one professing to be an Arian priest, seemed clear from the watchman's story. For the originator of the plot, Basil had not far to look. This was the vengeance of Petronilla. But whither the two captives would be conveyed, was less easy to conjecture. Perhaps to Cumae. The thought stung Basil to frenzy, for, if Veranilda once fell into the hands of the Greeks, what hope had he of ever seeing her again?

'Did Petronilla know?' he asked of Marcian.

'Who can say?' answered his friend, easily understanding the curtailed question. 'Like enough that she had sent to Cumae to learn all she could; and in that case, she found, you may be sure, ready instruments of her malice. Were it not better,' Marcian added in an aside, 'to tell Venantius what danger threatened Veranilda?'

The warlike Roman, who, aroused on an alarm, had instantly equipped himself with casque and sword, stood listening to what passed, sniffing the air and rolling his eyes about as if he desired nothing better than a conflict. The others now drew him aside into a more private place, and made known to him their reason for fearing that the Gothic maiden had been seized by emissaries from Cumae.

'Had I heard that story before,' said Venantius, all but laughing with angry surprise, 'Veranilda would now be safe in my castle; for, instead of lingering, I should have come straightway, to rescue her and you. Holy Peter and Paul! You sported here, day after day, knowing that the hounds of Justinian had scent of the maid you carried away? You, Basil, might commit such folly, for you were blinded to everything by your love. But, Marcian, how came you to let him loll in his dream of security? Why did you conceal this from me? By Castor! it was unfriendly as it was imprudent. You robbed me of a sweet morsel when you denied me the chance of balking the Greeks in such a matter as this. Nay, the bird is caged at Cumae, be sure.'

Marcian's brows were knit, and his eyes cast down as he listened to this reproof.

'I had not thought of Petronilla,' he murmured. 'But for her, the danger was not pressing. That thick-skulled Hun at Cumae easily let himself be blinded, as I told you.'

'How could I forget,' cried Basil, 'that Petronilla would risk damnation rather than lose her vengeance upon Aurelia But,' he added, with sudden change from gloom to vehemence, 'that woman is not beyond our reach. Only yesterday did she set forth for Rome, and she may have passed the night at Neapolis. A horseman will easily overtake her. Felix!' he shouted. 'Our horses!—she shall pay for this if my hands can get at her throat!'

Felix appeared, but not in answer to his master's summons; he came precipitately, followed by a swarm of frightened slaves, to announce another surprise. Before the villa stood a hostile multitude, folk of Surrentum, who demanded admittance, and, if denied, would enter by force. At this news Venantius hastened to muster his troop of archers and spearmen. Basil and Marcian, having made sure that all entrances were locked and barred, went to the front gate, and through a wicket surveyed the assailants. These seemed to be mainly of the baser class; they had armed themselves with all sorts of rude weapons, which they brandished menacingly, shouting confused maledictions. From the porter Basil learned that those who had first presented themselves at the door had demanded that 'the heretics' should be given up to them; and by listening to the cries, he understood that the wrath of these people was directed against the Arian servants brought hither by Aurelia. Through the wicket he held colloquy with certain leaders of the throng.

'The heretics! Yield to us the accursed heretics!' shouted a burly fellow armed with an ox-goad.

'For what usage?' asked Basil.

'That's as they choose. If they like to come before the bishop and turn Christian—why, a little correction shall suffice. If not, they have only themselves and the devil to blame.'

By this time Venantius and his retainers stood in the forecourt. To him, the routing of such a rabble seemed a task not worth speaking of, but some few would no doubt be slain, and Basil shrank from such extremities.

'Would you give up these trembling wretches?' asked Venantius scornfully, pointing to the four slaves, male and female, Arians either by origin or by conversion to please Aurelia, whom she had brought from Cumae. On their knees they were imploring protection.

'Nay, I will fight for their safety,' Basil answered. 'But if we can frighten off this tag-rag without bloodshed so much the better.'

Venantius consented to make the attempt. On the upper villa was an open gallery looking over the entrance, and fully visible from where the invaders stood. Hither the armed men ascended and stood in line, the bowmen with arrows on string. Their lord, advancing to the parapet, made a signal demanding silence, and spoke in a audible to every ear in the throng.

'Dogs! You came on this errand thinking that the villa was defenceless. See your mistake! Each one of these behind me has more arrows in store than all your number, and never shot bolt from bow without piercing the mark. Off! Away with your foul odours and your yelping throats! And if, when you have turned tail, any cur among you dares to bark back that I, Venantius of Nuceria, am no true Catholic, he shall pay for the lie with an arrow through chine and gizzard!' This threat he confirmed with a terrific oath of indisputable orthodoxy.

The effect was immediate. Back fell the first rank of rioters, pressing against those in the rear; and without another cry, with only a low, terrified growling and snarling, the crowd scattered in flight.

'There again I see Petronilla,' declared Basil, watching the rout with fierce eyes. 'I'll swear that, before starting, she set this game afoot. I must after her, Venantius.'

'Alone?'

'Mother of God! if I had your men! But I will make soldiers of my own. Some of the likeliest from our folk here shall follow me; enough to stay that she-wolf's journey till I can choke the truth out of her.'

Venantius, his eyes fixed on the descending road by which the rabble had disappeared, caught sight of something which held him mute for a moment. Then he gave a snort of surprise.

'What's this? There are no Greek soldiers in Surrentum.'

Yet unmistakable soldiers of the Imperial army were approaching. First came into sight a commanding officer; he rode a little in advance of the troop, which soon showed itself to consist of some two score mounted men, armed with bows and swords. And in the rear came the rabble of Surrentines, encouraged to return by this arrival of armed authority.

'That is Chorsoman,' said Marcian, as soon as he could distinguish the captain's feature, 'the commander at Cumae.'

'Then it is not to Cumae that they have carried her!' exclaimed Basil, surmising at once that the Hun was come in pursuit of Veranilda.

'Time enough to think of that,' growled Venantius, as he glared from under black brows at the advancing horsemen. 'What are we to do? To resist is war, and this villa cannot be held for an hour. Yet to yield is most likely to be made prisoners. Marcian!'

Marcian was watching and listening with a look of anxious thought. Appealed to for his counsel, he spoke decidedly.

'Withdraw your men and go down. Resistance is impossible. Chorsoman must enter, but trust me to manage him. I answer for your liberty.'

Venantius led his men down to the inner court. Basil, careless of everything but the thought that Veranilda was being borne far from him, he knew not whither, went to get horses ready, that he might pursue Petronilla as soon as the road was free. Marcian, having spoken with the porter, waited till a thundering at the gate announced Chorsoman's arrival, then had the doors thrown open, and stood with a calm smile to meet the commander.

'Fair greeting to your Magnificence!' he began with courtesy. 'Be welcome to this villa, where, in absence of its mistress, I take upon myself to offer you hospitality.'

Chorsoman had dismounted, and stood with half a dozen of his followers behind him in the portico. At sight of Marcian his face became suspicious.

'By mistress,' he replied gruffly, stepping forward, 'I suppose you mean the daughter of Maximus. Where is she?'

Marcian would have continued the conversation within, but the Hun chose to remain standing in the for-court, the gate wide open. From the Surrentines he had already heard the story of Aurelia's disappearance, which puzzled and angered him, for no one professed to be able to explain what had happened, yet his informants declared that the Roman lady and the Gothic maiden had been carried away without the knowledge of the men who were their protectors. This was now repeated by Marcian, who professed himself overwhelmed by the event.

'You have here one Basilius,' said Chorsoman.

'The same whom your greatness saw on a certain occasion at Cumae.'

'They tell me he was about to wed with Veranilda. What does that mean?'

'An idle rumour,' replied Marcian, 'springing from vulgar gossip, and from the spiteful anger of the lady sister of Maximus, who hoped to inherit what has fallen to her niece. Let your valorous magnificence be assured that there is no truth in it. Can you imagine that I, whose mission is known to you, should have looked on at such an audacity? I think your perspicuity will not require better proof of the powers with which I am intrusted than that I gave you at Cumae?'

Of the profound contempt proclaimed, rather than disguised, by Marcian's extravagant courtesy, Chorsoman had no inkling; but his barbaric mind resented the complexity of things with which it was confronted, and he felt a strong inclination to take this smooth-tongued Latin by the throat, so as to choke the plain truth out of him. Why, he demanded fiercely, had not Aurelia and her companion travelled straight on to Rome, as he had been assured they were to do?

'For a simple reason,' answered Marcian. 'I judged an escort necessary, and only yesterday did I obtain it. This very day should we have set forth.'

'You speak of one Venantius and his followers—he who just now, I am told, threatened to massacre the harmless citizens of Surrentum.'

'I would rather say the most noble Venantius, a senator, but for whose presence this villa would have been sacked by a thievish rabble from below.'

'Let me see him,' said the Hun, his eyes like those of a boar at bay.

'Will it please your Illustrious Magnanimity to eat with us?'

'I will eat when I choose. Fetch here Venantius.'

Marcian despatched the porter, and in a few moments Venantius appeared, behind him his armed men. A hand lightly on his sword, as though he played with the hilt, his head proudly erect, the Roman noble paused at a few paces from the Hun, and regarded him with bold steadfastness.

'You serve the Emperor?' said Chorsoman, somewhat less overbearingly than he had spoken hitherto.

'When occasion offers,' was the dry response.

On the Hun's countenance grew legible the calculation busying his thought. At a glance he had taken the measure of Venantius, and gauged the worth of the men behind him. A smile, which could not mask its cunning, came on to his lips, and all of a sudden he exchanged his truculence for amiability.

'Lord Venantius,' he said, laying an open palm on his own breast, and then motioning with it towards the Roman, 'you and I, two men of valour, can understand each other in few words. I am no talker'—his narrow eyes glanced at Marcian—'nor are you. Tell me, if you can, what has become of the lady Aurelia and of the Gothic maiden who attended upon her.'

'Lord Chorsoman,' replied Venantius, 'I thought it was you who could have answered that question. The ladies Aurelia and Veranilda have this morning disappeared, and we judged it likely that they had been enticed from the villa to be captured and borne to Cumae.'

'Who should have done that?'

'Emissaries of your own, we supposed.'

The Hun reflected.

'This man of words'—he nodded sideways at Marcian—'spoke of a woman's malice. Explain to me.'

Venantius told what he knew of Petronilla's enmity, and the listener had no difficulty in coming to the conclusion which to Basil had been evident from the first. It was possible moreover, that Cumae might be the place to which the captives had been conveyed, for Chorsoman had left the fortress yesterday to come hither by way of Neapolis, his reason for the expedition being news of Veranilda's approaching marriage, brought to him by a fisherman who said he had been paid by a person unknown. Did Petronilla, he next inquired, know that Veranilda was to be sent to the East? To this Marcian replied with a negative, adding:

'Unless your Illustrious Discretion have seen fit to spread abroad what I imparted to your private ear.'

'My tongue is not so loose as yours,' was the Hun's rejoinder.

Again he reflected, with the result that he decided to send a messenger at once to Cumae. Until news could be brought back he should remain here in the villa. This intention he announced in a tone abundantly significant, his hearers understanding that Aurelia's property was now in hands not accustomed to relax their grasp.

'Lord Venantius,' he added, 'as your escort is no longer needed, you will wish, no doubt, to return forthwith to your own abode. It will not be long before you have the occasion you desire of proving your loyalty to the Emperor. Brave men both, we may presently fight side by side. Let us sit at table together, and then good-speed!'

With a haughty glare Venantius heard this dismissal. A reply surged into his throat, but he swallowed it again, remembering that more than his personal safety was at stake.

'You will pardon me, lord,' he replied, 'if I do not stay to break my fast. I am of impatient humour, and never willingly linger when a journey is before me.'

'As you will,' said Chorsoman, with a slight knitting of his brows. 'You ride alone, I suppose?'

'The lord Basil, who starts for Rome, will give me his company as far as our ways are one.'

Chorsoman gave a glance at the soldiers in his rear, then at Marcian, and smiled grimly.

'I fear you must go without lord Basil. I shall have need of him.'

There was a very short silence; then Marcian spoke, with bland decision.

'Commander, this cannot be. Basil carries letters of urgency to Rome and Ravenna; letters which I would not intrust to any one else. Your Sublimity will see that it is impossible to delay him.'

Teeth hard set, and eyes aflame, the Hun took a step forward. In the same instant, Venantius laid a hand upon his sword, and, at the gesture, his armed men looked to their weapons.

'Where is this Basil?' demanded Chorsoman.

'I will let him know if you wish to speak with him,' replied Marcian.

'You shall be spared the trouble. Lord Venantius, bid your followers retire and get their horses ready, whilst you and I go in search of lord Basil. You will not refuse me your company for a few minutes?'

Cunning had again subdued the Hun's violence, and discretion prevailed with the Roman. Together they passed through the atrium, Chorsoman casting eager glances about him, and to the inner court; but the followers of Venantius, obedient to a silent order, still kept their position in face of the Greek soldiers, and this Chorsoman knew.

'You understand,' said the Hun, when they were alone together, you, a brave and honourable man, how my duty to the Emperor obliges me to act. I, of course, take possession of this villa until Aurelia is discovered. And, however important his mission, I cannot allow Basil to depart without some security—you will understand that.'

The barbarous accent with which these sentences were uttered caused Venantius almost as much disgust as the plundering purpose they avowed.

'What security?' he asked.

Chorsoman named a large sum of money. As he spoke, Basil himself appeared; and with brief preface, the matter under debate was reported to him. He glanced at Venantius but could find no counsel in the dark, stern face. Foreseeing the result of the Hun's visit, Basil had hastened to conceal on his own person a considerable weight of coin, and had intrusted something like the same amount to Felix. In the treasure chamber lay a mass of wealth now belonging to Aurelia, and the mere fact of this being under lock and key by no means secured it against the commander's greed. Marcian came forward, and hearing the talk of ransom, endeavoured to awe the Hun into moderation, but with less success than he had had at Cumae. So he led Basil aside, told him of the messenger sent to Cumae, as well as of the inventions by which Chorsoman had been beguiled, and counselled mere inaction until news came. Marcian then inquired of the commander whether, in case Veranilda were found at Cumae, he would permit her to be sent on to Rome under the escort already provided; but to this Chorsoman vouchsafed no direct reply: he would consider the matter.

Negotiations had reached this point when new visitors arrived, the Bishop of Surrentum and presbyter Joannes. Though suffering much, the good bishop had risen from bed as soon as the exciting events of this morning had reached his ear His innocence of complicity in the plot against Aurelia and Veranilda, no one who saw him could doubt; with astonishment he had heard of the priests and their armed attendants, and with indignation of the citizens' tumultuous behaviour. What right or reason had folk to proclaim that Aurelia was still a heretic, and that she should not have been allowed to inherit property? Who, he asked severely, could read her heart? And when inquiry made it too certain that all this angry feeling had originated with Petronilla, the prelate shook his head sadly, thinking more than he cared to say. Arrived at the villa, he first of all learnt all he could as to the position of things (declaring total ignorance when the Hun sought to examine him as to the relations of Basil and Veranilda), then made earnest inquiry whether there really were slaves here who professed Arianism. The four were summoned; overcome with dread, they prostrated them selves, and entreated the bishop to make them Catholics Having heard from them that they all had been baptized (the Roman Church held the baptism of Arians valid), he sent them apart for summary instruction by Joannes, and afterwards laid his reconciling hands upon them. Thus had the Church gained four members, and the good folk of Surrentum lost a heretic-baiting.

With the proceedings of the Imperial commander the worthy cleric could not interfere. He spoke privately with Basil, and betrayed, in a gentle severity of mien, his suspicion of the young noble's state of mind, but of this not a word fell from him; his concern seemed to be solely with the lady Aurelia, regarding whom he would set every possible inquiry on foot. He advised Basil not to leave the neighbourhood for a day or two, and to communicate with him before he went far. Gratefully Basil kissed the old man's hand. They never met again. A week later the bishop was dead.

After all, Venantius sat at table with Chorsoman. Fuming, he waited till the next morning, when, if the news could be believed, it became certain that Aurelia and her companion were not at Cumae. Basil, having no choice, then paid for ransom nearly all the money he had secreted, and rode away with Venantius, purposing to remain at Nuceria until joined by Marcian. Three days later Marcian appeared at the castle He brought no intelligence of the lost ladies. As for their abode, it had been thoroughly pillaged; the treasure chamber was discovered and broken open; not a coin, not a vessel or ornament which had its price, not a piece of silk, had escaped the clutches of the Hun.

Chorsoman's departure was followed by an invasion of the Surrentines, who robbed more grossly. A fire broke out in the house of Proba, and much of that building was destroyed. In the once magnificent villa there lurked but a few slaves, who knew not whether their owner lived.

CHAPTER X
THE ANICIANS

Not many days after, in a still noontide of mellow autumn, Basil and Marcian drew towards Rome. They rode along the Via Appia, between the tombs of ancient men; all about them, undulant to the far horizon, a brown wilderness dotted with ruins. Ruins of villas, of farms, of temples, with here and there a church or a monastery that told of the newer time. Olives in scant patches, a lost vineyard, a speck of tilled soil, proved that men still laboured amid this vast and awful silence, but rarely was a human figure visible. As they approached the city, marshy ground and stagnant pools lay on either hand, causing them to glance sadly at those great aqueducts, which for ages had brought water into Rome from the hills and now stood idle, cleft by the Goths during the siege four years ago.

They rode in silence, tired with their journey, occupied with heavy or anxious thoughts. Basil, impatient to arrive, was generally a little ahead. Their attendants numbered half a dozen men, among them Felix and Sagaris, and two mules laden with packs came in the rear. Earthworks and rough buildings of military purpose, again recalling the twelve months' blockade, presently appeared; churches and oratories told them they were passing the sacred ground of the catacombs; then they crossed the little Almo, rode at a trot along a hollow way, and saw before them the Appian Gate. Only a couple of soldiers were on guard; these took a careless view of the travellers, and let them pass without speaking.

Marcian rode up to his friend's side, and spoke softly.

'You have promised to be advised by me.'

Basil answered only with a dull nod.

'I will see her to-day,' continued the other, 'and will bring you the news before I sleep.'

'Do so.'

No more words passed between them. On their left hand they saw the Thermae of Caracalla, their external magnificence scarce touched by decay, but waterless, desolate; in front rose the Caelian, covered with edifices, many in ruin, and with neglected or altogether wild gardens; the road along which they went was almost as silent as that without the walls. Arrived at a certain point, the two looked at each other and waved a hand; then Marcian, with Sagaris and one other servant, pushed forward, whilst Basil, followed by the rest of the train, took an ascending road to the right.

The house in which he was born, and where he alone now ruled, stood on the summit of the Caelian. Before it stood the ruined temple of Claudius, overlooking the Flavian Amphitheatre; behind it ranged the great arches of the Neronian aqueduct; hard by were the round church of St. Stephen and a monastery dedicated to St. Erasmus. By a narrow, grass-grown road, between walls overhung with ivy, Basil ascended the hill; but for the occasional bark of a dog, nothing showed that these buildings of old time were inhabited; and when he drew rein before his own portico, the cessation of the sound of hoofs made a stillness like that among the Appian sepulchres. Eyeless, hoary, with vegetation rooted here and there, the front of the house gave no welcome. Having knocked, Basil had to wait for some moments before there came a sign of opening. With drooped head, he seemed to watch the lizards playing in the sunshine upon a marble column.

A wicket opened, and at once there sounded from within an exclamation of joyful surprise. After much clanking, the door yielded, and an elderly servant, the freedman Eugenius, offered greeting to his lord. Basil's first question was whether Decius had been there; he learnt that his kinsman was now in the house, having come yesterday to reside here from the Anician palace beyond the Tiber.

'Tell him at once that I am here. Stay; I dare say he is in the library. I will go to him.'

He passed through the atrium, adorned with ancestral busts and with the consular fasces which for centuries had signified nothing, through a room hung with tapestry and floored with fine mosaic, through the central court, where the fountain was dry, and by a colonnade reached the secluded room which was called library, though few books remained out of the large collection once guarded here. In a sunny embrasure, a codex open on his knees, sat the pale student; seeing Basil, he started up in great surprise, and, when they had embraced, regarded him anxiously.

'How is this? What has happened? Some calamity, I see.'

'Seek some word, O Decius, to utter more than that. I have suffered worse than many deaths.'

'My best, my dearest Basil!' murmured the other tenderly. 'You have lost her?'

'Lost her? yes; but not as you mean it. Is Petronilla in Rome?'

'She arrived the day before yesterday, two hours after sunset.'

'And you have seen her, talked with her?'

'I was at the house yonder when she came.'

'And she behaved ill to you?' asked Basil.

'Far from that, Petronilla overwhelmed me with affection and courtesy. I knew not,' proceeded Decius smiling, 'how I had all at once merited such attention. I came away merely because this situation better suits my health. Down by the river I have never been at ease. But let me hear what has befallen you.'

Basil told his story, beginning with the explanation of Veranilda's importance in the eyes of the Greek commander. After learning from the Hun that nothing was known of the lost ladies at Cumae, he had impatiently lingered for three days in the castle of Venantius, on the chance that Marcian might be able to test the truth of Chorsoman's report; but his friend made no discovery, and in despair he set out for Rome. To all this Decius listened with wonder and with sympathy. He had no difficulty in crediting Petronilla with such a plot, but thought she could scarce have executed it without the help of some one in authority. Such a person, he added cautiously, as a deacon of the Roman Church. Hereupon Basil exclaimed that he and Marcian had had the same suspicion.

'I will find her,' he cried, 'if it cost me my life! And I will be revenged upon those who have robbed me of her. She may at this moment be in Rome. The ship that carried her off was large enough, they say, to make the voyage, and winds have been favourable. My good Decius, I am so overcome with misery that I forget even to ask how you sped on the sea.'

'A smooth and rapid voyage. I had only time to reperuse with care the *Silvae* of Statius—his Epicedion being appropriate to my mood. Arrived at Portus, I sent a post to those who awaited the ship's coming, and the remains of Maximus were brought with all due honour to their resting place.'

'Was the deacon Leander here to receive you?' asked Basil.

'I learnt that he had not yet been heard of.'

They exchanged a significant look, and Basil remarked that he would soon discover the deacon's movements since his leaving Surrentum. Marcian was even now on his way to visit Petronilla, and would come with news this evening.

'If I could know,' he cried, 'whether she has been delivered to the Greeks, or is kept imprisoned by that Megaera! It may be that Petronilla is ignorant of what I have told you; yet, if so, I fear she will soon learn it, for Chorsoman will write—if the barbarian can write—to Bessas, and cannot but mention her. There are prisons in Rome for those who offend the tyrant of Byzantium.'

'It troubles me to hear you say that,' said Decius, with an anxious glance.

'I, too, may be in peril, you think,' replied his kinsman gloomily. 'True, all the more that I am known to have just inherited. Bessas takes a peculiar interest in such people. Be that as it will. Let us turn for a moment to other things.'

They spoke of the duties that had to be discharged by Basil as his uncle's heir. On the morrow he must assemble such of his kinsfolk as were in Rome, and exhibit to them the testament. Aurelia's part in it would of course excite discussion, perhaps serious objection; whereas her disappearance would probably be regarded as a matter of small moment, and Petronilla, even if suspected, could count on sympathy. When he left the library, Basil found all the members of his household, from the old nurse Aguella, whose privilege it was to treat him with motherly affection, to the men who groomed his horse, assembled outside to give him welcome. His character and bearing were such as earn the good-will of dependents; though proud and impatient, he never behaved harshly, and a service well rendered often had its recognition. Among the young men of his rank, he was notable for temperance in pleasures; his slaves regarded him as above common temptations of the flesh, and, though this might be a loss to them in one way, they boasted of it when talking to the slaves of masters less exceptional. Having learnt from Felix that their lord was heir of Maximus, the servants received him with even more than wonted respect. One of them was the steward of his estate in Picenum, who had arrived at Rome a few days ago; with him Basil had private talk, received money which the man had brought, heard of the multitudinous swine in his oak forest, and of the yield of his fruit trees. That strip of the Adriatic coast south of Ancona had always been famous for its pears and apples, and choice examples of the fruit lay on Basil's table to-day. When he had supped, he anxiously awaited the coming of Marcian. It was two hours after nightfall before his friend appeared, having come in a litter, with torch-bearing attendants, from the Palatine, where he had supped with Bessas, the Greek commander.

The news he brought was disquieting. Bessas had just received despatches from Cumae, which acquainted him with the story of Veranilda's disappearance, so far as it was known to Chorsoman; he wore a heavy brow about the business, swore that the Gothic damsel should be found, if it cost the skins of all who had had anything to do with her.

'I partly soothed the brute,' concluded Marcian, 'by telling him that Petronilla was within such easy reach. Her he will summon to-morrow.'

'You promised to see her,' said Basil impatiently.

'Do I often break my promises? I saw her before going even to my own house, with the dust of the journey still upon me.'

'Ever kind Marcian?'

'Why so hasty to think me less than kind?' returned the other, with his smile of sad irony. 'I saw her, though with difficulty. She kept me waiting like an importunate poor kinsman, and when I was received, she sat like the Empress giving audience. I did not touch the earth with my forehead; nay, I stood looking at her with a look she did not easily bear. That she is guilty, I am sure; I read triumph in her eyes as soon as I spoke of Aurelia. That she would deny all knowledge of the affair was only to be expected. Moreover, she has taken possession of the great house yonder, and declares that Aurelia, as a heretic, can claim nothing under her father's will. You, of course, the heir, can expel her, if you think it worth the trouble. But let us see the result of her conversation with Bessas. She smiled disdainfully when I mentioned his name, and tried to continue smiling when I carelessly explained the interest he had in finding Veranilda; but she was frightened, I heard it in her hoarse voice when she began to speak evil of Veranilda.'

'What!' cried Basil. 'Evil of Veranilda!'

'Such as naturally comes to the tongue of an angry woman.'

The lover raged, Marcian listening with a sad, half-absent look. Their talk continued for a long time, arid, because of the lateness of the hour, Marcian stayed to sleep in his friend's house. Before sunrise on the morrow, Basil sent forth his invitations to all of the Anician blood in Rome. The first to respond was Gordianus, whose dwelling on the Clivus Scauri stood but a few minutes' walk away. Though but a little older than Basil, Gordian had been for several years a husband and a father; he was in much esteem for his worldly qualities, and more highly regarded for the fervour of his religious faith. A tall, handsome, dignified man, he looked straight before him with frank eyes, and his lips told of spirit tempered by kindliness. Between him and his relative no great intimacy existed, for their modes of life and of thought were too dissimilar, but each saw the good in the other, and was attracted by it. Not long ago Gordian had conceived the project of giving his young sister Aemiliana as wife to Basil. Maximus favoured this design, but his nephew showed no eagerness to carry it out, and Roman gossip presently found a reason for that. Among the leaders of fashion and of pleasure—for fashion and pleasure did not fail to revive in Rome soon after the horrors of the siege—shone a lady named Heliodora, the Greek wife of a little-respected senator, who, favoured by Bessas, rose to the position of City Prefect. With Heliodora's character rumour made very free; the captives of her beauty were said to be numerous, and one of the names mentioned by those who loved such scandal was that of the young Basil. Gordian, finding that there was some ground for this suspicion, spoke no more of the suggested marriage, and it was at his instance that Maximus, ill in Campania, summoned Basil away from the city. Reports from Surrentum gave reason to hope that this measure had succeeded. But to-day, as he entered Basil's house, Gordian's face wore a troubled look, and there was no warmth in his response to the greeting which met him.

'You have sent for me, my dear lord,' he began with grave and distant courtesy, 'to speak of the matter of your inheritance. Forgive me if I first of all ask you a question—of more intimate concern. Is it true that you have taken a wife?'

Basil, in whom fatigue and misery had left little patience, began quivering in every nerve, and made blunt answer:

'It is not true, arid she who told you contrived the lie.'

'You speak of the lady Petronilla,' pursued Gordian gently. 'Can I think that she has wilfully deceived me?'

'Think it not, my lord Gordian,' returned the other; 'if Petronilla told you I was married, she lied.'

'That is strange indeed. Listen, I pray you, to the story heard in Rome since Petronilla returned. It is right that you should hear it just as it comes from her own lips.'

Thereupon Gordian repeated a narrative which would have been substantially true had it not crowned Basil's love with marriage. The listener, shaken with violent passion, could scarce wait till the end.

'And now hear *me*,' he cried. 'If I were prudent, I also should lie, for the truth may be dangerous. But you shall know it, O Gordian, and if you choose to harm me—'

The other raised a hand, and so full of dignity was this gesture, so solemn the look which accompanied it, that Basil's vehemence felt itself rebuked; he grew silent and listened.

'Basil, check your tongue, which I see will be your greatest peril. Do not confide in me, for I know not whether I can respect your confidence. Let us speak of other things.'

The younger man stood for a moment in hesitancy, his cheeks aflame, his eyes fiercely gleaming.

'As you will,' he exclaimed, mastering himself. 'When the others are here, you will learn all that it concerns you to know. Remember, Gordian, that I would have opened my heart to you, for, whatever I said, I know well that you are no betrayer. As for that woman—'

He was interrupted by the arrival of several persons, old and young, who appeared in answer to his summons. Having received them with colder courtesy than was natural to him, Basil produced the testament of Maximus, and submitted it to his kinsmen's inspection. The tablets passed from hand to hand; the signatures and seals of the seven witnesses were examined, the contents read and discussed. Meanwhile guests continued to arrive, until a considerable gathering, which included several ladies, had assembled in the great hall. Here was represented all that deemed itself best and most illustrious in the society of Rome. More came than were expressly invited; for, beyond the legitimate interest of the occasion, curiosity had been aroused by the gossip of Petronilla, and some whose connection with the Anician house was of the very slightest, hastened to present themselves at Basil's door. Hither came men whose names recalled the glories of the Republic; others who were addressed by appellations which told of Greek dominion; alike they claimed the dignity of Roman optimates, and deemed themselves ornaments of an empire which would endure as long as the world. Several ranked as senators; two or three were ex-consuls; ten years ago the last consul of Rome had laid down his shadowy honours; one had held the office of Praetorian Prefect when Theodoric was king; yet, from the political point of view, all were now as powerless as their own slaves. Wealth a few of them still possessed, but with no security; a rapacious Byzantine official, the accident of war, might at any moment strip them of all they had. For the most part they had already sunk to poverty, if not to indigence; among these aristocratic faces were more than one which bore the mark of privation. Those who had little means or none lived as parasites of more fortunate relatives; though beggars, they housed in palaces—palaces, it is true, which had often no more comfort within their marble walls than the insulae where the ignoble laid their heads.

When all had perused the will, Basil rose up and addressed them. He began by a seemingly careless allusion to the tattle about himself, which, as it appeared, had been started in Rome by some one who wished him ill. The serious matter of which he had to speak regarded the daughter of Maximus. No one here, of course, would be inclined to take up the defence of Aurelia, whose history was known to all, he would merely make known to them that after having abjured her religious errors, and when living quietly in the Surrentine villa, she had been treacherously seized and carried off he knew not whither. It was not difficult to surmise by whom this plot had been laid, but he would leave that point for his hearers' discussion. Him it chiefly concerned to make known the strange facts so far as he knew them; and this he proceeded to do. Basil concluded with sarcastic reference to the possibility that he, as heir, might be openly or secretly suspected of having laid hands upon Aurelia; that point also he left to be debated by such as thought it worth while.

Only some two or three of those who listened had any personal interest in the will, and few cared at all for the fate of Aurelia; but the lady at whom

Basil's innuendo pointed enjoyed no great favour, and her absence from this family gathering made it possible to discuss with all freedom the likelihood of her culpability. At Basil himself no suspicion glanced, but the rumour of his marriage with a Goth had excited much curiosity, hardly appeased by a whisper that Gordian declared the story false. Having spoken all he thought fit to say, Basil was going apart with the persons to whom legacies had been left, he, as heir, being charged with the execution of the will, when Gordian approached him, and begged for a word in private.

'I would not have you think me unkind, dear Basil,' he said, in a gentle voice. 'It was neither the place nor the moment to hear secrets from you, and I am glad now that I refused to listen; but be assured that I put faith in what you have declared to us.'

'It is well, dear Gordian,' replied Basil frankly.

'One word I will add,' continued the other. 'If you are troubled about things of the world, if you lack counsel such as you think a friend might give, delay not in coming to me. I should not speak thus confidently did I speak of myself alone; but there is one ever at my side, who with her wisdom— sometimes I think it divinely bestowed—supplies the weakness of my own understanding. Guided by her, I cannot counsel you amiss.'

They parted with an embrace, and Basil turned to the business of the moment. This occupied him until nearly mid-day. As he took leave of the last of his guests, there entered Marcian; his coming surprised Basil, for they had parted at early morning not to meet again before the morrow.

'I bring you an invitation,' said Marcian, in a careless tone, which was not quite natural. 'It is to the Palatine, after dinner.'

'To the Palatine? I am summoned by Bessas?'

'In a friendly way. Have no anxiety. Petronilla has been examined this morning, and, from what I can gather, she seems to have betrayed herself. Bessas wore the smile which means that he has over-reached somebody.'

'Then we shall find her,' exclaimed Basil.

'They will find her, I doubt not,' was the reply.

The meal being ready, they sat down to eat together, but their appetite was small. Decius, who had wearied himself this morning in finding discreet answers to the questions with which he was privately assailed by his kinsfolk, did not come to table. Having dined, Basil and his friend set forth on foot, half a dozen servants walking behind them. Midway in the descent of the Caelian, they were met by an odd procession: a beautiful boy of some twelve years old, clad in yellow, riding upon a small white ass with rich housings, and behind him three slaves, dark-visaged men of the East, on mules of great size, caparisoned with yellow cloth, to which hung innumerable tinkling bells. At sight of Basil, the child drew rein; jumped down, and ran forward with smiling demonstrations of respect.

'What is it, Laetus?' asked Basil, with no welcome upon his sombre countenance. 'I cannot talk with you now.'

The boy, who had been sold into slavery from the far island of the Angles, did but smatter the Roman tongue. With a few words to signify that his message was important, he delivered a letter, and Basil, turning aside impatiently, broke the seal. Upon the blank side of a slip of papyrus cut from some old manuscript were written lines which seemed to be in Greek, and proved to be Latin in Greek characters, a foppery beginning to be used by the modish at Rome.

'Heliodora to Basil. You are bidden to supper. Come if you will. If you come not, I care not.'

'Say that I gave you no reply,' were Basil's blunt words, as he walked on past the ass and the mules.

CHAPTER XI
SEEKING

They passed beneath the walls of the amphitheatre and by Constantine's triumphal arch. Like all the innumerable fountains of the city, the Meta Sudans stood dry; around the base of the rayed colossus of Apollo, goats were browsing. Thence they went along by the Temple of Venus and Rome, its giant columns yet unshaken, its roof gleaming with gilded bronze; and so under the Arch of Titus, when, with a sharp turn to the left, they began the ascent of the Palatine.

The vast buildings which covered the Imperial hill, though discoloured by the lapse of ages and hung with ivy, had suffered little diminution of their external majesty; time had made them venerable, but had not shattered their walls. For two centuries and a half, they had stood all but desolate, and within that time had thrice been sacked by barbarians, yet something of the riches and art which made their ancient glory was still discoverable in the countless halls and chambers; statues, busts, mural paintings, triumphs of mosaic, pictured hangings, had in many parts escaped the spoiler and survived ruin; whilst everywhere appeared the magnificence of rare stones, the splendours of royal architecture, the beauty of unsurpassed carving. Though owls nested where empresses were wont to sleep, and nettles pierced where the lord of the world feasted his courtiers, this was still the Palace of those who styled themselves Ever August; each echo seemed to repeat an immortal name, and in every gallery seemed to move the shadows of a majestic presence.

Belisarius had not resided here, preferring for his abode the palace of the Pincian. His successor in the military government of Rome chose a habitation on the deserted hill, in that portion of its complex structures which had been raised by Vespasian and his sons. Thither the two visitors were now directing their steps. Having passed a gateway, where Marcian answered with a watchword the challenge of the guard, they ascended a broad flight of stairs, and stood before an entrance flanked with two great pillars of Numidian marble, toned by time to a hue of richest orange. Here stood soldiers, to whom again the password was given. Entering, they beheld a great hall, surrounded by a colonnade of the Corinthian order, whereon had been lavished exquisite carving; in niches behind the columns stood statues in basalt, thrice the size of life, representing Roman emperors, and at the far end was a tribune with a marble throne. This, once the hall of audience, at present served as a sort of antechamber; here and there loitered a little group of citizens, some of whom had been waiting since early morning for speech with the commander; in one corner, soldiers played at dice, in another a notary was writing at a table before which stood two ecclesiastics. Voices and footsteps made a faint, confused reverberation under the immense vault.

Anxiously glancing about him, Basil followed his conductor across the hall and out into a peristyle, its pavement richly tesselated, and the portico, still elaborately adorned with work in metal and in marble, giving proof of still greater magnificence in bygone time; pedestals had lost their statues, and blank spaces on the wall told of precious panelling torn off. Beyond, they came to a curtained doorway, where they were detained for some moments by the sentry; then the curtain was drawn aside, and Basil found himself in the triclinium of the Flavian palace, now used by the Greek general as his public reception room. Its size was not much less than that of the hall of audience; its decoration in the same grandiose style. Enormous pillars of granite supported the roof; statues stood, or had stood, all around; the pavement, composed of serpentine, porphyry, and Numidian marble in many hues, was a superb work of art. But Basil saw only the human figures before him. In a chair covered with furs sat a man of middle age, robust, fair-complexioned, with a keen look in his pale blue eyes and something of the wolfish about his mouth. Bessas had long ago given proof of valour, and enjoyed repute as a general, but since his holding command in Rome, his vices, chief of which was avarice, showed much more prominently than the virtues which had advanced him; he used the Imperial authority chiefly to enrich himself, in this respect, it is true, merely acting in harmony with the Emperor's representative at Ravenna, and with: the other Greek generals scattered about Italy, but exhibiting in his methods a shrewdness and an inhumanity not easily rivalled. Behind his chair stood several subordinates, and on a stool before him sat a noble recently arrived as envoy from Byzantium.

Having been previously instructed as to his behaviour in this redoubtable presence, Basil followed the example of Marcian in approaching with bent head to within a distance of three paces, then dropping to his knees, and bowing so as almost to touch the ground with his forehead. He heard a gruff voice command him to rise.

'So this is the heir of the Senator Maximus,' said Bessas, much as he might have spoken of viewing a horse that interested him. 'What is his name?'

'Basilius, my lord,' replied Marcian, with grave respect.

'And what is he doing? Why does not a limber lad like that serve the Emperor?'

'Your Magnanimity will recollect that the lord Basil had permission to attend Maximus into Campania, whence he is but now returned.'

'Can't he speak for himself?' growled Bessas, turning sharply upon Marcian. 'You have a tongue, lord Basil? Do you only use it among the wenches?'

A subdued laugh sounded behind the commander's chair. The envoy from Byzantium showed more discreet appreciation of the jest. And Basil, his head bowed, would fain have concealed a face burning with angry shame.

'I will do my best,' he replied in a steady voice, 'to answer any question your excellence may put to me.'

'Come, that's better,' said the general, with that affectation of bluff good-nature which always veiled his designs. 'I like the look of you, my good Basil; who knows but we may be friends? By the bye, was there not some special reason for your coming to see me?'

'Your excellence summoned me.'

'Yes, yes, I remember. That affair of the Gothic wench.' Bessas checked himself, glanced at the envoy, and corrected his phrase. 'The Gothic lady, I would say, who has somehow been spirited out of sight. What can you tell us of her, lord Basil? It has been whispered to me that if you cannot lead us to this beauty's hiding-place, nobody can.'

Basil answered in the only way consistent with prudence: he not only denied all knowledge of where Veranilda was to be found, but spoke as though her fate had little or no interest for him, whereas he professed himself greatly troubled by the disappearance of his cousin Aurelia. It seemed that Petronilla did not purpose delivering Veranilda to the Greeks. Perhaps she did not yet understand the import of their inquiry. That it was she who held Veranilda prisoner he had less doubt than ever, and boldly he declared his conviction. But even, whilst speaking, he thought with dread of the possibility of Veranilda's being delivered to Bessas; for who could assure him that this sinister-looking Thracian would respect the mandate received from Byzantium? On the other hand, who could say to what sufferings and perils his beloved was exposed whilst Petronilla's captive? He preferred the risks to follow upon her surrender. Did he but know where she was there would at least be a hope of rescuing her.

'By Christ!' exclaimed Bessas, when he had listened intently to all Basil's replies, 'this is a strange business. I begin to think, excellent lord Basil, that you are as much deceived in your suspicions of the lady Petronilla as she is in her suspicions of you. These two wenches—ladies, I would say—may have reasons of their own for hiding; or somebody of whom you know nothing may have carried them off. How is this Aurelia to look upon? Young and comely, I warrant.'

Basil briefly described his cousin; whereupon the listener gave a shrug.

'We will talk of it again, to-morrow or the day after. Hold yourself in readiness, lord Basil—you hear?—to come when bidden. And, hark you, bring the senator's will, that I may look it over myself. Trust me, I will see that this lady Aurelia suffers no wrong; if necessary, I will myself hold her property in trust. They tell me she is a heretic—that must be inquired into. But take no thought for the matter, my good Basil; trust me, you shall be relieved from all responsibilities. Go in peace!'

Bessas rose, impatient to have done with business. In the little hippodrome, hard by, an entertainment had been prepared for this afternoon: female equestrians were to perform perilous feats; there was to be a fight between a man and a boar; with other trifles, such as served to pass the time till dinner. In the entrance hall waited messengers from Ravenna, who for hours had urgently requested audience; but, partly because he knew that their despatches would be disagreeable, in part because he liked playing at royalty, the commander put them off till to-morrow. Even so did he postpone an inspection of a certain part of the city wall, repeatedly suggested to him by one of his subordinates. Leisure and accumulation of wealth were obscuring the man's soldierly qualities. He gave little heed to the progress of the war, and scoffed at the fear that Totila might ere long march against Rome.

Basil walked in gloomy silence. The interview had inflamed his pride. Mentally he repeated the oath never to acquiesce in this Byzantine tyranny, and he burned for the opportunity of open war against it. When they were at a safe distance from the Palatine, Marcian warned his friend against the Greek's indulgent manner; let him not suppose that Bessas spoke one word sincerely.

'His aim at present, I see, is to put you off your guard; and doubtless he is playing the like game with Petronilla. You will be spied upon, day and night—I myself, you understand, being one of the spies, but only one, unfortunately. This Thracian is not so easy to deal with as the Hun at Cumae. There have been moments when I thought he suspected me. If ever I vanish, Basil—'

He ceased with a significant look.

'Why does Totila delay?' exclaimed Basil, with a passionate gesture.

'He delays not. It is wisdom to conquer Campania before coming hither. Another month will see him before Neapolis.'

'Could I but find Veranilda, make her my own, and put her in safety, I would go straight to the king's camp, and serve him as best I might.'

Marcian looked steadily at the speaker, smiling strangely.

'Why do you look at me so?' cried Basil. 'You doubt me? You distrust my courage?'

'Not for a moment. But why should this depend upon the finding of Veranilda, my best Basil? Having found her, having made her your own, will it be easier than now to take your chance of death or of captivity? When was a Roman wont to let his country's good wait upon his amorous desire?'

They were on the Sacred Way, between the Basilica of Constantine and the Atrium of Vesta. Struck to the heart by his friend's words, words such as Marcian had never yet addressed to him, Basil stood mute and let his eyes wander: he gazed at the Forum, at the temples beyond it, at the Capitol with its desecrated sanctuary of Jupiter towering above. Here, where the citizens once thronged about their business and their pleasure, only a few idlers were in view, a few peasants with carts, and a drove of bullocks just come in from the country.

'You would have me forget her?' he said at length, in a voice distressfully subdued.

'I spoke only as I thought.'

'And your thought condemned me—despised me, Marcian?'

'Not so. Pitied you rather, as one whose noble nature has fallen into trammels. Have you not long known, O Basil, how I think of the thing called love?'

'Because you have never known it!' exclaimed Basil. 'My love is my life. Having lost Veranilda, I have lost myself; without her I can do nothing. Were she dead I could fling myself into the struggle with our enemies, all the fiercer because I should care not whether I lived or died; but to lose her thus, to know that she may be in Rome, longing for me as I for her—to think that we may never hold each other's hands again—oh, it tears my heart, and makes me weak as a child. You cannot understand me; you have never loved!'

'May such knowledge be far from me!' said Marcian, with unwonted vehemence. 'Do you feel no shame in being so subdued to the flesh?'

'Shame? Shame in the thought that I love Veranilda?'

Marcian seemed to make an effort to control a passion that wrought in him; he was paler than of wont, and, instead of the familiar irony, a cold, if not cruel, austerity appeared in his eyes and on his lips. He shunned Basil's astonished gaze.

'Let us not speak of this,' broke from him impatiently. 'You understand me as little as I you. Forgive me, Basil—I have been talking idly—I scarce know what I said. It is sometimes thus with me. Something takes hold upon me, and I speak at random. Come, come, dear friend of my heart, we will find your Veranilda; trust me, we will.'

Three days went by, then Basil was summoned again to the Palatine, where he had an interview with Bessas alone. This time the commander hardly spoke of Veranilda; his talk was of the possessions left by Maximus, whose testament, when he had read it, he said that he would take care of until the lost daughter was discovered; he inquired closely, too, as to Basil's own wealth, and let fall a remark that the Roman nobles would soon be called upon to support the army fighting for their liberties against the barbarians. When next called, let Basil have ready and bring with him an exact statement of the money in his hands, and of the income he expected to derive from his property during the present year. Thereupon he was dismissed with a nod and a smile, which made him quiver in rage for an hour after. This happened in early morning. The day was overcast, and a cold wind blew from the mountains; Basil had never known such misery as fell upon him when he reentered his gloomy, silent house. On the way home he had passed two funerals—their hurried aspect proving that the dead were victims of the plague, that *lues inguinaria* which had broken out in Italy two years ago, and with varying intensity continued throughout the land. Throwing himself down upon a couch, he moaned in utter wretchedness, fearful of the pestilence, yet saying to himself that he cared not if it seized upon him. His moans became sobs; he wept for a long time, then lay, half soothed by the burst of hysterical passion, with eyes turned blankly to the ceiling and a hand clenched upon his breast.

In his solitude he often talked with Felix, and more intimately perhaps than with either Decius or Marcian. This trusty servant held communication with a man in the household of Petronilla, and from him learnt what he could as to the lady's movements; but nothing was as yet discoverable which threw light on the mystery of Aurelia and Veranilda. To-day, however, Felix returned from the other side of the Tiber with what sounded like important news. Petronilla had left home this morning in her carriage, had gone forth from the city by one of the southern gates, and, after an absence of two or three hours, had returned, bringing with her some one, a woman, whom she took into her house and kept there in privacy. He who related this to Felix declared that his mistress had only visited the church of her patron saint on the Via Ardeatina, but who the woman might be that she had brought back with her, he did not pretend to know. This story so excited Basil that he would have hastened forthwith across the Tiber, had not Felix persuaded him that at this late hour nothing could be done. After a sleepless night he set out at sunrise, accompanied by Felix alone. Whether he would be admitted at Petronilla's door was quite uncertain; in any case, it would serve no purpose to go thither with a band of attendants, for the Anician house was sure to be strongly guarded. All he could do was to present himself in the hope of seeing Petronilla, and take his chance of learning something from her when they stood face to face.

On horseback he went down by the Clivus Scauri, followed the road between the Circus Maximus and the Aventine, crossed the river by the Aemilian bridge (the nearer bridge of Probus was falling into ruins), and then turned to the left. This part of the transtiberine district was inhabited by poor folk. Something unusual seemed to have happened among them just now: groups stood about in eager talk, and a little further on, in front of a church, a noisy crowd was assembled, with soldiers among them. Having made inquiry, Felix explained the disturbance to his master. It was due to the rapacity of the Greek commander, who, scorning no gain, however small, was seizing upon the funds of the trade guilds; this morning the common chest of the potters had been pillaged, not without resistance, which resulted in the death of a soldier; the slayer had fled to St. Cecilia's church, and taken sanctuary. Basil's feeling, as he listened, was one of renewed bitterness against the Greeks; but to the potters themselves he gave little thought, such folk and their wrongs appearing of small moment to one of his birth.

Pursuing the road towards the Portuensian Gate, he was soon in sight of the palace where for generations had dwelt the heads of the Anician family. It lay on a gentle slope above the river, at the foot of the Janiculan Hill; around it spread public porticoes, much decayed, and what had once been ornamental gardens, now the pasture of goats. As Basil had expected, he was kept waiting without the doors until the porter had received orders regarding him. Permitted at length to enter, he passed by a number of slaves who stood, as if on guard, in the atrium, and, though seeming to be alone in the room beyond, he heard subdued voices from behind the curtains of the doorways, which told him that he was under observation. All parts of this great house were perfectly familiar to him, and had it been possible to conduct a search, he would soon have ascertained whether she he sought was kept imprisoned here; but, unless he took the place by storm, how could he hope to make any discovery? Whilst he was impatiently reflecting, Petronilla entered. She moved towards him with her wonted dignity of mien, but in the look with which she examined him, as she paused at two paces' distance, it was easy to perceive distrust, and a certain inquietude.

'Your leisure at length permits you to visit me, dear lord Basil,' she began coldly.

'My leisure, indeed,' he replied, 'has not been great since the day on which you left Surrentum. But the more plainly we speak to each other the better. I come now to ask whether you will release Veranilda to me, instead of waiting until you are compelled to release her to the Greeks.'

Before replying, Petronilla clapped her hands, then stood waiting for a moment, and said at length:

'You can now speak without hearers. I did not think you would be so imprudent in your words. Go on: say what you will.'

She seated herself, and looked at Basil with a contemptuous smile. He, surprised by her behaviour, spoke on with angry carelessness.

'I neither cared before, nor do I now, if any of your servants overhear me. No more credit would be given to anything they told of me than is given to what you yourself say. I might begin by warning you of the dangers to which you are exposed, but no doubt you have calculated them, and think the price not too much to pay for your revenge. Well, with your revenge I have no wish to interfere. Hold Aurelia prisoner as long as you will, or as long as you can. I speak only of Veranilda, against whom you can feel no enmity. Will you release her to me? It will only be anticipating by a few days her release to Bessas. Veranilda in his hands, trust me, he will care little what becomes of Aurelia.'

'I listen to you,' replied Petronilla, 'because I am curious to learn into what extravagances your ignoble passion drives you. I had been told, but could hardly believe, that you charged me with having seized these women. Now I see that you really are foolish enough to think it.' She threw her head back in a silent laugh of scorn. 'Child—for you are a child in wit though man in years—do you not live at large in Rome, free to come and go as you will?'

'What of that?'

'Am not I also a free woman? Did I not yesterday visit the church of the blessed Petronilla, and might I not, if so I had willed, have escaped instead of returning to the city?'

'What has this to do with the matter?' demanded Basil.

'Child! child!' cried the other, as if with boundless contempt. 'You ask that, knowing why this Veranilda is sought by the Greeks? Were they truly still in search of her, and were you, were I, suspected of keeping her hidden, do you suppose we should be free, and not rather locked as close as any prison in Rome could hold us?'

The listener stood mute. So vehement was Petronilla's speech, and so convincing, thus delivered, seemed her argument, that Basil felt his heart sink. Had she, then, outwitted him? Was he really playing the part of a simpleton, at whom people laughed? He remembered the seeming indifference of Bessas touching Veranilda at the second interview, natural enough if the maiden had already passed into the Greek's hands. Two days ago Marcian had told him that Petronilla must needs be aware of Veranilda's importance, seeing that it was now common knowledge in Roman society. But a thought flashed into his mind, and he lifted up his head again.

'This is not true!' he exclaimed. 'If Bessas had found her, I should have known it.'

'Pray, how? Does your foolish little lordship imagine that Bessas must needs have told you all he has done?'

'Bessas? no,' he answered, his eyes burning with hatred as they searched her face. 'But I have other means of learning the truth. You try vainly to deceive me.'

'As you will, good nephew,' said the lady, as if indulgently. 'Believe as you list, and talk on, for you entertain me.'

'One thing I have to say,' pursued Basil, 'which you will perhaps find less amusing.' He had lost control of himself, and spoke in a low tone of fierce menace, all his body quivering. 'If I learn that Veranilda is in the hands of the Greeks, and that *you* delivered her to them—by the God above us, your life shall pay for it.'

Petronilla's face hardened till its cruel sternness outdid any expression of hatred possible to Basil's features.

'Keep your ruffian threats for more suitable occasion, such as you will find among your friends the Goths.' She spoke coldly and deliberately. 'If enslavement to a yellow-haired barbarian had not muddled your wits, you would long ago have seen who it was that has played you false.'

Basil stared at her, his passion chilled with surprise and alarm.

'Played me false!' he echoed involuntarily.

'Who is it,' continued Petronilla with slow scorn, 'that you have trusted blindly? To whom have you looked for guidance and protection? Who has fostered your suspicion against *me*?'

An intolerable pang went through the listener's heart.

'That's but another lie!' he exclaimed furiously. 'O basest of women born!'

A hand was upon his dagger. Petronilla rose and stepped back a little, glancing towards one of the drawn curtains.

'You have threatened my life,' she said in an undertone. 'Remember that it is you who are in my power. If I raise my voice on one word, the next moment you will lie pierced by a score of weapons. Moderate your insults: my temper is not meek.'

Basil thought for a moment with painful intentness.

'Speak plainly,' he said at length. 'You would have me suspect—? I am ashamed to utter the name.'

'Keep it to yourself and muse upon it.'

'You dare bid me think that he, my dearest and most loyal friend, has infamously betrayed me? Now I know indeed that you have lied to me in every word, for this is the last audacity of baseness. You hope to poison my soul against him, and so, whilst guarding yourself, bring more evil upon those you hate. But you have overreached yourself. Only cunning driven desperate could have devised this trick. Listen to me again, before it is too late. Give me Veranilda. I take upon myself all the peril. It shall be made to appear that I have all along kept her in hiding, and that you knew nothing of her. Be advised before the worst comes upon you. I will escape with her to a place of safety that I know of; *you* will be declared innocent, and no one will care to ask what has become of Aurelia. Think well; you spoke of prisons, but the Greeks have worse than imprisonment for those who incur their wrath. Will Bessas forego revenge when, after much trouble, he has wrested the captive from your hands? Think!'

Petronilla's countenance, fixed as a face in marble, still suggested no thought save one of scorn; but there was a brief silence before she replied.

'I would not have believed,' she said calmly, 'that a man could be so besotted with foolish passions. Listen, you in turn. Where those women are, I know as little as do you yourself. I think, and have good reason for thinking, that the Goth is already on her way to Constantinople, but I have no certainty of it. The one thing I do surely know, is that you are hoodwinked and baffled by the man you trust.'

A groan of rage and anguish broke from Basil. He wrung his bands together.

'You lie! A thousand times you lie! Either Veranilda or Aurelia is in this house. Who was it you brought back with you yesterday when you returned from beyond the walls?'

The listener uttered a short, fierce laugh.

'So that is what brought you here? O fool! Think you I should have no more wisdom than that? Since you must needs pry into my doings yesterday, you shall hear them. I went to the church of the holy Petronilla, to pray there against all the dangers that environ me—against the wiles of the wicked, the cruelty of violent men, the sickness which is rife about us. And when I rose from before the altar, the servant of God who passes his life there, who is pleased to regard me with kindness, led me apart into the sacristy, where sat a woman who had lost her sight. She had travelled, he told me, from Mediolanum, because of a vision in which she had been bidden to seek the tomb of the daughter of the chief Apostle; and, whilst praying in the church, her darkness had been illumined by a vision of the saint herself, who bade her go into the city, and abide in the house of the first who offered her welcome, and there at length she would surely receive her sight. So I spoke with the woman, who, though in poverty, is of noble blood, and when I had offered to make her welcome, she gladly came with me, and straightway we returned to Rome. And I brought with me oil from the lamp of the saint, wherewith, at the hours of prayer, I cross my forehead, that no evil may befall me. So, you have heard. Believe or not, as you list, O Basil.'

Whether true or not, Basil had no choice but to accept the story. He looked helplessly about him. If by killing this woman he could have obtained liberty to search through every chamber of the great house, his dagger would have leapt at her breast; and that Petronilla well knew; whence the defiant look in her eyes as they watched his slightest movement.

'What is your next question?' she said. 'I am at leisure for a little longer.'

'If Veranilda is in the hands of the Greeks, where is Aurelia?'

'I should be glad to think,' replied the lady, 'that she has withdrawn from the world to expiate her sins.'

'Would you have me believe that Marcian knows that secret also?'

'I respect your innocence,' answered Petronilla, with a smile, 'and will say no more.'

Again Basil stood for a moment voiceless in wrath. Then he threw up an arm, and spoke with terrible vehemence.

'Woman, if you have lied to me, wickedly seeking to put enmity between me and my friend, may the pest smite you, and may you perish unforgiven of man and God!'

Petronilla blanched not. For one instant he glared at her, and was gone.

CHAPTER XII
HELIODORA

Marcian's abode was in the Via Lata, the thoroughfare which ran straight and broad, directly northwards, from the Capitoline Hill to the Flaminian Gate. Hard by were the headquarters of the city watch, a vast building, now tenanted by a few functionaries whose authority had fallen into contempt; and that long colonnade of Hadrian, called the Septa, where merchants once exposed their jewels and fabrics to the crowd of sauntering wealthy, and where nowadays a few vendors of slaves did their business amid the crumbling columns. Surrounded by these monuments of antiquity, the few private residences still inhabited had a dreary, if not a mean, aspect. Some of them—and Marcian's dwelling was one—had been built in latter times with material taken from temple or portico or palace in ruins; thus they combined richness of detail with insignificant or clumsy architecture. An earthquake of a few years ago, followed by a great inundation of the Tiber, had wrought disaster among these modern structures. A pillar of Marcian's porch, broken into three pieces, had ever since been lying before the house, and a marble frieze, superb carving of the Antonine age, which ran across the facade, showed gaps where pieces had been shattered away.

His family, active in public services under Theodoric, had suffered great losses in the early years of the war; and Marcian, who, as a very young man, held a post under the Praetorian Prefect at Ravenna, found himself reduced to narrow circumstances. After the fall of Ravenna, he came to Rome (accompanied on the journey by Basil, with whom his intimacy then began), and ere long, necessity driving him to expedients for which he had no natural inclination, he entered upon that life of double treachery which he had avowed to his friend. As the world went, Marcian was an honest man: he kept before him an ideal of personal rectitude; he believed himself, and hitherto with reason, incapable of falsity to those who trusted him in the relations of private life. Moreover, he had a sense of religion, which at times, taking the form of an overpowering sense of sin, plunged him into gloom. Though burdened in conscience with no crime, he was subject in a notable degree to that malady of his world, the disposition to regard all human kind, and himself especially, as impure, depraved. Often at the mercy of his passions, he refrained from marriage chiefly on this very account, the married state seeming to him a mere compromise with the evil of the flesh; but in his house were two children, born to him by a slave now dead, and these he would already have sent into a monastery, but that human affection struggled against what he deemed duty. The man lived in dread of eternal judgment; he could not look at a setting sun without having his thought turned to the fires of hell, and a night of wakefulness, common enough in his imperfect health, shook him with horrors unutterable. Being of such mind and temper, it was strange that he had not long ago joined the multitude of those who day by day fled from worldly life into ascetic seclusion; what withheld him was a spark of the ancestral spirit, some drops of the old Roman blood, prompting his human nature to assert and justify itself. Hence the sympathy between him and Basil, both being capable of patriotism, and feeling a desire in the depths of their hearts to live as they would have lived had they been born in an earlier time. But whereas Basil nursed this disposition, regarding it as altogether laudable, Marcian could only see in it an outcome of original sin, and after every indulgence of such mundane thoughts did penance as for something worse than weakness. His father had died in an anguish of compunction for a life stained with sensuality; his mother had killed herself by excessive rigours of penitence; these examples were ever before his mind. Yet he seldom spoke, save to spiritual counsellors, of this haunting trouble, and only the bitterness of envy, an envy entirely human, had drawn from him the words which so astonished Basil in their last conversation. Indeed, the loves of Basil and Veranilda made a tumult in his soul; at times it seemed to him that he hated his friend, so intolerable was the jealousy that racked him. Veranilda he had never seen, but the lover's rapture had created in his imagination a face and form of matchless beauty which he could not cease from worshipping. He took this for a persecution of the fiend, and strove against it by all methods known to him. About his body he wore things that tortured; he fasted to the point of exhaustion; he slept—if sleep came to him—on a bare stone floor; some hours of each day he spent in visiting churches, where he prayed ardently.

Basil, when he had rushed forth from the Anicianum, rode straightway to the Via Lata, and presented himself at Marcian's door. The porter said that his master had been absent since dawn, but Basil none the less entered, and, in the room where he and his friend were wont to talk, threw himself upon a couch to wait. He lay sunk in the most sombre thoughts, until at the door appeared Sagaris, who with the wonted suave servility, begged permission to speak to him.

'Speak on,' said Basil gloomily, fixing his eyes upon the oriental visage, so little reassuring to one harassed by suspicions.

'It is regarding my dear lord, Illustrious, that I would say a humble word, if your nobility will bear with me.'

'What can that be?'

'I am guilty, I know, of much presumption, but I entreat your nobility's patience, for in truth it is only my love and my fears that embolden me to speak. What I would make known to you, Illustrious, is that for more than two whole days my dear lord has not broken bread. Since our return to Rome he has fasted all but continuously, at the same time inflicting upon himself many other penances of the severest kind. For this, I well know, he will have his reward in the eternal life; but when I note his aspect, I am overcome with fear lest we should lose him too soon. This morning, when I was helping him to dress, he sank down, and lay for a time as one dead. My lord would rebuke me severely if he knew that I had ventured to speak of these things; but with you, Illustrious, I feel that I am in no danger. You will understand me, and pardon me.'

Basil had raised himself to a sitting position. Supporting himself on one hand, he stared straight before him, and only spoke when a movement on the part of the servant betrayed impatience.

'This has gone on, you say, since your return to Rome? Was it your lord's habit to do such penance on his travels?'

'Never in this extreme, though I have always marvelled at his piety.'

Again Basil kept a long silence.

'You have done well to tell me,' he said at length; then, with a wave of the hand, dismissed the Syrian.

It was nearly mid-day when Marcian returned. At the sight of Basil his pale, weary countenance assumed a troubled smile. He embraced his friend, kissing him affectionately on both cheeks, and sat down by him with a sigh of fatigue.

'What makes you so wan?' asked Basil, peering into his eyes.

'I sleep ill.'

'Why so? Is it pain or thought that keeps you wakeful?'

'Both, perhaps,' answered Marcian. He paused, reflected gloomily, and went on in a subdued voice. 'Do you think often, Basil, of the eternal fire?'

'Not often. Sometimes, of course.'

'Last night I had a dream, which assuredly was a temptation of the evil one. My father stood before me, and said, "Fear not, Marcian, for there is no Gehenna. It is but the vision of man's tormented conscience." And I awoke with a great joy. But at once the truth came upon me; and until dawn I prayed for strength to resist that perilous solace. This morning I have talked long with a holy man, opening my heart to him, that he might finally resolve my doubts. I said to him: "Slaves who have committed a fault are punished that they may amend. To what purpose is the punishment of the wicked after death, since there can be no amendment?" and he replied: "My son, the wicked are punished in Gehenna that the just may feel gratitude to the divine grace which has preserved them from such a doom." "But," I objected, "ought not the just to pray for their enemies in such evil case?" His answer was prompt: "The time for prayer is past. The blessed concur in the judgment of God!"'

Basil listened with bent head.

'Maximus,' he said presently, 'often doubted of eternal torment; and my cousin Decius has more than once confessed to me that he believes it not at all, being strengthened therein by his friend the philosopher Simplicius. I, O Marcian, would fain think it a dream—yet there are evil doings in this world which make me fear that it may be true.'

'You have seen Bessas again?'

'Yes. And I have seen Petronilla.'

His eyes on the listener, Basil recounted his conversation of this morning, all save that part of it which related to Marcian. He could detect no sign of guilty uneasiness in his friend's face, but saw that Marcian grew very thoughtful.

'Is not this a shamelessness in falsehood which passes belief?' were his last words.

'If indeed it be falsehood,' replied Marcian, meeting the other's eyes. 'I will confess that, this day or two, I have suspected Bessas of knowing more than he pretends.'

'What?' Basil exclaimed. 'You think Veranilda is really in his power?'

Marcian answered with a return to the old irony.

'I would not venture to set bounds to the hypocrisy and the mendacity and the pertinacity of woman, but, after another conversation with Petronilla, I am shaken in my belief that she still holds her prisoners. She may, in truth, have surrendered them. What makes me inclined to think it, is the fierceness with which she now turns on *me*, accusing me of the whole plot from the first. That, look you, would be sweet revenge to a woman defeated. Why,' he added, with a piercing but kindly look, 'do you hide from me that she sought to persuade you of my treachery? Is it, O Basil, because you feared lest she spoke the truth?'

Flushing under that honest gaze, Basil sprang up and seized his friend's hand. Tears came into his eyes as he avowed the truth and entreated pardon.

'It was only because misery has made me all but mad. Nay, I *knew* that she lied, but I could not rest till I had the assurance of it from your own lips. You think, then, dearest Marcian, that Veranilda is lost to me for ever? You believe it is true that she is already on the way to Constantinople?'

Marcian hoped it with all his heart, for with the disappearance of Veranilda this strange, evil jealousy of his would fade away; and he had many reasons for thinking that the loss of his Gothic love would be the best thing that could happen to Basil. At the same time, he felt his friend's suffering, and could not bring himself to inflict another wound.

'If so,' he replied, 'the Greek has less confidence in me than I thought, and I must take it as a warning. It may be. On the other hand, there is the possibility that Petronilla's effrontery outwits us all. Of course she has done her best to ruin both of us, and perhaps is still trying to persuade Bessas that you keep Veranilda in hiding, whilst I act as your accomplice. If this be the case, we shall both of us know the smell of a prison before long, and perchance the taste of torture. What say you? Shall we wait for that chance, or speed away into Campania, and march with the king against Neapolis?'

Though he smiled, there was no mistaking Marcian's earnestness. For the moment he had shaken off his visions of Tartarus, and was his saner self once more.

'If I knew that she has gone!' cried Basil wretchedly. 'If I knew!'

'So you take your chance?'

'Listen! You speak of prison, of torture. Marcian, can you not help, me to capture that woman, and to get from her the truth?'

Basil's face grew terrible as he spoke. He quivered, his teeth ground together.

'I, too, have thought of it,' replied the other coldly. 'But it is difficult and dangerous.'

They talked yet awhile, until Marcian, who looked cadaverous, declared his need of food, and they went to the mid-day meal.

A few days went by. Basil was occupied with the business of his inheritance. He had messengers to despatch to estates in Lucania and Apulia. Then came news that a possession of Maximus' in the south had been invaded and seized by a neighbour; for which outrage there was little hope of legal remedy in the present state of affairs; only by the strong hand could Basil vindicate his right. Trouble was caused him by a dispute with one of the legatees, a poor kinsman who put an unexpected interpretation upon the item of the will which concerned him. Another poor kinsman, to whom Maximus had bequeathed a share in certain property in Rome, wished to raise money on this security. Basil himself could not lend the desired sum, for, though lord of great estates, he found himself after Chorsoman's pillage of the strong room at Surrentum, scarcely able to meet immediate claims upon him under the will; but he consented to accompany his relative to a certain moneychanger, of whom perchance a loan might be obtained. This man of business, an Alexandrian, had his office on the Capitoline Hill, in that open space between the Capitol and the Arx, where merchants were still found; he sat in a shadowed corner of a portico, before him a little table on which coins were displayed, and at his back a small dark shop, whence came a confused odour of stuffs and spices. Long and difficult were the negotiations. To Basil's surprise, the Alexandrian, though treating him with the utmost respect, evidently gave little weight to his guarantee in money matters; as to property in Rome, he seemed to regard it as the most insubstantial of securities. Only on gems and precious metals would he consent to lend a sum of any importance.

Whilst this debate was in progress, a litter, gaudy and luxurious, borne by eight slaves clad in yellow, with others like them before and behind, came to a stop close by, and from it alighted a lady whose gorgeous costume matched the brilliance of her vehicle and retinue. She was young and beautiful, with dark, oriental features, and a bearing which aimed at supremity of arrogance. Having stepped down, she stood at the edge of the portico, languidly gazing this way and that, with the plain intention of exhibiting herself to the loiterers whom her appearance drew together; at every slightest movement, the clink of metal sounded from her neck, her arms, her ankles; stones glistened on her brow and on her hands; about her she shed a perfume like that wafted from the Arabian shore.

The Greek merchant, as soon as he was aware of her arrival, ran forward and stood obsequiously before her, until she deigned to notice him.

'I would speak with you. See that we are private.'

'Noble lady,' he replied, 'the lord Basilius, heir of the Senator Maximus, is within. I will straightway beg him to defer his business.'

The lady turned and gazed into the dusky shop.

'He is not alone, I see.'

'A kinsman is with him, noble lady.'

'Then bid the kinsman go his way, and keep apart, you, until you are summoned. I will speak for a moment with the lord Basilius.'

The Alexandrian, masking a smile, drew near to Basil, and whispered that the lady Heliodora demanded to see him alone. A gesture of annoyance was the first reply, but, after an instant's reflection, Basil begged his kinsman to withdraw. Heliodora then entered the shop, which was nothing more than an open recess, with a stone counter half across the entrance, and behind it a couple of wooden stools. Upon one of these the lady seated herself, and Basil, who had greeted her only with a movement of the head, stood waiting.

'So you will not sup with me?' began Heliodora, in a voice of bantering indifference. 'You will not come to see me? You will not write to me? It is well. I care less than the clipping of a finger-nail.'

'So I would have it,' Basil replied coldly.

'Good. Then we are both satisfied. This is much better than making pretence of what we don't feel, and playing a comedy with our two selves for spectators. You amused me for a while; that is over; now you amuse me in another way. Turn a little towards the light. Let me have a look at your pretty face, Basilidion.'

She spoke with a Greek accent, mingling now and then with the Roman speech a Greek word or exclamation, and her voice, sonorous rather than melodious, one moment seemed about to strike the note of anger, at another seemed softening to tenderness.

'With your leave,' said Basil, 'I will be gone. I have matters of some importance to attend to.'

'With your leave,' echoed Heliodora, 'I will detain you yet a little. For you, Basilidion, there is only one matter of importance, and it may be that I can serve you better therein than any you esteem your graver friends. There, now, I see your face. Holy Mary ! how wan and worn it is. From my heart I pity you, Basilidion. Come now, tell me the story. I have heard fifty versions, some credible, some plain fable. Confide in me; who knows but I may help you.'

'Scoff as you will,' was his answer. 'It is your privilege. But in truth, lady, I have little time to waste.'

'And in truth, lord, your courtesy has suffered since you began to peck and pine for this little Hun.'

'Hun?'

'Oh, I cry pardon! Goth, I should have said. Indeed, there are degrees of barbarism—but, as you will. I say again, I care not the clipping of my smallest nail.' She held her hand towards him; very white it was, and soft and shapely, but burdened with too many rings. 'Tell me all, and I will help you. Tell me nothing, and have nothing for your pains.'

'Help me?' exclaimed Basil, in scornful impatience. 'Am I such a fool as to think you would wish to help me, even if you could?'

'Listen to me, Basil.' She spoke in a deep note which was half friendliness, half menace. 'I am not wont to have my requests refused. Leave me thus, and you have one more enemy—an enemy more to be dreaded than all the rest. Already I know something of this story, and I can know the whole of it as soon as I will; but what I want now is to hear the truth about your part in it. You have lost your little Goth; of that I need no assurance. But tell me how it came about.'

Basil stood with bent head. In the portico, at a little distance, there began to sound the notes of a flute played by some itinerant musician.

'You dare refuse me?' said Heliodora, after waiting a moment. 'You are a bolder man than I thought.'

'Ask what you wish to know,' broke from the other. 'Recount to you I will not. Put questions, and I will reply if I think fit.'

'Good.'

Heliodora smiled, with a movement which made all her trappings of precious metal jingle as though triumphantly. And she began to question, tracking out all Basil's relations with Veranilda from their first meeting at Cumae to the day of the maiden's disappearance. His answers, forced from him partly by vague fear, partly by as vague a hope, were the briefest possible, but in every case he told the truth.

'It is well,' said Heliodora, when the interrogation was over. 'Poor, poor Basilidion! How ill he has been used! And not even a kiss from the little Goth. Or am I mistaken? Perhaps—'

'Be silent!' exclaimed Basil harshly.

'Oh, I will not pry into chaste secrets. For the present, enough. Go your ways, Basil, and take courage. I keep faith, as you know; and that I am disposed to be your friend is not your standing here, alive and well, a sufficient proof?'

She had risen, and, as she uttered these words, her eyes gleamed large in the dusk.

'When you wish to see me,' she added, 'come to my house. To you it is always open. I may perchance send you a message. If so, pay heed to it.'

Basil was turning away.

'What! Not even the formal courtesy? Your manners have indeed declined, my poor Basil.'

With an abrupt, awkward movement, he took her half offered hand, and touched the rings with his lips; then hastened away.

On the edge of the cluster of idlers who were listening to the flute player stood his needy kinsman. Basil spoke with him for a moment, postponed their business, and, with a sign to the two slaves in attendance, walked on. By the Clivus Argentarius he descended to the Forum. In front of the Curia stood the state' carriage of the City Prefect, for the Senate had been called together this morning to hear read some decree newly arrived from Byzantium; and as Basil drew near he saw the Prefect, with senators about him, come forth and descend the steps. These dignitaries, who wore with but ill grace the ancient toga, were evidently little pleased by what they had heard; they talked under their breath together, many of them, no doubt, recalling sadly the honour they were wont to receive from King Theodoric. As their president drove away, Basil, gazing idly after the *carpentum*, felt himself touched on the arm; he looked round and saw Decius, whose panting breath declared his haste, whilst his countenance was eloquent of ill.

'I come from the Anicianum,' Decius whispered, 'and bring terrible news. Petronilla lies dying of the pest.'

Dazed as if under a violent blow, Basil stretched out his hand. It touched the wall of the little temple of Janus, in the shadow of which they were standing.

'The pest?' he echoed faintly.

'She was seized in the night. Some one in the house—some woman, they tell me, whom she brought with her a few days ago, I know not whence—is just dead. I have sped hither in search of any one with whom I could speak of it; God be thanked that I have met you! I went to fetch away books, as you know.'

'I must go there,' said Basil, gazing about him to find his slaves. 'I must go straightway.'

'Why? The danger is great.'

'It may be'—this was spoken into Decius' ear—'that Veranilda is imprisoned there. I have proof now, awful proof, that Petronilla lied to me. I must enter, and seek.'

Hard by were litters for public hire. Bidding his slaves follow, Basil had himself carried, fast as bearers could run, towards the Anicianum. Not even fear of the pestilence could withhold him. His curse upon Petronilla had been heard; the Almighty God had smitten her; would not the same Power protect him? He prayed mentally, beseeching the intercession of the Virgin, of the saints. He made a vow that, did he recover Veranilda, he would not rest until he had won her conversion to the Catholic faith.

Without the Anicianum, nothing indicated disturbance, but as soon as he had knocked at the door it was thrown wide open, and he saw, gathered in the vestibule, a crowd of dismayed servants. Two or three of them, whom he knew well, hurried forward, eager to speak. He learnt that physicians were with the sick lady, and that the presbyter of St. Cecilia, for whom she had sent in the early morning, remained by her side. No member of the family (save Decius) had yet come, though messages had been despatched to several. Unopposed, Basil entered the atrium, and there spoke with Petronilla's confidential freedman.

'Leo, your mistress is dying. Speak the truth to me, and you shall be rewarded; refuse to answer, or lie to me, and I swear by the Cross that you shall suffer. Who was the woman that died here yesterday?'

The freedman answered without hesitation, telling the same story Basil had already heard from Petronilla.

'Good. She has been buried?'

'She was carried out before dawn.'

'Tell me now, upon your salvation, is any one kept prisoner here?'

Leo, an elderly man, his eyes red with tears and his hands tremulous, gazed meaningly at the questioner.

'No one; no one,' he answered under his breath. 'I swear it to you, O lord Basil.'

'Come with me through the house.'

'But Leo, moving nearer, begged that he might be heard and believed. He understood the meaning of these inquiries, for he had been with his mistress at Surrentum. They whom Basil sought were not here; all search would be useless; in proof of this Leo offered the evidence of his wife, who could reveal something of moment which she had learnt only a few hours ago. The woman was called, and Basil spoke apart with her; he learnt that Petronilla, as soon as her pains began, sent a messenger to the deacon Leander, entreating him to come; but Leander had only yesterday set out on a journey, and would not be back for a week or more. Hearing this, the stricken lady fell into an anguish of mind worse even than that of the body; she uttered words signifying repentance for some ill-doing, and, after a while, said to those who were beside her—a physician and the speaker—that, if she died, they were to make known to Bessas that the deacon Leander, he and he alone, could tell all. Having said this, Petronilla became for a time calmer; but her sufferings increased, and suddenly she bade summon the presbyter of St. Cecilia's church. With him she spoke alone, and for a long time. Since, she had uttered no word touching worldly matters; the woman believed that she was now unconscious.

'And you swear to me,' said Basil, who quivered as he listened, 'that this is the truth and all you know?'

Leo's wife swore by everything sacred on earth, and by all the powers of heaven, that she had falsified nothing, concealed nothing. Thereupon Basil turned to go away. In the vestibule, the slaves knelt weeping before him, some with entreaties to be permitted to leave this stricken house, some imploring advice against the plague; men and women alike, all were beside themselves with terror. In this moment there came a knocking at the entrance; the porter ran to open, and admitted Gordian. Basil and he, who had not met since the day of the family gathering, spoke together in the portico. He had come, said Gordian, in the fear that Petronilla had been forsaken by all her household, as sometimes happened to those infected. Had it been so, he would have held it a duty to approach her with what solace he could. As it was, physician and priest and servants being here, he durst not risk harm to his own family; but he would hold himself in readiness, if grave occasion summoned him. So Gordian remounted his horse, and rode back home.

Basil lingered. He no longer entertained the suspicion that Veranilda might be here, but he thought that, could he speak with Petronilla herself, penitence might prompt her to tell him where the captive lay hidden. It surprised him not at all to hear Leander's name as that of her confidant in the matter, though hitherto his thought had not turned in that direction. Leander signified the Church, and what hope was there that he could gain his end against such an opponent?—more formidable than Bessas, more powerful, perhaps, than Justinian. Were Veranilda imprisoned in some monastery, he might abandon hope of beholding her again on this side of the grave.

Yet it was something to know that she had not passed into the hands of the Greeks; that she was not journeying to the Byzantine court, there to be wedded against her will. Cheered by this, he felt an impulse of daring; he would see Petronilla.

'Leo! Lead me to the chamber.'

The freedman besought him not to be so rash, but Basil was possessed with furious resolve. He drove the servant before him, through the atrium, into a long corridor. Suddenly the silence was broken by a shriek of agony, so terrible that Basil felt his blood chilled to the very heart. This cry came again, echoing fearfully through the halls and galleries of this palace of marble. The servants had fled; Basil dropped to his knees, crossed himself, prayed, the sweat standing upon his forehead. A footstep approached him; he rose, and saw the physician who had been with Maximus at Surrentum.

'Does she still live?' he asked.

'If life it can be called. What do you here, lord Basil?'

'Can she hear and speak?'

'I understand you,' replied the physician. 'But it is useless. She has confessed to the priest, and will utter no word more. Look to yourself; the air you breathe is deadly.'

And Basil, weak as a child, suffered himself to be led away.

CHAPTER XIII
THE SOUL OF ROME

The library in Basil's house was a spacious, graceful room, offering at this day very much the same aspect as in the time of that ancestral Anician, who, when Aurelian ruled, first laid rolls and codices upon its shelves. Against the walls stood closed presses of wood, with bronze panelling, on which were seen in relief the portraits of poets and historians; from the key of each hung a strip of parchment, with a catalogue of the works within. Between the presses, on pedestals of dark green serpentine, ranged busts of the Greek philosophers: Zeno with his brows knitted, Epicurus bland, Aratus gazing upward, Heraclitus in tears, Democritus laughing. These were attributed to ancient artists, and by all who still cared for such things were much admired. In the middle stood a dancing faun in blood red marble, also esteemed a precious work of art. Light entered by an arched window, once glazed, now only barred with ornamental iron, too high in the wall to allow of any view; below this, serving as table, was an old marble sarcophagus carved with the Calydonian hunt.

Here, one day of spring, Decius sat over his studies. Long ago he had transferred hither all the books from the great house across the Tiber, and had made his home on the Caelian. As he read or wrote a hard cough frequently interrupted him. During the past half year his health had grown worse, and he talked at times of returning to the Surrentine villa, if perchance that sweeter air might soothe him, but in the present state of things—Totila had just laid siege to Neapolis—the removal did not seem feasible. Moreover, Decius loved Rome, and thought painfully of dying elsewhere than within her walls.

There was a footfall at the door, and Basil entered. He was carelessly clad, walked with head bent, and had the look of one who spends his life in wearisome idleness. Without speaking, however, he threw himself upon a couch and lay staring with vacant eye at the bronze panels of the vaulted ceiling. For some minutes silence continued; then Decius, a roll in his hand, stepped to his kinsman's side and indicated with his finger a passage of the manuscript. What Basil read might be rendered thus:

'I am hateful to myself. For though born to do something worthy of a man, I am now not only incapable of action, but even of thought.'

'Who says that?' he asked, too indolent to glance at the beginning of the roll.

'A certain Marcus Tullius, in one of his letters,' replied the other, smiling, and returned to his own couch.

Basil moved uneasily, sighed, and at length spoke in a serious tone.

'I understand you, best Decius. You are right. Many a time I have used to myself almost those very words. When I was young—how old I feel!—I looked forward to a life full of achievements. I felt capable of great things. But in our time, what can we do, we who are born Romans, yet have never learnt to lead an army or to govern a state?'

He let his arm fall despondently, and sank again into brooding silence.

At root, Basil's was a healthy and vigorous nature. Sound of body, he needed to put forth his physical energies, yet had never found more scope for them than in the exercise of the gymnasium, or the fatigue of travel; mentally well-balanced, he would have made an excellent administrator, such as his line had furnished in profusion, but that career was no longer open. Of Marcian's ascetic gloom he knew nothing: not all the misery he had undergone in these last six months could so warp his wholesome instincts. Owning himself, in the phrases he had repeated from childhood, a miserable sinner, a vile clot of animated dust, at heart he felt himself one with all the beautiful and joyous things that the sun illumined. With pleasure and sympathy he looked upon an ancient statue of god or hero; only a sense of duty turned his eyes upon the images of Christian art.

And this natural tendency was encouraged by his education, which, like that of all well-born Romans, even in the sixth century after Christ, had savoured much more of paganism than of Christianity. Like his ancestors, before the age of Constantine, he had been taught grammar and rhetoric; grammar which was supposed to include all sciences, meaning practically a comment on a few classical texts, and rhetoric presumed a preparation for the life of the Forum, having become an art of declamation which had no reference to realities. Attempts had been made—the last, only a few years ago, by Cassiodorus—to establish Christian schools in Rome, but without success, so profoundly were the ancient intellectual habits rooted in this degenerate people. The long resistance to the new religion was at an end, but Romans, even while confessing that the gods were demons, could not cast off their affection for the mythology and history of their glorious time. Thus Basil had spent his schooldays mostly in the practice of sophistic argument, and the delivery of harangues on traditional subjects. Other youths had shown greater aptitude for this kind of eloquence; he did not often carry off a prize; but among his proud recollections was a success he had achieved in the form of a rebuke to an impious voluptuary who set up a statue of Diana in the room which beheld his debauches. Here was the nemesis of a system of education which had aimed solely at the practical, the useful; having always laboured to produce the man perfectly equipped for public affairs, and nothing else whatever. Rome found herself tottering with senile steps in the same path when the Empire and the ancient world lay in ruins about her. Basil was not studious. Long ago he had forgotten his 'grammatical' learning—except, of course, a few important matters known to all educated men, such as the fact that the alphabet was invented by Mercury, who designed the letters from figures made in their flight by the cranes of Strymon. Though so ardent a lover, he had composed no lyric or elegy in Veranilda's honour; his last poetical effort was made in his sixteenth year, when, to his own joy, and to the admiration of his friends, he wrote a distich, the verses of which read the same whether you began from the left hand or the right. Nowadays if he ever opened a book it was some historian of antiquity. Livy, by choice, who reminded him of his country's greatness, and reawakened in him the desire to live a not inglorious life.

Of his latter boyhood part had been spent at Ravenna, where his father Probus, a friend as well as kinsman of the wise minister Cassiodorus, now and then made a long sojourn; and he had thus become accustomed to the society of the more cultivated Goths, especially of those who were the intimates of the learned Queen Amalasuntha. Here, too, he learned a certain liberality in religious matters; for it was Cassiodorus who, in one of the rescripts given from the Gothic court, wrote those memorable words: 'Religious faith we have no power to impose, seeing that no man can be made to believe against his will.' Upon the murder of Amalasuntha, when the base Theodahad ruled alone, and ruin lay before the Gothic monarchy, Probus, despairing of Italy, following the example of numerous Roman nobles, migrated to Byzantium. His wife being dead, and his daughter having entered a convent, he was accompanied only by Basil, then eighteen years of age. A new world thus opened before Basil's mind; its brilliancy at first dazzled and delighted him, but very soon he perceived the difference between a noble's life at Rome or Ravenna under the mild rule of the Goths, and that led by so-called Romans in the fear of Justinian and of Theodora. His father, disappointed in hopes of preferment which had been held out to him, gladly accepted a mission which would take him back to Italy: he was one of the envoys sent to Belisarius during the siege of Ravenna, to urge the conclusion of the Gothic war and command the return of the Patricius as soon as might be for service against the Persians; and with him came Basil. On the journey Probus fell ill; he was able to cross the Adriatic, but no sooner touched Italian Soil than he breathed his last.

Then it was that Basil, representing his father in the Imperial mission, came face to face with Belisarius, and conceived a boundless enthusiasm for the great commander, whose personal qualities—the large courtesy, the ready kindliness, the frequent laugh—made intimate appeal to one of his disposition. He stayed in the camp before Ravenna until the city surrendered, and no one listened with more ardent approval to the suggestion which began as a whisper between Italians and Goths that Belisarius should accept the purple of the Western Empire. This, to be sure, would have been treachery, but treachery against Justinian seemed a small thing to Basil, and a thing of no moment at all when one thought of Rome as once more an Imperial city, and Italy with such a ruler as the laurelled Patricius. Treachery the general did commit, but not against Byzantium. Having made pretence of accepting the crown which the Goths offered him, he entered into Ravenna, took possession in Justinian's name, and presently sailed for the East, carrying with him the King Vitiges and his wife Matasuntha, grand-daughter of Theodoric. It was a bitter disappointment to Basil, who had imagined for himself a brilliant career under the auspices of the new Roman Emperor, and who now saw himself merely a conquered Italian, set under the authority of Byzantine governors. He had no temptation to remain in the North, for Cassiodorus was no longer here, having withdrawn a twelvemonth ago to his own country by the Ionian Sea, and there entered the monastery founded by himself; at Ravenna ruled the logothete Alexandros, soon to win a surname from his cleverness in coin-clipping. So Basil journeyed to Rome, where his kinsfolk met him with news of deaths and miseries. The city was but raising her head after the long agony of the Gothic siege. He entered his silent home on the Caelian, and began a life of dispirited idleness.

Vast was the change produced in the Roman's daily existence by the destruction of the aqueducts. The Thermae being henceforth unsupplied with water, those magnificent resorts of every class of citizen lost their attraction, and soon ceased to be frequented; for all the Roman's exercises and amusements were associated with the practice of luxurious bathing, and without that refreshment the gymnasium, the tennis-court, the lounge, no longer charmed as before. Rome became dependent upon wells and the Tiber, wretched resource compared with the never-failing and abundant streams which once poured through every region of the city and threw up fountains in all but every street. Belisarius, as soon as the Goths retreated, ordered the repairing of an aqueduct, that which served the transtiberine district, and was indispensable to the working of the Janiculan mills, where corn was ground; but, after his departure, there was neither enough energy nor sufficient sense of security in Rome for the restoration of even one of the greater conduits. Nobles and populace alike lived without the bath, grew accustomed to more or less uncleanliness, and in a certain quarter suffered worse than inconvenience from the lack of good water.

Formerly a young Roman of Basil's rank, occupied or not by any serious pursuit, would have spent several hours of the day at one or other of the Thermae still in use; if inclined to display, he would have gone thither with a train of domestic attendants, and probably of parasites; were the season hot, here he found coolness; were it cold, here he warmed himself. Society never failed; opportunity for clandestine meetings could always be found; all the business and the pleasure of a day were regulated with reference to this immemorial habit. Now, to enter the Thermae was to hear one's footsteps resound in a marble wilderness; to have statues for companions and a sense of ruin for one's solace. Basil, who thought more than the average Roman about these changes, and who could not often amuse himself with such spectacles as the theatres or the circus offered, grew something of a solitary in his habits, and was supposed by those who did not know him intimately, to pass most of his time in religious meditation, the preface, perhaps, to retirement from the world. Indolence bringing its wonted temptations, he fell into acquaintance with Heliodora, a Neapolitan Greek of uncertain origin, whose husband that year held the office of City Prefect. Acquaintance with Heliodora was, in his case, sure to be a dangerous thing, and might well prove fatal, for many and fierce were the jealousies excited by that brilliant lady, whose husband alone regarded with equanimity her amorous adventures. Happily, Basil did not take the matter very much to heart; he scarce pretended to himself that he cared whether Heliodora was his for a day only or for a month; and he had already turned his thoughts to the sweetness of Aemiliana, that young sister of Gordian, whom, if he chose, he might make his wife.

Now again had sluggishness taken possession of him, and with it came those promptings of the flesh which, but a few months ago, he easily subdued, but which the lapse of time had once more made perilous. To any who should have ventured to taunt him with forgetfulness of Veranilda, he would have fiercely given the lie; and with reason, for Veranilda's image was as vivid to him as on the day when he lost her, and she alone of women had the power to excite his deepest and tenderest emotions. Nevertheless, he had more than once of late visited Heliodora, and though these visits were in appearance only such as he might have paid to any lady of his acquaintance, Basil knew very well whither they tended. As yet Heliodora affected a total forgetfulness of the past; she talked of Veranilda, and confessed that her efforts to make any discovery regarding the captive were still fruitless, though she by no means gave up hope; therewithal, she treated Basil only half seriously, with good-naturedly mocking smiles, as a mere boy, a disdain to her mature womanhood. Of this was he thinking as he tossed on the couch in the library; he had thought of it too much since leaving Heliodora yesterday afternoon. It began to nettle him that his grief should be for her merely an amusement. Never having seen the Gothic maiden, whose beauty outshone hers as sunrise outdoes the lighting of a candle, this wanton Greek was capable of despising him in good earnest, and Basil had never been of those who sit easy under scorn. He felt something chafe and grow hot within him, and recalled the days when he, and not Heliodora, had indulged contempt—to his mind a much more natural posture of affairs, The animal that is in every man had begun to stir; it urged him to master and crush and tame this woman, whom, indeed, he held rather in hate than in any semblance of love.

Her beauty, her sensuality, had power over him still; he resented such danger of subjection, and encouraged himself in a barbarism of mood, which permitted him to think that even in yielding he might find the way of his revenge.

There had been a long silence since his reply to the hint offered by Decius. The student spoke again.

'Basil, leave Rome.'

'It is forbidden,' answered the other dully, his face averted.

'Many things are forbidden which none the less are done. Did you learn that Veranilda awaited you at Asculum, how long would it be before you set forth?'

'Not one hour, good Decius.'

'Even so. You would pass the gates disguised as a peasant or as a woman— no matter how. Will you do less to save all that makes life dear to an honourable man? Be gone, be gone, I entreat you.'

'Whither?'

'To Picenum, which is not yet subject to the Goths. There gather your capable men and arm them, and send to the King Totila, offering to serve him where he will, and how he will. You know,' pursued Decius earnestly, 'that I speak this something against my conscience, but, alas! we can only choose between evils, and I think Totila is less of a tyrant than Justinian. You will not go to Constantinople, nor would I bid you, for there, assuredly, is nothing to be done worthy of a man; but you must act, or you perish. For me, a weakling and a dreamer, there is solace in the *vita umbratilis*; to you, it is naught. Arise, then, O Basil, ere it be too late.'

The listener rose from his recumbent attitude; he was stirred by this unwonted vigour in Decius, but not yet did resolve appear on his countenance.

'Did I but know,' he murmured, 'that Veranilda is not in Rome!'

Innumerable times had he said it; the thought alone held him inert. Impossible to discover, spite of all his efforts, whether Veranilda had been delivered to the Greeks, or still lay captive in some place known to the deacon Leander. From the behaviour of Bessas nothing could be certainly deduced: it was now a long time since he had sent for Basil, and Marcian, though believing that the commander's search was still futile, had no more certainty than his friend. Soon after Petronilla's death, the Anician mansion had been thoroughly pillaged and everything of value removed to the Palatine. Bessas condescended to justify this proceeding: having learnt, he said, that the question of Aurelia's orthodoxy lay in doubt, some declaring that she was a heretic, some that she had returned to orthodoxy before her father's death, he took charge of the property which might be hers until she appeared to claim it, when, having the testament of Maximus in his hand, he would see that justice was done. With Leander, Basil had succeeded in obtaining an interview, which was altogether fruitless. The deacon would answer no question, and contented himself with warning his visitor of the dangers incurred by one who openly sought to defeat the will of the Emperor.

'Is it farewell?' asked Decius, stepping towards his kinsman, who seemed about to leave the room.

'I will think.'

'Go speak with Gordian. He says that he can obtain you permission to leave the city.'

'I doubt it,' replied Basil. 'But I will see him—ere long.'

Decius went forth for his morning's exercise, which sometimes took the form of a gentle game of ball, but was generally a ramble on foot and unaccompanied, for he never felt at ease when an attendant followed him. His habits were solitary; ever absorbed in thought, or lost in dreams, he avoided the ways where he would be likely to encounter an acquaintance, and strayed among ruins in deserted gardens, such as were easily found in the remoter parts of the Caelian. To-day, tempted on by the delicious air, and the bright but not ardent sunshine, he wandered by such unfrequented paths till a sound of voices broke upon his meditation, and he found himself in view of the Lateran. Numbers of poor people were streaming away from the open space by the Pope's palace, loud in angry talk, its purpose intelligible enough to any one who caught a few words. Decius heard maledictions upon the Holy Father, mingled with curses no less hearty upon the Greeks who held Rome.

'It was not thus,' cried an old man, 'in the time of King Theodoric, heretic though he might be. We had our bread and our hog's flesh, prime quality both, and plenty for all.'

'Ay,' cried a woman, 'and our oil too. Since these Greek dogs came, not a drop of oil has there been in my cruse. Heretics, forsooth! What better is the Holy Father who lets Christians die of hunger while he eats and drinks his fill?'

'Evil go with thee, O Vigilius! The pest seize thee, O Vigilius! May'st thou perish eternally, O Vigilius!' shrilled and shouted all manner of voices, while fists were shaken towards the pontifical abode.

Decius hastened away. The sight of suffering was painful to him, and the cries of the vulgar offended his ear; he felt indignant that these people should not be fed, as Rome for so many ages had fed her multitude, but above all, he dreaded uproar, confusion, violence. His hurried pace did not relax until he was lost again amid a wilderness of ruins, where browsing goats and darting lizards were the only life.

Later in the day, when he sat alone in the peristyle, a visitor was introduced, whom he rose to welcome cordially and respectfully. This was a man of some threescore years, vigorous in frame, with dry, wrinkled visage and a thin, grey beard that fell to his girdle. As he approached, Decius saw that he was bleeding from a wound on the head and that his cloak was torn.

'What means this, dear master?' he exclaimed. 'What has befallen you?'

'Nothing worth your notice, gentle Decius,' the philosopher replied, calmly and gravely. 'Let us rather examine this rare treatise of Plotinus, which by good fortune I yesterday discovered among rubbish thrown aside.'

'Nay,' insisted Decius, 'but your wound must be washed and dressed; it may else prove dangerous. I fear this was no accident?'

'If you must know,' answered the other with good-natured peevishness, 'I am accused of magic. The honest folk who are my neighbours, prompted, I think it likely, by a certain senator who takes it ill that his son is my disciple, have shown me of late more attention than I care for, and to-day as I came forth, they pursued me with cries of "Sorcerer!" and the like, whereupon followed sticks and stones, and other such popular arguments. It is no matter. Plotinus begins—'

Simplicius was one of the last philosophers who taught in Athens, one of the seven who were driven forth when Justinian, in his zeal for Christianity, closed the schools. Guided by a rumour that supreme wisdom was to be found in Persia, the sages journeyed to that kingdom, where disappointment awaited them. After long wanderings and many hardships, Simplicius came to Rome, and now had sojourned here for a year or two, teaching such few as in these days gave any thought to philosophy. Poor, and perhaps unduly proud, he preferred his own very humble lodging to the hospitality which more than one friend had offered him; and his open disregard for religious practices, together with singularities of life and demeanour, sufficiently explained the trouble that had come upon him. Charges of sorcery were not uncommon in Rome at this time. Some few years ago a commission of senators had sat in judgment upon two nobles accused of magic, a leading article of proof against one of them being that he had a horse which, when stroked, gave off sparks of fire. On this account Decius was much troubled by the philosopher's story. When the wound had been attended to, he besought Simplicius not to go forth again to-day, and with some difficulty prevailed.

'Why should it perturb you, O most excellent Decius,' said the sage, 'that a lover of wisdom is an offence to the untaught and the foolish? Was it not ever thus? If philosophy may no longer find peace at Athens, is it likely that she will be suffered to dwell at ease in Rome?'

'Alas, no!' admitted Decius. 'But why, dear master, should you invite the attacks of the ignorant?'

'I do no such thing. I live and act as seems good to me, that is all. Should no one have the courage to do that, what hope would there be, O Decius, for that most glorious liberty, the liberty of the mind?'

The listener bent his head abashed. Then Simplicius began to read from the manuscript, and Decius, who knew Greek fairly well—he had lately completed certain translations from Plato, left unfinished by Boethius—gave reverent attention. At a certain point the philosopher paused to comment, for the subject was difficult—nothing less than the nature of God. In God, according to the system here expounded, there are three principles or hypostases, united but unequal—the One, the Intelligence, the Soul; which correspond, respectively, to the God of Plato, the God of Aristotle, the God of Zeno. Usually curt and rather dry in his utterances, Simplicius rose to a fervid eloquence as he expounded this mysticism of Alexandria. Not that he accepted it as the final truth, it was merely a step, though an important one, towards that entire and absolute knowledge of which he believed that a glimpse had been vouchsafed to him, even to him, in his more sublime hours. As for Decius, the utmost effort never enabled him to attain familiarity with these profound speculations: he was soon lost, and found his brain whirling with words that had little or no significance. At home in literature, in philosophy he did but strive and falter and lose himself. When at length there came a silence, he sighed deeply, his hand propping his forehead.

'Master, how few men can ever know God!'

'Few, few,' admitted the philosopher, his gaze upwards.

'I think I should be content,' said Decius, 'to love and praise Him. Yet that meseems is no less hard.'

'No less,' was the reply. 'For, without knowledge, love and praise are vain.'

But Decius' thought had another meaning.

CHAPTER XIV
SILVIA'S DREAM

It was the Paschal season, and Basil, careless at most times of religious observances, did not neglect this supreme solemnity of his faith. On Passion Day he fasted and received the Eucharist, Decius doing the like, though with a half-smiling dreaminess which contrasted with the other's troubled devotion. Since the death of Petronilla, Basil had known moments of awe-stricken wonder or of gloomy fear such as never before had visited him; for he entertained no doubt that his imprecation had brought upon Petronilla her dreadful doom, and this was a thought which had power to break his rest. Neither to Marcian nor to Decius did he speak of it in plain terms, merely hinting his belief that the cruel and treacherous woman had provoked divine anger.

But the inclination to piety which resulted from such brooding was in some measure counteracted by his hostile feeling towards all the Church. Petronilla might have conceived the thought of imprisoning Aurelia and Veranilda, but only with the aid of an influential cleric such as Leander could she have carried it out so successfully. The Church it was that held Veranilda captive; unless, indeed, it had handed her over to the Greeks. This conviction made his heart burn with wrath, which he could scarce subdue even whilst worshipping the crucified Christ. His victim's heresy would of course be Leander's excuse for what he had done; the daughter of Maximus and the Gothic maiden were held in restraint for their souls' good. Not long after Petronilla's death Basil had been driven by his distress of mind to visit Gordian and Silvia, and to speak with them of this suspicion. He saw that, for all their human kindness, they were disposed rather, to approve than condemn the deacon's supposed action, and he had gone forth from them in scarce concealed bitterness.

Now, in the festival days of Easter, his thoughts again turned to that house on the Clivus Scauri, so near to his own dwelling, yet so remote from the world of turbid passions in which his lot was cast. The household of Gordian seemed untouched by common cares; though thoroughly human its domestic life, it had something of the calm, the silence, of a monastery. None entered save those whom husband and wife held in affection or in respect; idle gaiety was unknown beneath their roof, and worldly ambition had no part in their counsels. Because of the reverence these things inspired in him, and because of his longing to speak with a pure-hearted woman who held him in kindness, Basil again presented himself at his kinsman's door. He was led directly to an inner room, where sat Silvia.

The severe fasts of Lent had left their mark upon the young face, yet it was fresh and smooth in its delicate pallor, and almost maidenly in its gentle smile. Silvia had blue eyes, and hair of the chestnut hue; a simple, white fillet lay above her forehead; her robe was of pale russet, adorned with the usual purple stripes and edged with embroidery; on each hand she wore but one ring. When the visitor entered, she was nursing her child, a boy of four years old, named Gregorius, but at once she put him to sit upon a little stool beside her.

'Welcome, dear cousin Basil,' was her greeting. 'We hoped this time of gladness would turn your thoughts to us. My husband has been called forth; but you will await his return?'

'It was you, lady cousin, whom I wished to see,' Basil replied. As he spoke, he touched the curly head of the boy, who looked up at him with large, grave eyes. 'Why is he so pale?'

'He has had a sickness,' answered the mother, in a low, tender voice. 'Not many days ago, one might have feared he would be taken from us. Our prayers prevailed, thanks to the intercession of the holy Cosma and Damian, and of the blessed Theodore. When he seemed to be dying, I bore him to the church in the Velabrum, and laid him before the altar; and scarcely had I finished my prayer, when a light seemed to shine upon his face, and he knew me again, and smiled at me.'

Listening, the child took his mother's hand, and pressed it against his wan little cheek. Then Silvia rang a bell that was beside her, and a woman came to take the child away, he, as he walked in silence from the room, looking back and smiling wistfully.

'I know not,' pursued Silvia, when they were alone, 'how we dare to pray for any young life in times so dark as ours. But that we are selfish in our human love, we should rather thank the Omnipotent when it pleases Him to call one of these little ones, whom Christ blessed, from a world against which His wrath is so manifestly kindled. And yet,' she added, 'it must be right that we should entreat for a life in danger; who can know to what it may be destined?—what service it may render to God and man? One night when I watched by Gregorius, weariness overcame me, and in a short slumber I dreamt. That dream I shall never forget. It kept me in heart and hope through the worst.'

'May I hear your dream?' asked Basil.

'Nay,' was the gentle reply, with a smile and a shake of the head, 'to you it would seem but foolishness. Let us speak of other things, and first of yourself. You, too, are pale, good cousin. What have you to tell me? What has come to pass since I saw you?'

With difficulty Basil found words to utter the thought which had led him hither. He came to it by a roundabout way, and Silvia presently understood: he was indirectly begging her to use her influence with eminent churchmen at Rome, to discover whether Veranilda was yet detained in Italy, or had been sent to the East. At their previous interview he had kept up the pretence of being chiefly interested in the fate of Aurelia, barely mentioning the Gothic maiden; but that was in the presence of Gordian. Now he spoke not of Aurelia at all, and so dwelt on Veranilda's name that his implied confession could not be misunderstood. And Silvia listened with head bent, interested, secretly moved, at heart troubled.

'What you ask,' she began, after a short silence, 'is not easy. If I make inquiries of such of the clergy as I know, I must needs tell them why I am doing so; and would they, in that case, think it well to answer me?'

'You know the deacon Leander,' urged Basil. 'Can you not plead for me with him, O Silvia?'

'Plead for you? Remember that it is impossible for me to assume that the holy deacon knows anything of this matter. And, were that difficulty removed, dare I plead for your union with one who is not of our faith—one, moreover, whom you cannot wed without putting yourself in grave peril?'

'Listen, gentle cousin!' exclaimed Basil eagerly. 'It may be that Veranilda has already renounced the heresy of Anus. If not, she would assuredly do so at my persuasion. So, that objection you may dismiss. As for the danger to which our marriage might expose us, our love would dare that—ay, and things much worse.'

'You speak so confidently of the Gothic maiden?' said Silvia, with a look half-timid, half-amused. 'Was there, then, a veritable plighting of troth between you?'

'There was, dear cousin. From you I will conceal nothing, for you are good, you are compassionate.'

And whilst he poured forth the story of his love, not without tears, Silvia gave sympathetic attention. The lady Petronilla had never been one of her intimates, nor was the deacon Leander among those ecclesiastics whom she most reverenced. When Basil had told all, her reply was ready. All she could do would be to endeavour to learn whether Veranilda remained in the charge of Petronilla's confederate, or had been given up to the Greeks. From conversation she had heard, Silvia inclined to this belief, that Bessas and his subordinates were still vainly seeking.

'I can make you no promise, good Basil; but I will take counsel with my husband (whom you can trust as you trust me), and see if indeed anything may be learnt.'

The lover kissed her hands in ardent gratitude. Whilst they were still talking confidentially, another visitor was announced, the deacon Pelagius. Basil begged permission to withdraw before the cleric entered; he was in no mood for conversation with deacons; and Silvia pointed smilingly to the door by which he could retreat.

The hour was still early. Basil passed a day of hopefulness, and his mood became exultant when, about sunset, a letter was brought to him from Silvia.

'To-morrow morning, at the third hour,' she wrote, 'certain of our kinsfolk and friends will assemble in this house to hear the reverend man Arator read his poem on the Acts of the Holy Apostles. This is an honour done to us, for only two or three persons have as yet heard portions of the poem, which will soon be read publicly in the church of the Holy Petrus ad Vincula. Let me welcome your Amiability among my guests. After the reading, I shall beg you to be acquainted with one who may perchance serve you.'

Scarcely had Basil read this, when another missive was put into his hands. It was from Heliodora, and written, as usual, in Greek characters.

'To-morrow, after the ninth hour, you are bidden hither. Come if you choose. If you do not, I shall have forgotten something I have learnt.'

To this he paid little heed; it might have significance, it might have none. If the morning sustained his hope, he would be able to resist the temptation of the afternoon. So he cherished Silvia's letter, and flung Heliodora's contemptuously aside.

Reaching Gordian's house next morning a little before the appointed hour, he found the members of the family and one or two guests assembled in a circular room, with a dome pierced to admit light: marble seats, covered with cushions, rose amphitheatre-wise on one half of the circle, and opposite was a chair for the reader. In this hall Sidonius Apollinaris had declaimed his panegyric on the Emperor Avitus; here the noble Boethius had been heard, and, in earlier days, the poet Claudian. Beside Silvia stood her husband's two sisters, Tarsilla and Aemiliana, both of whom, it had begun to be rumoured, though still in the flower of their youth, desired to enter the monastic life. At the younger, who was beautiful, Basil glanced diffidently, remembering that she might have been his wife; but Aemiliana knew nothing of the thought her brother had entertained, and her eyes were calm as those of a little child. When other guests appeared, Basil drew aside, for most of the persons who entered were strangers to him. Ecclesiastics grew numerous; among them might be distinguished a tall, meagre, bald-headed man, the sub-deacon

Arator, who held in his hand the manuscript from which he was to read. Among the latest to arrive was a lady, stricken in years and bowed with much grief, upon whom all eyes were respectfully bent as Gordian conducted her to a place of honour. This was Rusticiana, the daughter of Symmachus, the widow of Boethius. When Basil looked at her, and thought of the anguish through which her life had passed in that gloomy evening of the reign of Theodoric, he felt himself for a moment at one with those who rejected and scorned the Gothic dominion. A great unhappiness flooded his heart and mind; he forgot what was passing about him, and only returned to himself when there sounded the voice of the reader.

Arator's poetic version of the Acts of the Apostles was written in hexameters; whether good or ill, Basil felt unable to decide, and he wished Decius had been here to whisper a critical comment. In any case he would have found the reading wearisome; that monotonous, indistinct voice soon irritated him, and at length made him drowsy. But admiration frequently broke out from the audience, and at the end applause became enthusiasm. Unspeakably glad that the ceremony was over, Basil mingled with the moving crowd, and drew towards Silvia. At length their eyes met; the lady thereupon spoke a word to a cleric who was standing by her, and in the next moment summoned Basil with a movement of the head. There was a brief formality, then Basil found himself led aside by the deacon Pelagius, who spoke to him in a grave, kind voice very pleasant to the ear, with the courtesy of a finished man of the world, and at the same time with a firmness of note, a directness of purpose, which did not fail to impress the listener.

Aged about five-and-thirty, bearing upon his countenance the signature of noble birth, Pelagius was at this moment the most accomplished diplomat that the Church of Rome possessed. He had spent some years at Byzantium, as papal emissary; had engaged the confidence of Justinian; and, on his return, had brought an Imperial invitation to Vigilius, who was requested to set forth for the East as soon as possible. Pope Vigilius had the misfortune to differ on certain dogmatic questions with that pious and acute theologian the Empress Theodora; being a man of little energy or courage, he durst not defy Byzantium, as he gladly would have done, nor yet knew how to deal subtly for his own ends with the Eastern despots; he lingered his departure, and in the meantime earned hatred at Rome because of his inability to feed the populace. It was already decided that, during his absence, the Holy Father should be represented by Pelagius, an arrangement very agreeable to that party in the Church which upheld Imperial supremacy, but less so to those ecclesiastics—a majority—who desired the independence of Rome in religious matters, and the recognition of Peter's successor as Patriarch of Christendom. In speaking to such a personage as this on Basil's behalf, Silvia had not reflected that the friend of Justinian was little likely to take the part of one who desired to frustrate an Imperial command; she thought only of his great influence, and of the fact that he looked with no favour on the deacon Leander, an anti-imperialist. What was again unfortunate for Basil, Pelagius had heard, before leaving Byzantium, of the Emperor's wish to discover Veranilda, and had already made inquiries on this subject in Rome. He was glad, then, to speak with this young noble, whose mind he found it very easy to read, and whom, without the least harshness, he resolved to deter from his pursuit of a Gothic bride.

The colloquy was not long. Buoyed by his ardour, Basil interpreted the first words of courteous preamble in the most hopeful sense. What followed gave him pause; he saw a shadow of obstacle arise. Another moment, and the obstacle had become very real; it grew to vastness, to insuperability He stood, as it were, looking into the very eyes of the Serene Majesty of Byzantium. Not that the speaker used a tone of peremptory discouragement. Granting the indispensable condition that Veranilda became a Catholic, it was not an impossible thing, said Pelagius, that Basil should obtain her as a wife; *but* it could only be by the grace of the Emperor. Veranilda had been summoned to Byzantium. If Basil chose to follow her thither, and sue for her before the throne, why, this was open to him, as to any other Roman of noble birth. It would have been idle indeed to seek to learn from Pelagius whether Veranilda had already left Italy, his tone was that of omniscience, but his brow altogether forbade interrogation. Basil, in despair, ventured one inquiry. If he desired to go to Byzantium, could he obtain leave of departure from the Greek commandant, under whose ban he lay? The reply was unhesitating; at any moment, permission could be granted. Therewith the conversation came to an end, and Basil, hating the face of man, stole away into solitude.

Entering his own house, he learnt that Marcian was within. For a month they had not seen each other, Marcian having been absent on missions of the wonted double tenor; they met affectionately as ever, then Basil flung himself down, like one crushed by sudden calamity.

'What now?' asked his friend, with a rallying rather than a sympathetic air.

'No matter,' Basil replied. 'You are weary of my troubles, and I can no longer talk of them.'

'What troubles? The old story still? I thought you had found solace?'

Basil looked an indignant wonder. His friend, sitting on the couch beside him, continued in the same half-bantering tone:

'When were you last at the house of a certain disconsolate widow, on the Quirinal?'

'What mean you?' cried the other, starting up, with sudden fury in his eyes. 'Are you vowed with my enemies to drive me mad?'

'Not I, dear Basil; but hear the truth. Only late last night I entered the gates of Rome, and since I rose this morning three several persons have spoken your name to me together with that of Heliodora.'

'They are black and villainous liars! And you, Marcian, so ready to believe them? Tell me their names, their names!'

'Peace! One would think you mad indeed. You know the son of Opilio, young Vivian?'

'I know him!' answered Basil scornfully, 'as I know the lousy beggar who sits before St. Clement's Church, or the African who tumbles in Trajan's forum.'

'Even so. This same spark of fashion stops me in the Vicus Longus. "You are the friend of Basil," quoth he. "Give him this warning. If ever I chance to find him near the portico of Heliodora, I will drive my dagger into his heart," and on he struts, leaving me so amazed that I forgot even to fetch the cub a box o' the ear. But I had not long to wait for an explanation of his insolence. Whom should I next meet but the solemn-visaged Opilio. "So your friend Basil," he began, "has forgotten his Gothic love?" We talked, and I learnt from him that you were the hot rival of Vivian for Heliodora's favour. Nay, I do but repeat what you ought to hear. Can such gossip begin without cause? Tell me now, how often have you been yonder since I left Rome?'

Basil could scarce contain himself. He had visited Heliodora, yes, but merely because he would neglect no chance of learning where Veranilda was imprisoned; it was not impossible that through this woman such a secret might be discovered. He the rival of that debauched boy! He the lover of Heliodora! Had he sunk so low in the esteem of his best friend? Why, then, it was time indeed to be gone: befall him what might, he could not be unhappier in Constantinople than here in Rome.

At these words, Marcian checked him with a surprised inquiry. What had turned his thoughts to Constantinople? Basil related the events of yesterday and of this morning.

'What other counsel could you have expected from Pelagius?' said Marcian, after listening attentively. 'But on one point I can reassure you. Veranilda has not yet fallen into the hands of the Greeks.'

'How do you know that?' exclaimed Basil eagerly.

'Enough that I do know it. Whilst you have been idling here—forgive me, good Basil—I have travelled far and conversed with many men. And I have something else to tell you, which will perchance fall less agreeably upon your ear. The fame of Veranilda promises to go forth over all lands. King Totila himself has heard of her, and would fain behold this ornament of his race.'

'Totila!'

'When Cumae was besieged by the Goths three months ago, Chorsoman—whom you have not forgotten—made terms with Totila, and was allowed to keep some portion of the plunder he had amassed. Thinking to do the king a pleasure, he told him of Veranilda, of the commands regarding her which had come from the East, and of her vanishing no one knew whither. And of these things, O Basil, did Totila himself, with his royal mouth, speak unto me not many days gone by.'

'I see not how that concerns me,' said Basil wearily.

'True, it may not. Yet, if I were wooing a wife, I had rather seek her at the hands of Totila than at those of Justinian. To be sure, I did not speak of you to the king; that would have been less than discreet. But Totila will ere long be lord of all Italy, and who knows but the deacon Leander, no friend of Constantinople, might see his interest and his satisfaction in yielding Veranilda rather to the Goth than to the Greek?'

Basil started. Such a thought had never entered his mind, yet he saw probability in the suggestion.

'You assure me,' he said, 'that she has not yet been surrendered. I find that hard to believe. Knowing in whose power she is, how comes it that Bessas does not seize the insolent Leander, and force the truth from him? Were I the commander, would I be baffled for an hour by that sleek deacon?'

'Were you commander, O best Basil,' replied Marcian, smiling, 'you would see things in another light. Bessas does not lay hands upon the deacon because it is much more to his profit to have the clergy of Rome for his friends than for his enemies. Whether Veranilda be discovered or not, he cares little; I began to suspect that when I saw that you came off so easily from your dealings with him. 'Tis a long road to Constantinople, and the Thracian well knows that he may perchance never travel it again. His one care is to heap up treasure for to-day; the morrow may look after itself. But let us return to the point from which we started. Do you think in earnest of voyaging to the Bosporus?'

'I should only choose a hazard so desperate were it the sole chance that remained of recovering Veranilda.'

'Wait, then, yet awhile. But take my counsel, and do not wait in Rome.'

To this advice Basil gave willing ear. Since he had heard from Pelagius that he was free to quit the city, he was all but resolved to be gone. One thought alone detained him; he still imagined that Heliodora might have means such as she professed of aiding him in his search, and that, no matter how, he might subdue her will to his own. She, of course, aimed only at enslaving him, and he knew her capable of any wickedness in the pursuit of her ends; for this very reason was he tempted into the conflict with her, a conflict in which his passions would have no small part, and whether for or against him could not be foreseen. Once more he would visit Heliodora; if fruitlessly, then for the last time.

But of this decision he did not speak to Marcian.

CHAPTER XV
YOUNG ROME

At the hour named by Heliodora, Basil set forth alone and rode by unfrequented ways towards the street on the Quirinal named Alta Semita. A sense of shame forbade him to make known even to his slaves whither he was going. He kept repeating to himself that it was for the last time; and perhaps a nobler motive would have withheld him altogether, had not the story told by Marcian of his 'rival's' insolent menace rankled in him and urged him to show that he felt no fear. Chance led him past the little church of St. Agatha, which belonged to the Arians; it helped him to fix his thoughts upon Veranilda, and silently he swore that no temptation should prevail against the fidelity due to his beloved.

Not far from the Thermae of Constantine, and over against that long-ruined sanctuary of ancient Rome, the Temple of Quirinus, he drew rein at a great house with a semicircular portico of Carystian columns, before which stood a bronze bull, the ornament of a fountain now waterless; on either side of the doorway was a Molossian hound in marble. A carriage and a litter waiting here showed that Heliodora had visitors. This caused Basil to hesitate for a moment but he decided to enter none the less. At his knock he was at once admitted, and a slave was sent to look after his horse.

Few houses in Rome contained so many fine works of ancient sculpture as this, for its master had been distinguished by his love of such things in a time when few cared for them. Some he had purchased at a great price; more than one masterpiece he had saved from oblivion amid ruins, or from the common fate of destruction in a lime-kiln. Well for him had he been content to pass his latter years with the cold creations of the sculptor; but he turned his eyes upon consummate beauty in flesh and blood, and this, the last of his purchases, proved the costliest of all.

The atrium was richly adorned. A colossal bust of Berenice faced the great head of an Amazon, whilst numerous statues, busts, and vases stood between the pillars; mosaics on the floor represented hunting scenes, the excellence of the work no less than its worn condition showing it to be of a time long gone by. Following his conductor, Basil passed along a corridor, and into a peristyle with a double colonnade. In the midst of a little garden, planted with flowering shrubs, rose the statue which its late owner had most prized, an admirable copy of the Aphrodite of Cnidos; it stood upon a pedestal of black basalt and was protected by a light canopy with slender columns in all but transparent alabaster. Round about it were marble seats, and here, shielded from the sun by little silken awnings, sat Heliodora and her guests. At once Basil became aware of the young Vivian, whose boyish form (he was but some eighteen years old) lounged among cushions on the seat nearest to Heliodora, his eyes fixed upon her beauty in a languishing gaze, which, as soon as he beheld the new comer, flashed into fierceness. The others were two women, young and comely, whose extravagant costume and the attitudes in which they reclined proved them suitable companions of the lady of the house. Whilst yet at some distance, Basil had heard a feminine voice rising to shrillness, and as he approached the group he found a discussion going on which threatened to become more than vivacious. The shrill speaker he had met here before, who she was, he knew not, save that she bore the name of Muscula.

'You—you—you!' this lady was exclaiming contemptuously. 'You say this, and you say that! Mother of God! What do *you* know about racing? When were you last in the circus at Constantinople? At eight years old you once told me. You have a good memory if you can remember as far back as that!'

She shrieked a laugh, which no one else joined in. Heliodora, to whom the speech was addressed, affected to smile as in lofty tolerance of infantine pettishness. At this moment Basil stepped up to her, and kissed her hand; As though for contrast with Muscula's utterance, she greeted him in the softest tone her voice could compass, inviting him with a gesture to take a place at her side, or rather at her feet, for she was reclining on a long couch. Heliodora's robe was of hyacinth blue, broidered in silver thread with elaborate designs. Bracelets, chains, and rings shone about her in the wonted profusion. Above the flat coils of her hair lay a little bunch of grapes between two vine leaves, wrought in gold, and at her waist hung a dagger, the silver sheath chased with forms of animals. Standing behind her the little Anglian slave Laetus gently fanned her with a peacock's tail, or sprinkled her with perfume from a vial; the air was heavy with Sabaean odours.

'Ah, here is lord Basil!' pursued Muscula with a mischievous glance at Vivian. 'He has lived at Constantinople lately—not thirty or forty years ago. Tell us, sweet lord'—she bent towards him with large, rolling eyes—'was it not Helladius who won for the Greens when Thomas the Blue was overturned and killed?'

'For all I know it may have been,' replied Basil carelessly; he had scarce heard the question.

'I swear you are wrong, Muscula,' put in the third lady. 'The lord Basil cares naught for such things, and would not contradict you lest you should scratch his face—so dangerous you look, much more like a cat than a mouse. By the beard of Holy Peter! should not Heliodora know, who, though she is too young to remember it herself, has heard of it many a time from her father. You think too much of yourself, O Muscula, since you ate crumbs from the hands of Bessas.'

The boy Vivian gave a loud laugh, rolling on his cushions.

'O witty Galla!' he exclaimed. 'Crumbs from the hand of Bessas. Say on, say on; I love your spicy wit, O Galla! Cannot you find something sharp, for the most grave, the most virtuous Basil?'

'Hold your saucy tongue, child,' said Heliodora with a pouting smile. 'But it is true that Muscula has won advancement. One doesn't need to have a very long memory to recall her arrival in Rome. There are who say that she came as suckling nurse in a lady's train, with the promise of marriage to a freedman when her mistress's baby was weaned. That is malice, of course; poor Muscula has had many enemies. For my part, I have never doubted that she was suckling her own child, nor that its father was a man of honourable name, and not a slave of the Circus stables as some said.'

Again Vivian rolled on the cushions in mirth, until he caught Basil's eye as it glanced at him with infinite scorn. Then he started to a sitting posture, fingered the handle of his dagger, and glared at Heliodora's neighbour with all the insolent ferocity of which his face was capable. This youth was the son of a man whose name sounded ill to any Roman patriot,—of that Opilio, who, having advanced to high rank under King Theodoric, was guilty of frauds, fell from his eminence, and, in hope of regaining the king's favour, forged evidence of treachery against Boethius. His attire followed the latest model from Byzantium: a loose, long-sleeved tunic, descending to the feet, its hue a dark yellow, and over that a long mantle of white silk, held together upon one shoulder by a great silver buckle in the form of a running horse; silken shoes, gold embroidered, with leather soles dyed purple; and on each wrist a bracelet. His black hair was short, and crisped into multitudinous curls with a narrow band of gold pressing it from the forehead to the ears.

'Oh, look at little Vivian!' cried Muscula. 'He has the eyes of an angry rat. What vexes him? Is it because he saw Basil touch Heliodora's slipper?'

'If I had!' sputtered the boy. 'By the devil, if I had!'

'Oh, he affrights me!' went on the mocking woman. 'Heliodora, stroke his curls, and give him a kiss, I beseech you. Who knows what dreadful thing may happen else?'

'I have had enough of this,' said Galla, rising with a careless laugh. 'Your house has been intolerable, most dear Heliodora, since you made friends with Muscula. Why you did, I'm sure I don't know; but for my part I take a respectful leave, noble lady, until I hear that this mouse of the Palatine has ceased to amuse you with its pretty pranks. May I never be saved if she is fit company for women who respect themselves.'

'Why such hurry, O chaste Galla!' exclaimed Muscula. 'Is your husband at home for once? I can answer for it he is not there very often; the wiser man he.'

'Slap her face, Galla,' cried Vivian. 'At her! She will run before you.'

Galla moved as if to act upon this advice, but the voice of Heliodora, peremptory, resonant, checked her step.

'None of that! Get you gone, both of you, and try conclusions if you will in the open street. Off! Pack! By the Virgin Mother, if you linger I will have you flung out of doors.'

In her amazement and indignation, Galla rose to the tips of her feet.

'This to *me*!' she screamed. 'To me, the only woman of noble birth and honest life who still remained your friend! Wanton! witch! poisoner!'

Basil sprang up and walked aside, overcome with shame at the scene enacted before him, and fearing it would end in ignoble violence. He heard Muscula's shriek of laughter, a shout of anger from Vivian, and the continued railing of Galla; then, ere he had taken a dozen steps, a hand touched him, and Heliodora's voice sounded low at his ear.

'You are right, dear Basil. Only an accident prevented me from being alone at your hour. Forgive me. We will go apart from these base-tongued creatures.'

But almost in the same moment sounded another voice, that of Muscula, who had sprung after them.

'Sweet lord Basil,' she murmured at his ear, 'a moment's patience, for I have that to say which is worth your hearing.'

Heliodora stepped aside. Pale with fury, she held herself in an attitude of contemptuous indifference.

'Speak and have done!' exclaimed Basil harshly.

'But a word, Illustrious. I know well why you are here. Not for this woman's painted cheeks and essence-soaked hair: you had enough of that long ago. You come because she pretends to know a secret which concerns you nearly. It was to discover this secret that she sought friendship with me. But do not imagine, sweet lord, that I tell all I know to Heliodora. I have played with her curiosity and fooled her. From me she has learnt nothing true. Even if she desired to tell you the truth—and be sure she does not—she could only mislead you.'

Basil was standing between the two women, his eyes on the ground. Had he watched Heliodora at this moment, he would have understood the sudden start with which Muscula sprang nearer to him as if for protection.

'I alone,' she continued, in a voice not so subdued but that Heliodora could hear every word. 'I alone can discover for you what you wish to know. Give yourself no more trouble in suing to a woman of whom you are weary—a woman evil and dangerous as a serpent. When you choose to seek me, dear lord, I will befriend you. Till that day, fare you well, and beware of other things than the silver-hilted dagger—which she would draw upon me did she dare. But she knows that I too have my little bosom friend—' she touched her waist—'though it does not glitter before every eye.'

Therewith Muscula turned and tripped off, looking back to laugh aloud before she disappeared in the corridor. Galla was already gone, half persuaded, half threatened away by Vivian, who now stood with knitted brows glaring at Basil.

'I must get rid of this boy,' said Heliodora to her companion. 'In a moment we shall be alone.'

Basil was held from taking curt leave only by Vivian's insolent eyes; when Heliodora moved, he stepped slowly after her.

'Your company is precious, dear Vivian,' he heard her say, 'but you must not spoil me with too much of it. Why did you not go away with Galla, whose wit so charms you, and whose husband is so complaisant? There, kiss my little finger, and say good-bye.'

'That shall be when it pleases me,' was Vivian's reply. 'To-day I have a mind to sup with you, Heliodora. Let that intruder know it; or I will do so myself.'

Heliodora had the air of humouring a jest. Putting forth a hand, she caught the stripling's ear and pinched it shrewdly.

'Little lord,' she said, 'you take too large a liberty.'

Whereto Vivian replied with a pleasantry so broad and so significant that Heliodora's cheek fired; for she saw that Basil stood within hearing.

'Nay, I must be brief with you, young monkey!' she exclaimed. 'Away! When I am at leisure for your tricks I will send for you. Be off!'

'And leave you with that...?' cried the other, using a villainous word.

Hereupon Basil addressed him.

'Whether you stay or go, foul mouth, is naught to me. I am myself in haste to be gone, but I will not leave you without a lesson by which, perchance, you may profit.'

As he uttered the last word, he dealt Vivian such a buffet on the side of the head with his open hand that the youngster staggered. The result of this, Basil had well foreseen; he stood watchful, and in an instant, as a dagger gleamed before his eyes, grasped the descending arm that wielded it. Vivian struggled furiously, but was overcome by the other's strength. Flung violently to the ground, his head struck against the edge of a marble seat, and he lay senseless.

Heliodora looked on with the eyes with which she had often followed a fight between man and beast in the amphitheatre. Pride, and something more, lit up her countenance as she turned to Basil.

'Brave generous!' she exclaimed, her hands clasped against her bosom. 'Not even to draw your dagger! Noble Basil!'

'Have him looked to,' was the reply; 'and console him as you choose. Lady, I bid you farewell.'

For a moment Heliodora stood as though she would let him thus depart. Basil was nearing the entrance to the corridor, when she sprang after him. Her arms were about his neck; her body clung against his; she breathed hotly into his eyes as she panted forth words, Latin, Greek, all burning with shameless desire. But Basil was not thus to be subdued. The things that he had heard and seen, and now at last the hand-to-hand conflict, had put far from him all temptation of the flesh; his senses were cold as the marbles round about him. This woman, who had never been anything to him but a lure and a peril, whom he had regarded with the contempt natural in one of his birth towards all but a very few of her sex, now disgusted him. He freed himself from her embrace with little ceremony.

'Have I deceived you?' he asked. 'Have I pretended to come here for anything but my own purpose, which you pretended to serve?'

Heliodora stood in a strange attitude, her arms thrown back, her body leaning forward—much like some fierce and beautiful animal watching the moment to spring.

'Do you believe what that harlot said?' she asked in a thick voice.

'Enough of it to understand my folly in hoping to learn anything through you. Let us part, and think of each other no more.'

She caught his arm and put her face close to his.

'Leave me thus, and your life shall pay for it.'

Basil laughed scornfully.

'That cockerel,' he replied, pointing to Vivian, who was just stirring, 'sent me a message this morning, that if I valued my life I should not come here. I heed your threat no more than his.'

They looked into each other's eyes, and Heliodora, deep read in the looks of men, knew that her desire was frustrate.

'Go then,' she said. 'Go quickly, lest the boy pursue you His second aim might be surer.'

Basil deigned no reply. He went into the vestibule, waited there until his horse was brought up, and rode away.

His head bent, scarce noting the way he took, he found himself at the entrance to Trajan's Forum. Here he checked his horse, and seemed to be contemplating that scene which for centuries had excited the wonder and the awe of men. But when he rode on over the grass-grown pavement, he was as little observant of the arches, statues, galleries, and of that great column soaring between Basilica and Temple, as of the people who moved hither and thither, sparse, diminutive. Still brooding, he came into the Via Lata and to the house of Marcian.

Marcian, said the porter, was closeted with certain visitors.

'Make known to him,' said Basil, 'that I would speak but a word in private.'

They met in the atrium. Marcian smiled oddly.

'If you come to tell me what you have heard this afternoon,' he whispered, 'spare your breath. I know it already.'

'How can that be?'

'I have seen an angry woman. Angry women are always either very mischievous or very useful. In this case I hope to make use of her. But I can tell you nothing yet, and I would that you were far from Rome. Could I but persuade you to be gone, dear Basil.'

'I need no more persuading,' replied the other, with sudden resolve. 'If it be true that I am free to leave the city, I go hence to-morrow.'

Marcian's face lighted up.

'To Asculum, then?'

'Since here I have no hope. Can I trust you, Marcian?' he added, grasping his friend's hand.

'As yourself—nay, better.'

'Then, to Asculum.'

CHAPTER XVI
WHISPERS

The greater part of southern Italy was once more held by the Goths. Whilst the long blockade of Neapolis went on, Totila found time to subdue all that lay between that city and the Ionian Sea, meeting, indeed, with little resistance among the country-folk, or from the inhabitants of the mostly unwalled towns. The Imperial forces which should have been arrayed against him had wintered in various cities of the north, where their leaders found all they at present cared for, repose and plunder; their pay long in arrear, and hardly to be hoped for, the Greek soldiers grew insubordinate, lived as they would or could, and with the coming of spring deserted in numbers to the victorious enemy. Appeals to Byzantium for reinforcements had as yet resulted only in the sending of a small, ill-equipped fleet, which, after much delay in Sicilian ports, sailed for Neapolis, only to be surprised by a storm, and utterly wrecked on the shores of the great bay. Not long after the news of this disaster, it was reported in Rome that Neapolis, hopeless of relief, had opened her gates, and presently the report had strange confirmation. There arrived by the Appian Way officers of the garrison which had surrendered; not as harassed fugitives, but travelling with all convenience and security, the Gothic king himself having expedited their journey and sent guides with them lest they should miss the road. Nor was this the most wonderful of the things they had to relate. For they told of humanity on the part of the barbarian conqueror such as had no parallel in any story of warfare known to Greek or Roman; how the Neapolitans being so famine-stricken that they could scarce stand on their legs, King Totila would not at once send plentiful stores into the town, lest the sufferers should die of surfeit, but ministered to their needs even as a friendly physician would have done, giving them at first little food, and more as their strength revived. To be sure, there were partisans of the Empire in Rome who scoffed at those who narrated, and those who believed, a story so incredible. On the Palatine, it was at first received with roars of laughter, in which the lady Muscula's shrill voice had its part. When confirmation had put the thing beyond dispute, Bessas and his supporters made a standing joke of it; if any one fell sick their word was: 'Send for the learned Totila'; and when there was talk of a siege of Rome, they declared that their greatest fear, should the city fall, was of being dieted and physicked by the victor.

Romans there were, however, who heard all this in another spirit. The ill-fed populace had long ago become ready for any change which might benefit their stomachs, and the name of Totila was to them significant of all they lacked under the Greeks. 'Let the Goth come quickly!' passed from mouth to mouth wherever the vulgar durst speak what they thought. Among the nobles, prejudice of race and religion and immemorial pride ensured predominance to the Imperialists, but even here a Gothic party existed, and imprudent utterances had brought certain senators into suspicion. The most active friend of Totila, however, was one whom Bessas never thought of suspecting, having, as he thought, such evidence of the man's devotion to the Greek cause. Marcian had played his double part with extraordinary skill and with boldness which dared every risk. He was now exerting himself in manifold ways, subtly, persistently, for the supreme achievement of his intrigue, the delivery of Rome from Byzantine tyranny.

Among the many persons whom he made to serve his ends without admitting them to his confidence was Galla, the wife of a noble whom Amalasuntha had employed in her secret communications with Byzantium, and who was now one of the intimates of Bessas. A light woman, living as she pleased because of her husband's indifference, Galla knew and cared nothing about affairs of state, and on that account was the more useful to Marcian. She believed him in love with her, and he encouraged the belief; flattering her with pretence at timidity, as though he would fain have spoken but durst not. Regarding him as her slave, Galla amused herself by sometimes coming to his house, where, as if in the pride of chastity, she received his devotion, and meanwhile told him things he was glad to know. And thus it happened on that day of the quarrel between Heliodora and Muscula, wherein Galla unexpectedly found herself involved. Bubbling over with wrath against Heliodora, she at once sought out Marcian, acquainted him with all that had happened, and made evident her desire to be in some way avenged. Marcian saw in this trivial affair the opportunity for a scheme of the gravest import; difficult, perilous, perhaps impracticable, but so tempting in its possibilities that he soon resolved to hazard everything on the chance of success. Basil's departure from Rome, which he had desired for other reasons, fell pat for the device now shaping itself in his mind. A day or two after, early in the morning, he went to Heliodora's house, and sent in a message begging private speech with the lady. As he had expected, he was received forthwith, Heliodora being aware of his friendship with Basil. Between her and Marcian the acquaintance was but slight; he had hitherto regarded her as unserviceable, because too dangerous. It was because of her dangerous qualities that he now sought her, and his courage grew as the conversation became intimate.

He began with a confession. Head hanging, visage gloomy, in slow, indirect, abashed language, he let it be understood that though truly Basil's friend, he had all along been secretly doing his utmost to frustrate the lover's search for the Gothic maiden Veranilda, and, as part of this purpose, had striven to turn Basil's thoughts to Heliodora. That he had had no better success grieved him to the heart. All who wished Basil well, desired that he should marry a lady of his own rank, his own religion, and could he but have won a wife such as Heliodora!

'Alas!' sighed Marcian, 'it was too much to hope. How could you be other than cold to him? Had you deigned, thrice gracious lady, to set your beauty, your gifts, in contest with his memory of that other!'

In every man that approached her, Heliodora suspected a selfish aim, but it was seldom that she talked with one whose subtlety seemed the equal of her own. The little she knew of Marcian had predisposed her to regard him as a cold and melancholy nature, quite uninteresting; she eyed him now with her keenest scrutiny, puzzled by his story, vainly seeking its significance.

'Your friend complained to you of my coldness?' she said distantly.

'He scarce spoke of you. I knew too well with what hope he came here. When he found it vain, he turned away in bitterness.'

This sounded like truth to one who knew Basil. After a moment's reflection, Heliodora made another inquiry, and in a tone of less indifference.

'Why, lord Marcian, do you come to tell me this? Basil has quitted Rome. You can scarce ask me to pursue him.'

'Lady,' was the sad reply, 'I will not even yet abandon hope. But this is not the moment to plead his cause with you, and indeed I came with a thought more selfish.'

Ready to believe whatever might be uttered with such preface, Heliodora smiled and bade the speaker continue. Again Marcian's head drooped; again his words became hesitant, vague. But their purpose at length grew unmistakable; unhappy that he was, he himself loved Veranilda, and the vehemence of his passion overcame his loyalty in friendship; never whilst he lived should Basil wed the Gothic maiden. This revelation astonished Heliodora; she inquired when and how Marcian had become enamoured, and heard in reply a detailed narrative, part truth, part false, of the events at Surrentum, known to her as yet only in outline and without any mention of Marcian's part in them. Upon her surprise followed malicious joy. Was there no means, she asked, of discovering Veranilda? And the other in a low voice made answer that he knew where she was—knew but too well.

'I shall not ask you to tell me the secret,' said Heliodora, with a smile.

'Gracious lady,' pursued Marcian, 'it is for the purpose of revealing it to you that I am here. Veranilda is in the palace, held in guard by Bessas till she can have escort to Constantinople.'

'Ha! You are sure of that?'

'I have it on testimony that cannot be doubted.'

'Why then,' exclaimed Heliodora, all but betraying her exultation in the thought, 'there is little chance that Basil's love will prosper.'

'Little chance, dear lady, I hope and believe, but I have confessed to you that I speak as a self-seeker and a faithless friend. It is not enough that Basil may not wed her; I would fain have her for myself.'

The listener laughed. She began to think this man something of a simpleton.

'Why, my excellent Marcian, I will give you all my sympathy and wish you good fortune. But that any one may do. What more do you expect of me?'

Marcian looked towards the open doorway. They were seated in a luxurious little room, lighted from the peristyle, its adornments in sculpture a sleeping Hermaphrodite and a drunken satyr; on the wall were certain marble low-reliefs, that behind Heliodora representing Hylas drawn down by the Naiads.

'Speak without fear,' she reassured him. 'In this house, believe me, no one dare play the eavesdropper.'

'I have to speak,' said Marcian, bending forward, 'of things perilous—a life hanging on every word. Only to one of whose magnanimity I felt assured should I venture to disclose my thought. You have heard,' he proceeded after a pause, 'and, yet I am perchance wrong in supposing that such idle talk could reach your ears, let me make known to you then, that with Bessas in the palace dwells a fair woman (or so they say, for I have not seen her) named Muscula. She is said to have much power with the commander.'

The listener's countenance had darkened. Regarding Marcian with haughty coldness, she asked him how this could concern *her*. He, in appearance dismayed, falteringly entreated her pardon.

'Be not angered, O noble Heliodora! I did not presume to think that you yourself had any acquaintance with this woman. I wished to make known to you things that I have heard of her—things which I doubt not are true. But, as it is only in my own interest that I speak, I will say no more until I have your permission.'

This having been disdainfully granted, Marcian proceeded with seeming timid boldness, marking in his listener's eyes the eager interest with which she followed him. Though every detail of the story was of his own invention, its plausibility had power upon one whose passions inclined her to believe it. He told then that Muscula, bribed by Basil, was secretly endeavouring to procure the release of Veranilda, which should be made to appear an escape of Basil's contriving. The lover's visits to Heliodora, he said, and his supposed ignorance as to where Veranilda was detained, were part of the plot. Already Muscula had so far wrought upon Bessas that success seemed within view, and Basil's departure from Rome was only a pretence; he waited near at hand, ready to carry off his beloved.

'How come you to know all this?' Heliodora asked bluntly at the first pause.

'That also I will tell you,' answered Marcian. 'It is through some one whom Muscula holds of more account than Bessas, and with whom she schemes against him.'

'By the Holy' Mother!' exclaimed Heliodora, 'that is yourself.'

Marcian shook his head.

'Not so, gracious lady.'

'Nay, why should you scruple to confess it? You love Veranilda, and do you think I could not pardon an intrigue which lay on your way to her?'

'Nevertheless it is not I,' persisted the other gravely.

'Be it so,' said Heliodora. 'And in all this, my good Marcian, what part have I? How does it regard me? What do you seek of me?'

Once more the man seemed overcome with confusion.

'Indeed I scarce know,' he murmured. 'I hardly dare to think what was in my mind when I sought you. I came to you, O Heliodora, as to one before whom men bow, one whose beauty is resistless, whose wish is a command. What gave me courage was a word that fell from Bessas himself when I sat at table with him yesterday. "Wore I the purple," he said, "Heliodora should be my Empress."'

'Bessas said that?'

'He did—and in the presence of Muscula, who heard it, I am bound to say, with a sour visage.'

Heliodora threw back her head and laughed. 'I think he has scarce seen me thrice,' fell from her musingly. 'Tell him from me,' she added, 'that it is indiscreet to talk of wearing the purple before those who may report his words.'

There was a silence. Marcian appeared to brood, and Heliodora did her best to read his face. If, she asked herself; he had told her falsehoods, to what end had he contrived them? Nothing that she could conjecture was for a moment satisfying. If he told the truth, what an opportunity were here for revenge on Muscula, and for the frustration of Basil's desire.

How that revenge was to be wrought, or, putting it the other way, how Marcian was to be helped, she saw as yet only in glimpses of ruthless purpose.

Of Bessas she did not think as of a man easy to subdue or to cajole; his soldierly rudeness, the common gossip of his inconstancy in love, and his well-known avarice, were not things likely to touch her imagination, nor had she ever desired to number him in the circle of her admirers. That it might be in her power to do what Marcian besought, she was very willing to persuade herself, but the undertaking had such colour of danger that she wished for more assurance of the truth of what she had heard.

'It seems to me,' she said at length, 'that the hour is of the latest. What if Veranilda escape this very day?'

'Some days must of necessity pass,' answered Marcian. 'The plot is not so far advanced.'

He rose hurriedly as if distracted by painful thoughts.

'Noble lady, forgive me for thus urging you with my foolish sorrows. You see how nearly I am distraught. If by any means you could aid me, were it only so far as to withhold her I love from the arms of Basil—'

So deep was Heliodora sunk in her thoughts that she allowed Marcian to leave her without another word. He, having carried his machination thus far, could only await the issue, counting securely on Heliodora's passions and her ruthlessness. He had but taken the first step towards the end for which he schemed; were this successful, with the result that Heliodora used her charms upon the Greek commander, and, as might well happen, obtained power over him, he could then proceed to the next stage of his plot, which had a scope far beyond the loves of Basil and Veranilda. That the Gothic maiden was really in the hands of Bessas he did not believe; moreover, time had soothed his jealousy of Basil, and, had he been able to further his friend's desire, he would now willingly have done so; but he scrupled not to incur all manner of risks, for himself and others, in pursuit of a great design. Marcian's convulsive piety, like the religion of most men in his day, regarded only the salvation of his soul from eternal torment, nor did he ever dream that this would be imperilled by the treacheries in which his life was now inured.

Only a few hours after his departure, Heliodora, by means familiar to her, had learnt that Marcian's confidential servant was a man named Sagaris, a conceited and talkative fellow, given to boasting of his light loves. Before sunset, Sagaris had received a mysterious message, bidding him repair that night to a certain place of public resort upon the Quirinal. He did so, was met by the same messenger, and bidden wait under a portico. Before long there approached through the darkness a muffled figure, followed by two attendants with lanterns; the Syrian heard his name whispered; a light touch drew him further away from the lantern-bearing slaves, and a woman's voice, low, caressing, began to utter endearments and reproaches. Not to-night, it said, should he know who she was; she could speak a name which would make his heart beat; but he should not hear it until he had abandoned the unworthy woman whose arts had won him. 'What woman?' asked Sagaris in astonishment. And the answer was whispered, 'Muscula.'

Now Muscula's name and position were well known to the Syrian. The reproach of the mysterious fair one made him swell with pride; he affected inability to deny the charge, and in the next breath declared that Muscula was but his sport, that in truth he cared nothing for her, he did but love her as he had loved women numberless, not only in Rome, but in Alexandria, Antioch, Constantinople. The muffled lady gave a deep sigh. Ah! and so it would be with *her*, were she weak enough to yield to *her* passion. Sagaris began to protest, to vow.

'It is vain,' replied the amorous voice. 'Only in one way can you convince me and win me.'

'Oh, how?'

'Let me hear that Muscula is dead.'

Sagaris stood mute. A hand touched his shoulder, his hair; perfumes loaded the air about him.

'Tell me your name and it shall be done.'

The warm mouth breathed against his cheek and a name was murmured.

The second day after this saw an event in the Palatine which was matter of talk for some two days more, and then passed into oblivion. Rumour said that Muscula had been detected plotting against the life of Bessas, that she had been examined under torture, found guilty, and executed. Certain gossips pretended that there was no plot at all, but that Bessas, weary of his mistress, had chosen this way of getting rid of her. Be that as it might, Muscula was dead.

CHAPTER XVII
LEANDER THE POLITIC

For most of his knowledge of private things that happened on the Palatine—and little that went on in the household of Bessas escaped him—Marcian depended upon his servant Sagaris. Exorbitant vanity and vagrant loves made the Syrian rather a dangerous agent; but it was largely owing to these weaknesses that he proved so serviceable. His master had hitherto found him faithful, and no one could have worked more cunningly and persistently when set to play the spy or worm for secrets. Notwithstanding all his efforts, this man failed to discover whether Veranilda had indeed passed into the guardianship of Bessas; good reason in Marcian's view for believing that she was still detained by Leander, and probably in some convent. But a rumour sprang up among those who still took interest in the matter that some one writing from Sicily professed to have seen the Gothic maiden on board a vessel which touched there on its way to the East. This came to the ears of Marcian on the day after his conversation with Heliodora. Whether it were true or not he cared little, but he was disturbed by its having become subject of talk at this moment, for Heliodora could not fail to hear the story.

The death of Muscula set him quivering with expectancy. That it resulted from his plotting he could not be assured. Sagaris, who wore a more than usually self-important air when speaking of the event, had all manner of inconsistent reports on his tongue Not many days passed before Marcian received a letter, worded like an ordinary invitation, summoning him to the house on the Quirinal.

He went at the third hour of the morning, and was this time led upstairs to a long and wide gallery, which at one side looked down upon the garden in the rear of the house, and at the other offered a view over a great part of Rome. Here was an aviary, constructed of fine lattice work in wood, over-trailed with creeping plants, large enough to allow of Heliodora's entering and walking about among the multitude of birds imprisoned. At this amusement Marcian found her. Upon her head perched a little songster; on her shoulder nestled a dove; two fledglings in the palm of her hand opened their beaks for food. Since her last visit a bird had died, and Heliodora's eyes were still moist from the tears she had shed over it.

'You do not love birds,' she said, after gazing fixedly at Marcian a moment through the trellis.

'I never thought,' was the reply, 'whether I loved them or not.'

'I had rather give my love to them than to any of mankind. They repay it better.'

She came forth, carefully closed the wicket behind her, and began to pace in the gallery as though she were alone. Presently she stood to gaze over the city spread before her, and her eyes rested upon the one vast building—so it seemed—which covered the Palatine Hill.

'Marcian!'

He drew near. Without looking at him, her eyes still on the distance, she said in an unimpassioned voice:

'Did you lie to me, or were you yourself deceived?'

'Lady, I know not of what you speak.'

'You know well.' Her dark eyes flashed a glance of rebuke, and turned scornfully away again. 'But it matters nothing. I sent for you to ask what more you have to say.'

Marcian affected surprise and embarrassment.

'It was my hope, gracious lady, that some good news awaited me on your lips. What can I say more than you have already heard from me?'

'Be it so,' was the careless reply. 'I have nothing to tell you except that Veranilda is not there.' She pointed towards the palace. 'And this I have no doubt you know.'

'Believe me, O Heliodora,' he exclaimed earnestly, 'I did not. I was perhaps misled by—'

Her eyes checked him.

'By whom?'

'By one who seemed to speak with honesty and assurance.'

'Let us say, then, that you were misled; whether deceived or not, concerns only yourself. And so, lord Marcian, having done what I can for you, though it be little, I entreat your kind remembrance, and God keep you.'

Her manner had changed to formal courtesy, and, with this dismissal, she moved away again. Marcian stood watching her for a moment, then turned to look at the wide prospect. A minute or two passed; he heard Heliodora's step approaching.

'What keeps you here?' she asked coldly.

'Lady, I am thinking.'

'Of what?'

'Of the day soon to come when Totila will be king in Rome.'

Heliodora's countenance relaxed in a smile.

'Yet you had nothing more to say to me,' she murmured in a significant tone.

'There were much to say, Heliodora, to one whom I knew my friend. I had dared to think you so.'

'What proof of friendship does your Amiability ask?' inquired the lady with a half-mocking, half-earnest look.

As if murmuring to himself, Marcian uttered the name 'Veranilda.'

'They say she is far on the way to Constantinople,' said Heliodora. 'If so, and if Bessas sent her, his craft is greater than I thought. For I have spoken with him, and'—she smiled—'he seems sincere when he denied all knowledge of the maiden.'

Marcian still gazed at the distance. Again he spoke as if unconsciously murmuring his thoughts:

'Totila advances. In Campania but a few towns still await his conquest. The Appian Way is open. Ere summer be past he will stand at the gates of Rome.'

'Rome is not easily taken,' let fall the listener, also speaking as though absently.

'It is more easily surrendered,' was the reply.

'What! You suspect Bessas of treachery?'

'We know him indolent and neglectful of duty. Does he not live here at his ease, getting into his own hands, little by little, all the wealth of the Romans, careless of what befall if only he may glut his avarice? He will hold the city as long as may be, only because the city is his possession. He is obstinate, bull-headed. Yet if one were found who could persuade him that the cause of the Greeks is hopeless—that, by holding out to the end, he will merely lose all, whereas, if he came to terms—'

Marcian was watching Heliodora's face. He paused. Their eyes met for an instant.

'Who can be assured,' asked Heliodora thoughtfully, 'that Totila will triumph? They say the Patricius will come again.'

'Too late. Not even Belisarius can undo the work of Alexandros and these devouring captains. From end to end of Italy, the name of the Greeks is abhorred; that of Totila is held in honour. He will renew the kingdom of Theodoric.'

Marcian saw straight before him the aim of all his intrigue. It was an aim unselfish, patriotic. Though peril of the gravest lay in every word he uttered, not this made him tremble, but the fear lest he had miscalculated, counting too securely on his power to excite this woman's imagination. For as yet her eye did not kindle. It might be that she distrusted herself, having learnt already that Bessas was no easy conquest. Or it might be that he himself was the subject of her distrust.

'What is it to *you*?' she suddenly asked, with a fierce gaze. 'Can the Goth bring Veranilda back to Italy?'

'I do not believe that she has gone.'

Marcian had knowledge enough of women, and of Heliodora, to harp on a personal desire rather than hint at high motive. But he was impelled by the turmoil of his fears and hopes to excite passions larger than jealousy. Throwing off all restraint, he spoke with hot eloquence of all that might be gained by one who could persuade the Greek commander to open the gates of Rome. Totila was renowned for his generosity, and desired above all things to reconcile, rather than subdue, the Roman people; scarce any reward would seem to him too great for service such as helped this end.

'Bessas lies before you. Ply your spells; make of him your creature; then whisper in his ear such promise of infinite gold as will make his liver melt. For *him* the baser guerdon; for *you*, O Heliodora, all the wishes of your noble heart, with power, power, power and glory unspeakable!'

Heliodora pondered. Then, without raising her head, she asked quietly:

'You speak for the King?'

'For the King,' was answered in like tone.

'Come to me again, Marcian, when I have had time for thought.'

With that they parted. On the same day, Sagaris was bidden as before to a meeting after nightfall, and again he conversed with a lady whose face was concealed from him. She began with a gentle reproof, for he had ventured to present himself at her door, and to beg audience. Let him be patient; his hour would come, but it must be when she chose. Many questions did she put to him, all seeming to be prompted by interest in the Gothic maiden of whom Sagaris had heard so much. With the simplicity of inordinate conceit, he assured her that here she had no ground for jealousy; Veranilda he had never beheld. Softly she corrected his error; her interest in the maiden was a friendly one. Only let him discover for her where Veranilda was concealed. Sagaris was led to avow that in this very search he and his master had been vainly occupied for many a day; it had carried them, he declared in a whisper, even to the camp of King Totila. With this the questioner appeared to be satisfied, and the Syrian was soon dismissed, promises in a caressing voice his sole reward.

When Marcian next held speech with Heliodora—it was after some days—she bore herself more openly. In the course of their talk, he learnt that she had consulted an astrologer, and with results wholly favourable to his design. Not only had this man foretold to her that Totila was destined to reign gloriously over the Italians for many years, but he saw in Heliodora's own fate a mysterious link with that of the triumphant king; her, under the Gothic conquest, great things awaited. 'Do,' was his counsel, 'that which thou hast in mind.' Hearing all this, Marcian's heart leaped with joy. He urged her to pursue their end with all the speed that prudence permitted. For his own part, he would make known to Totila as soon as might be the hope of his friends in Rome.

Again some days passed, and Marcian received one of those messages which at times reached him from the Gothic king. Totila's bidding was contained in a few words: Let Marcian seek speech with the deacon Leander. Surprised, but having full confidence in the messenger, Marcian presently wrote to the deacon in brief terms, saying that he wished to converse with him regarding a certain heretic of whom he had hopes. To this came prompt reply, which did not, however, invite Marcian, as he had expected, to a meeting in private; but merely said that, on the morrow, an hour after sunrise, Leander would be found in a certain public place.

Leander was busied just now in a matter peculiarly congenial to him, the destruction of an ancient building in order to enrich with its columns and precious marbles a new Christian church. At the hour appointed, Marcian found him in the temple of Minerva Chalcidica, directing workmen as to what they should remove; before him lay certain mouldings in green porphyry (the precious *lapis Lacedaemonius*), which had been carefully broken from their places, and he was regarding them with the eye of a lover. For the first few minutes of their conversation, Marcian felt mistrust, as the deacon appeared to have no intelligence of any secret purpose in this meeting; but presently, still gossiping of stones, Leander led him out of the temple and walked in the shadowy public place beside the Pantheon.

'That must be purified and consecrated,' he remarked, glancing from the granite columns of Agrippa's porch to the bronze-tiled dome. 'Too long it has been left to the demons.'

Marcian, preoccupied as he was, listened with awe. Since the ravage of the Vandals, no mortal had passed those vast doors, behind which all the gods of heathendom, known now for devils, lurked in retreat.

'I have urged it upon the Holy Father,' Leander added. 'But Vigilius is all absorbed in the dogmatics of Byzantium. A frown of the Empress Theodora is more to him than the glory of the Omnipotent and the weal of Christendom.'

The look which accompanied these words was the first hint to Marcian that he might speak in confidence. He inquired whether the Pope, as was reported, would shortly sail for Constantinople.

'Before another week has passed,' was the reply, 'he will embark. He would fain go forth'—a malicious smile was in the corner of Leander's eye—'without leave-taking of his beloved people but that can scarce be permitted.'

'Ere he return,' said Marcian, 'things of moment may happen.'

Again the deacon smiled. Seeing on the steps of the Pantheon a couple of idlers playing at flash-finger, they turned aside to be out of earshot.

'We are agreed, it seems,' remarked Leander quickly, 'that there is hope of the heretic. You had news of him yesterday? I, also. It may be in my power to render him some service—presently, presently. Meanwhile, what can you tell me of the lost maiden about whom there has been so much talk? Is it true that Bessas has sent her to the East?'

Marcian turned his eyes upon the speaker's face, and regarded him fixedly with a half smile. For a moment the deacon appeared to be unconscious of this; then he met the familiar look, averted his head again, and said in the same tone as before:

'The heretic, I learn, would gladly see her.'

'It would be as well, I think,' was the reply, 'if his wish were gratified.'

'Ah? But how would that please a friend of yours, dear lord?' asked Leander, with unaffected interest.

Marcian's answer was in a tone of entire sincerity, very unlike that he had used when speaking on this subject with Heliodora.

'It might please him well or ill. The King'—he lowered his voice a little—'would see with gladness this beautiful maiden of his own people, sprung too from the royal blood, and would look with favour upon those who delivered her in safety to him. Should he make her his queen, and I believe she is worthy of that, the greater his gratitude to those who prevented her marriage with a Roman. If, on the other hand, he found that she could not forget her first lover, Totila is large-hearted enough to yield her up in all honour, and politic enough to see advantage in her union with the heir of the Anician house. Between these things, Basil must take his chance. Had he carried off his love, he would have wedded her in disregard of every danger; and so long as it was only the Greeks that sought her, I should have done my best to aid and to protect him. It is different now. Basil I hold dearer than any friend; his place is in my very heart, and his happiness is dearer to me than my own; but I cannot help him to frustrate a desire of Totila. The King is noble; to serve him is to promote the weal of Italy, for which he fights, and in which name he will conquer.'

The deacon had paused in his walk. He looked thoughtfully about him. At this moment there came along the street an ox-drawn wagon, on which lay the marble statue of a deity; Leander stepped up to it, examined the marble, spoke with the men who were conveying it, and returned to Marcian with a shake of the head.

'It pains me to see such carven beauty burnt to lime. And yet how many thousands of her worshippers are now burning in Gehenna. Lord Marcian,' he resumed, 'you have spoken earnestly and well, and have given me good proof of your sincerity. I think with you, and willingly would work with you.'

'Reverend, does no opportunity present itself?'

'In this moment, none that I can see,' was the suave answer.

'Yet I perceive that you have made some offer of service to the King.'

'It is true; and perchance you shall hear more of it. Be not impatient; great things are not hastily achieved.'

With sundry other such remarks, so uttered that their triteness seemed to become the maturity of wisdom, Leander brought the colloquy to an end. It was his principle to trust no man unless he were assured of a motive strong enough to make him trustworthy, and that motive he had not yet discovered in Marcian. Nor, indeed, was he entirely sure of himself; for though he had gone so far as to communicate with the Gothic king, it was only in view of possibilities whose issue he still awaited. If the Pope set forth for Constantinople, he would leave as representative in Rome the deacon Pelagius, and from this brother cleric Leander had already received certain glances, which were not to be misunderstood. The moment might shortly come when he would need a friend more powerful than any he had within the city.

But Vigilius lingered, and Leander, save in his influence with the irresolute Pontiff, postponed the step he had in view.

CHAPTER XVIII
PELAGIUS

Rome waited. It had been thought that the fall of Neapolis would be followed by Totila's swift march along the Appian Way; but three months had passed, and the Gothic king was but little nearer to the city. He seemed resolved to leave nothing behind him that had not yielded to his arms; slowly and surely his rule was being established over all the South. Through the heats of summer, with pestilence still lurking in her palaces and her dens, no fountain plashing where the sun blazed on Forum and on street, Rome waited.

In June Bessas was joined by another of the Greek commanders, Joannes, famed for his ferocity, and nicknamed the Devourer. A show of activity in the garrison resulted from this arrival; soldiers were set to work upon parts of the city wall which needed strengthening; the Romans began to make ready for a siege; and some, remembering the horrors of a few years ago, took to flight. There was much talk of a conspiracy to open the gates to Totila; one or two senators were imprisoned, and a few Arian priests who still dwelt in Rome were sentenced to banishment. But when, after a few weeks, Joannes and his troop marched northward, commotion ceased; Bessas fell back into the life of indolent rapacity, work on the walls was soon neglected, and Rome found that she had still only to wait.

About this time Marcian fell sick. He had suffered much from disappointment of high hopes, neither Heliodora nor Leander aiding his schemes as he expected. The constant danger in which he lived tried his fortitude to the utmost, and at length he began to burn with fever. Agonies came upon him, for even the slightest disorder in these plague-stricken times filled men with fear. And whilst he lay thus wretched, his servants scarce daring to attend upon him—Sagaris refused to enter his chamber, and held himself ready for flight (with all he could lay hands on) as soon as the physician should have uttered the fatal word—whilst his brain was confused and his soul shaken with even worse than the wonted terrors, there came to visit him the deacon Pelagius. That the visit happened at this moment was mere chance, but Pelagius, hearing of Marcian's condition, felt that he could not have come more opportunely. A courageous man, strong in body as in mind, he was not to be alarmed by mere talk of the pest; bidding the porter conduct him, he came to Marcian's bedside, and there sat for half an hour. When he went away, his handsome countenance wore a smile of thoughtful satisfaction.

As though this conversation had relieved him, the sick man at once began to mend. But with his recovery came another torment. Lying in fear of death and hell, he had opened his soul to Pelagius, and had revealed secrets upon which depended all he cared for in this world. Not only he himself was ruined, but the lives of those he had betrayed were in jeopardy. That suspicion was busy with him he knew; the keen-sighted deacon had once already held long talk with him, whereupon followed troublesome interrogation by Bessas, who had since regarded him with somewhat a sullen eye. How would Pelagius use the knowledge he had gained? Even when quite recovered from the fever, Marcian did not venture to go forth, lest an enemy should be waiting for him without. In his weak, dejected and humbled state he thought of the peace of a monastery, and passed most of his time in prayer.

But when a few days had passed without event, and increasing strength enabled him to think less brain-sickly, he began to ask whether he himself had not peradventure been betrayed It was a long time since he had seen Heliodora, who appeared to be making no effort for the conquest of the Greek commander; had she merely failed, and lost courage, or did the change in her mean treachery? To trust Heliodora was to take a fool's risk; even a little wound to her vanity might suffice to turn her against him. At their last meeting she had sat with furrowed brows, brooding as if over some wrong, and when he urged her for an explanation of her mood, she was first petulant, then fiery, so that he took umbrage and left her. Happily she knew none of his graver secrets, much though she had tried to discover them. Were she traitorous, she could betray him alone.

But he, in the wreck of his manhood, had uttered many names besides hers—that of Basil, from whom he had recently heard news, that of the politic Leander, those of several nobles engaged in the Gothic cause. Scarcely could he believe that he had been guilty of such baseness; he would fain have persuaded himself that it was but a memory of delirium. He cursed the subtlety of Pelagius, which had led him on till everything was uttered. Pelagius, the bosom friend of Justinian, would know how to deal with plotters against the Empire. Why had he not already struck? What cunning held his hand?

Unable at length to sit in idleness, he tried to ease his conscience by sending a warning to Basil, using for this purpose the trustworthy slave who, in many disguises, was wont to travel with his secret messages. This man wore false hair so well fixed upon his head that it could not attract attention; the letter he had to deliver was laid beneath an artificial scalp.

'Be on your guard,' thus Marcian wrote. 'Some one has made known to the Greeks that you are arming men, and for what purpose. Delay no longer than you must in joining the King. In him is your only hope, if hope there still can be. I, too, shall soon be in the camp.'

These last words were for his friend's encouragement. As soon as the letter had been despatched, he went forth about Rome in his usual way, spoke with many persons, and returned home unscathed. Plainly, then, he was to be left at liberty yet awhile; Pelagius had purposes to serve. Next day, he betook himself to the Palatine; Bessas received him with bluff friendliness, joked about his escape from death (for every one believed that he had had the plague), and showed no sign of the mistrust which had marked their last meeting. In gossip with certain Romans who were wont to hang about the commander, flattering and fawning upon him for their base advantage, he learnt that no one had yet succeeded to the place left vacant by the hapless Muscula; only in casual amours, generally of the ignoblest, did Bessas bestow his affections. Of Heliodora there was no talk.

Another day he passed in sauntering; nothing that he could perceive in those with whom he talked gave hint of menace to his safety. Then, early the next morning, he turned his steps to the Quirinal. As usual, he was straightway admitted to Heliodora's house, but had to wait awhile until the lady could receive him. Gloomily thoughtful, standing with eyes fixed upon those of the great bust of Berenice, he was startled by a sudden cry from within the house, the hoarse yell of a man in agony; it was repeated, and became a long shriek, rising and falling in terrible undulation. He had stepped forward to seek an explanation, when Heliodora's eunuch smilingly came to meet him.

'What is that?' asked Marcian, his nerves a-quiver.

'The noble lady has ordered a slave to be punished,' was the cheerful reply.

'What is his fault?'

'Illustrious, I know not,' answered the eunuch more gravely.

The fearful sounds still continuing, Marcian turned as though to hurry away; but the eunuch, following, implored him not to go, for his departure would but increase Heliodora's wrath. So for a few more minutes he endured the horror of that unbroken yell. When it ceased, he could hear his heart beating.

Summoned at length to the lady's presence, he found her lying in the chamber of the Hermaphrodite. A strange odour floated in the air, overcoming that of wonted perfumes.

Faint with a sudden nausea, Marcian performed no courtesy, but stood regarding the living woman much as he had gazed at the face in marble, absent and sombre-browed.

'What now?' were Heliodora's first words, her smile fading in displeasure.

'Must we needs converse in your torture-chamber?' asked Marcian.

'Are your senses more delicate than mine?'

'It seems so. I could wish I had chosen another hour for visiting you.'

'It was well chosen,' said Heliodora, regarding him fixedly. 'This slave I have chastised, shall I tell you of what he was guilty? He has a blabbing tongue.'

'I see not how that concerns me,' was his cold reply, as he met her look with steady indifference.

From her lounging attitude Heliodora changed suddenly to one in which, whilst seated, she bent forward as though about to spring at him.

'How comes it that Bessas knows every word that has passed between us?' broke fiercely from her lips.

In an instant Marcian commanded himself, shrugged his shoulders, and laughed.

'That is a question,' he said, 'to put to your astrologer, your oneirocritic, your genethliac. I profess not to read mysteries.'

'Liar!' she shot out. 'How could he have had it but from your own lips?'

Marcian betook himself to his utmost dissimulation, and the talk of the next few minutes—on his part, deliberately provocative; on hers, recklessly vehement—instructed him in much that he had desired to learn. It was made clear to him that a long combat of wills and desires had been in progress between the crafty courtesan and the half wily and the half brutal soldier, with a baffling of Heliodora's devices which would never have come to his knowledge but for this outbreak of rage. How far the woman had gone in her lures, whether she had played her last stake, he could not even now determine; but he suspected that only such supreme defeat could account for the fury in which he beheld her. Bessas, having (as was evident) heard the secret from Pelagius, might perchance have played the part of a lover vanquished by his passions, and then, after winning his end by pretence of treachery to the Emperor, had broken into scoffing revelation. That were a triumph after the Thracian's heart. Having read thus far in the past, Marcian had to turn anxious thought upon the future, for his position of seeming security could not long continue. He bent himself to allay the wrath he had excited. Falling of a sudden into a show of profound distress, he kept silence for a little, then murmured bitterly:

'I see what has happened. When the fever was upon me, my mind wandered, and I talked.'

So convincing was the face, the tone, so plausible the explanation, that Heliodora drew slowly back, her fury all but quenched. She questioned him as to the likely betrayer, and the name of Sagaris having been mentioned, used the opportunity to learn what she could concerning the man.

'I cannot promise to give him up to you to be tortured,' said Marcian, with his characteristic smile of irony.

'That I do not ask. But,' she added significantly, 'will you send him here, and let me use gentler ways of discovering what I can?'

'That, willingly.'

And when Marcian went away, he reflected that all was not yet lost. For Heliodora still had faith in the prophecy of her astrologer; she was more resolute than ever in her resolve to triumph over Bessas; she could gain nothing to this end by helping her confederate's ruin. Before parting, they had agreed that Marcian would do well to affect ignorance of the discovery Bessas had made; time and events must instruct them as to the projects of their enemies, and guide their own course.

That same day, he despatched the Syrian with a letter to Heliodora, and on the man's return spoke with him as if carelessly of his commission. He remarked that the face of Sagaris shone as though exultantly, but no indiscreet word dropped from the vaunter's lips. A useful fellow, murmured Marcian within himself, and smiled contempt.

Another day or two of indecision, then in obedience to an impulse he could no longer resist, he sought speech with the deacon Pelagius. Not without trouble was this obtained, for Pelagius was at all times busy, always beset by suitors of every degree, the Romans holding him in high reverence, and making their appeals to him rather than to the Pope, for whom few had a good word. When at last Marcian was admitted to the deacon's presence, he found himself disconcerted by the long, silent scrutiny of eyes deep read in the souls of men. No word would reach his lips.

'I have been expecting you,' said the deacon at length, gravely, but without severity. 'You have made no haste to come.'

'Most reverend,' replied Marcian, in a tone of the deepest reproach, 'I knew not certainly whether I had indeed made confession to you, or if it was but a dream of fever.'

Pelagius smiled. He was standing by a table, and his hand lay upon an open volume.

'You are of noble blood, lord Marcian,' he continued, 'and the greatness of your ancestors is not unknown to you. Tell me by what motive you have been induced to play the traitor against Rome. I cannot think it was for the gain that perishes. Rather would I suppose you misled by the opinion of Cassiodorus, whose politics were as unsound as his theology. I read here, in his treatise *De Anima*, that there is neither bliss nor torment for the soul before the great Day of Judgment—a flagrant heresy, in utter contradiction of the Scriptures, and long ago refuted by the holy Augustine. Can you trust in worldly matters one who is so blinded to the clearest truths of eternity?'

'I confess,' murmured the listener, 'that I thought him justified in his support of the Gothic kingdom.'

'You are content, then, you whose ancestors have sat in the Senate, to be ruled by barbarians? You, a Catholic, revolt not against the dominions of Arians? And so little is your foresight, your speculation, that you dream of permanent conquest of Italy by this leader of a barbaric horde? I tell you, lord Marcian, that ere another twelvemonth has passed, the Goths will be defeated, scattered, lost. The Emperor is preparing a great army, and before the end of summer Belisarius will again land on our shores. Think you Totila can stand against him? Be warned; consider with yourself. Because your confession had indeed something of sickness in it, I have forborne to use it against you as another might have done. But not with impunity can you resume your traitorous practices; of that be assured.'

He paused, looking sternly into Marcian's face.

'I have no leisure to debate with you, to confute your errors. One thing only will I add, before dismissing you to ponder what I have uttered. It is in your power to prove your return to reason and the dignity of a Roman; I need not say how; the occasion will surely ere long present itself, and leave you in no doubt as to my meaning. Remember, then, how I have dealt with you; remember, also, that no such indulgence will be granted to a renewal of your crime against Rome, your sin against God.'

Marcian dropped to his knees; there was a moment of silence; then he arose and went forth.

A week passed, and there came the festival of St. Laurentius. All Rome streamed out to the basilica beyond the Tiburtine Gate, and among those who prayed most fervently at the shrine was Marcian. He besought guidance in an anguish of doubt. Not long ago, in the early days of summer, carnal temptation had once more overcome him, and the sufferings, the perils, of this last month he attributed to that lapse from purity. His illness was perhaps caused by excess of rigour in penitence. To-day he prayed with many tears that the Roman martyr would enlighten him, and make him understand his duty to Rome.

As he was leaving the church, a hand touched him; he turned, and beheld the deacon Leander, who led him apart.

'It is well that I have met you,' said the cleric, with less than his usual bland deliberation. 'A messenger is at your house to bid you come to me this evening. Can you leave Rome to-morrow?'

'On what mission?'

Leander pursed his lips for a moment, rolled his eyes hither and thither, and said with a cautious smile:

'That for which you have been waiting.'

With difficulty Marcian dissembled his agitation. Was this the saint's reply to his prayer? Or was it a temptation of the Evil Power, which it behoved him to resist?

'I am ready,' he said, off-hand.

'You will be alone for the first day's journey, and in the evening you will be met by such attendants as safety demands. Do you willingly undertake the charge? Or is there some new danger which you had not foreseen?'

'There is none,' replied Marcian, 'and I undertake the charge right willingly.'

'Come to me, then, at sunset. The travel is planned in every detail, and the letters ready. What follower goes with you?'

'The same as always—Sagaris.'

'Confide nothing to him until you are far from Rome. Better if you need not even then.'

Leander broke off the conference, and walked away at a step quicker than his wont. But Marcian, after lingering awhile in troubled thought, returned to the martyr's grave. Long he remained upon his knees, the conflict within him so violent that he could scarce find coherent words of prayer. Meanwhile the August sky had clouded, and thunder was beginning to roll. As he went forth again, a flash of lightning dazzled him. He saw that it was on the left hand, and took courage to follow the purpose that had shaped in his thoughts.

That evening, after an hour's close colloquy with Leander, he betook himself by circuitous way to the dwelling of Pelagius, and with him again held long talk. Then went home, through the dark, still streets, to such slumber as his conscience might permit.

CHAPTER XIX
THE PRISONER OF PRAENESTE

On the morrow of St. Laurentius, at that point of dawn when a man can recognise the face of one who passes, there issued from the Lateran a silent company equipped for travel. In a covered carriage drawn by two horses sat the Pope, beside him a churchman of his household; a second carriage conveyed the deacon Leander and another ecclesiastic; servants and a baggage vehicle brought up the rear. With what speed it could over the ill-paved roads, this procession made for the bank of the Tiber below the Aventine, where, hard by the empty public granaries, a ship lay ready to drop down stream. It was a flight rather than a departure. Having at length made up his mind to obey the Emperor's summons, Vigilius endeavoured to steal away whilst the Romans slept off their day of festival. But he was not suffered to escape thus. Before he had reached the place of embarkation, folk began to run shouting behind his carriage. Ere he could set foot on board the vessel a crowd had gathered. The farewell of the people to their supreme Pontiff was given in a volley of stones and potsherds, whilst the air rang with maledictions.

Notwithstanding his secret hostility, Leander had of late crept into Vigilius' confidence, thus protecting himself against his formidable adversary Pelagius. He was now the Pope's travelling companion as far as Sicily. Had he remained in Rome, the authority of Pelagius would have fallen heavily upon him, and he could scarce have escaped the humiliation of yielding his Gothic captive to Justinian's friend. Apprised only a day before of Vigilius' purpose, he had barely time to plot with Marcian for the conveyance of Veranilda to Totila's camp. This had long been his intention, for, convinced that Totila would rule over Italy, he saw in the favour of the king not only a personal advantage, but the hope of the Western Church in its struggle with Byzantium. Driven at length to act hurriedly, he persuaded himself that he could use no better agent than Marcian, who had so deeply pledged himself to the Gothic cause. Of what had passed between Marcian and Pelagius he of course knew nothing. So, as the ship moved seaward upon tawny Tiber, and day flamed upon the Alban hills, Leander laughed within himself. He enjoyed a plot for its own sake, and a plot, long savoured, which gave him triumph over ecclesiastical rivals, and even over the Emperor Justinian, was well worth the little risk that might ensue When he returned to Rome, it would doubtless be with the victorious Goth—safe, jubilant, and ere long to be seated in the chair of the Apostle.

At the same hour Marcian was riding along the Praenestine Way, the glory of summer sunrise straight before him. The thought most active in his mind had nothing to do with the contest of nations or with the fate of Rome: it was that on the morrow he should behold Veranilda. For a long time he had ceased to think of her; her name came to his lips in connection with artifice and intrigue, but the maiden herself had faded into nothingness, no longer touched his imagination. He wondered at that fantastic jealousy of Basil from which he had suffered. This morning, the caress of the warm air, the scents wafted about him as he rode over the great brown wilderness, revived his bygone mood. Again he mused on that ideal loveliness which he attributed to the unseen Veranilda For nearly a year she had been sought in vain by her lover, by Greek commanders, by powerful churchmen; she had been made the pretext of far-reaching plots and conspiracies; her name had excited passions vehement and perilous, had been the cause of death. Now he was at length to look upon her; nay, she was to pass into his guardianship, and be by him delivered into the hands of the warrior king. Dreaming, dreaming, he rode along the Praenestine Way.

Though the personal dignity of Pelagius and the calm force of his speech had awed and perturbed him, Marcian soon recovered his habitual mind. He had thought and felt too deeply regarding public affairs to be so easily converted from the cause for which he lived. A new treachery was imposed upon him. When, after receiving all his instructions from Leander, he went to see Pelagius, it was in order to secure his own safety and the fulfilment of his secret mission by a seeming betrayal of him he served. He knew that his every movement was watched; he could not hope to leave Rome without being stopped and interrogated. If he desired to carry out Leander's project—and he desired it the more ardently the longer he reflected—his only course was this. Why did it agitate him more than his treachery hitherto? Why did he shake and perspire when he left Pelagius, after promising to bring Veranilda to Rome? He knew not himself—unless it were due to a fear that he might perform his promise.

This fear it was, perhaps, which had filled his short sleep with dreams now terrible, now luxurious. This fear it was which caught hold of him, at length distinct and intelligible, when, on turning his head towards the city soon after sunrise, he became aware of a group of horsemen following him at a distance of half a mile or so. Thus had it been agreed with Pelagius. The men were to follow him, without approaching, to a certain point of his journey, then would close about him and his attendants, who would be inferior in number, and carry them, with the Gothic maiden, back to Rome. At the sight Marcian drew rein, and for a moment sat in his saddle with bent head, suffering strangely. Sagaris came up to his side, regarded him with anxious eye, and asked whether the heat of the sun's rays incommoded him; whereupon he made a negative sign and rode on.

He tried to laugh. Had he forgotten the subtlety of his plot for deceiving Pelagius? To have made known to the deacon where Veranilda really was, would have been a grave fault in strategy. These armed horsemen imagined that a two days' journey lay before them, whereas the place of Veranildas imprisonment would be reached this evening. The artifice he had elaborated was, to be sure, full of hazard; accident might disconcert everything; the instruments upon whom he reckoned might fail him. But not because of this possibility was his heart so miserably perturbed. It was himself that he dreaded—the failure of his own purpose, the treachery of his own will.

On he rode in the full eye of the August sun. The vast, undulant plain spread around him; its farms, villas, aqueducts no less eloquent of death than the tombs by the wayside its still air and the cloudless azure above speaking to a man's soul as with the voice of eternity. Marcian was very sensible of such solemn influence. More than once, in traversing this region, he had been moved to bow his head in devotion purer than that which commonly inspired his prayers, but to-day he knew not a moment's calm. All within him was turbid, subject to evil thoughts.

A little before noon he made his first halt. Amid the ruins of a spacious villa two or three peasant families had their miserable home, with a vineyard, a patch of tilled soil, and a flock of goats for their sustenance. Here the travellers, sheltered from the fierce sun, ate of the provisions they carried, and lay resting for a couple of hours. Marcian did not speak with the peasants, but he heard the voice of a woman loud in lamentation, and Sagaris told him that it was for the death of a child, who, straying yesterday at nightfall, had been killed by a wolf. Many hours had the mother wept and wailed, only interrupting her grief to vilify and curse the saint to whose protection her little one was confided.

When he resumed his journey, Marcian kept glancing back until he again caught sight of the company of horsemen; they continued to follow him at the same distance. On he rode, the Alban hills at his right hand, and before him, on its mountain side, the town for which he made. The sun was yet far from setting when he reached Praeneste. Its great walls and citadel towering on the height above told of ancient strength, and many a noble building, within the city and without, monuments of glory and luxury, resisted doom. Sulla's Temple of Fortune still looked down upon its columned terraces, but behind the portico was a Christian church, and where once abode the priests of the heathen sanctuary, the Bishop of Praeneste had now his dwelling. Thither did Marcian straightway betake himself. The bishop, a friend and ally of Leander, received him with cordiality, and eagerly read the letter he brought. Asked whether Vigilius had left Rome, Marcian was able to tell something of the Pope's departure, having heard the story just before his own setting forth; whereat the prelate, a man of jovial aspect, laughed unrestrainedly.

'To supper! to supper!' he exclaimed with hospitable note. 'Time enough for our business afterwards.'

But Marcian could not postpone what he had to say. Begging the bishop's patience, he told how all day long he had been followed by certain horsemen from Rome, who assuredly were sent to track him. His servant, he added, was watching for their entrance into the town, and would observe where they lodged. This, the bishop admitted, was a matter of some gravity.

'Your guard is ready,' he said. 'Six stout fellows on good horses. But these pursuers outman you. Let me think, let me think.'

Marcian had but to suggest his scheme. This was, to resume his journey as soon as the townsfolk were all asleep, and travel through the night, for there was a moon all but at the full. He might thus gain so much advance of his pursuers that they would not be able to overtake him before he came to the nearest outpost of the Gothic army. After reflection, the bishop gave his approval to this project, and undertook that all should be ready at the fitting hour. He himself would accompany them to the gate of the town, and see them safely on their way. To make surer, Marcian used another device. When he had learned the quarters of the pursuing horsemen he sent Sagaris privily to speak with their leader, warning him to be ready to ride at daybreak. Such a message had of course nothing unexpected for its recipient, who looked upon Marcian as secretly serving Pelagius. It put his mind at ease and released him from the necessity of keeping a night watch. Sagaris, totally ignorant of his master's mission, and of the plans that had just been formed, imagined himself an intermediary in some plot between Marcian and the leader of the horsemen, and performed the deceitful office in all good faith.

The bishop and his guest sat down to supper in an ancient room, of which the floor was a mosaic representing an Egyptian landscape, with a multitude of figures. Marcian would gladly have asked questions about Veranilda; how long she had been at Praeneste, whether the lady Aurelia was in the same convent, and many other things; but he did not venture to make known how little he had enjoyed of Leander's confidence. His reverend host spoke not at all on this subject, which evidently had no interest for him, but abounded in inquiries as to the state of things ecclesiastical at Rome. The supper was excellent; it pained the good prelate that his guest seemed to have so poor an appetite. He vaunted the quality of everything on the table, and was especially enthusiastic about a wine of the south, very aromatic, which had come to him as a present from his friend the Bishop of Rhegium, together with a certain cheese of Sila, exquisite in thymy savour, whereof he ate with prodigious gusto.

It was about the third hour of the night when Sagaris, to his astonishment, was aroused from a first sleep, and bidden prepare at once for travel.

Following his master and the bishop, who were not otherwise attended, he passed through a garden to a postern, where, by dim lantern light, he saw, in the street without, a small covered carriage drawn by four mules, and behind it several men on horseback; his master's horse and his own were also in readiness at the door. He mounted, the carriage moved forward; and by a steep descent which needed extreme caution, the gate of the city was soon reached. Here the bishop, who had walked beside Marcian, spoke a word with two drowsy watchmen sitting by the open gateway, bade his guest an affectionate farewell, and stood watching for a few minutes whilst vehicle and riders moved away in the moonlight.

Finding himself well sped from Praeneste, where his pursuers lay sound asleep, Marcian felt an extravagant joy; he could scarce command himself to speak a few necessary words, in an ordinary tone, to the leader of the guard with which he was provided; to shout, to sing, would have better suited his mood. Why he thrilled with such exultancy he could not have truly said; but a weight seemed to be lifted from his mind, and he told himself that the relief was due to knowing that he had done with treachery, done with double-dealing, done with the shame and the peril of such a life as he had led for years. Never could he return to Rome save with the Gothic King; in beguiling Pelagius, he had thrown in his lot irrevocably with the enemies of the Greeks. Now he would play the part of an honest man; his heart throbbed at the thought.

But all this time his eyes were fixed upon the closed vehicle, behind which he rode; and was it indeed the thought of having gained freedom which made his heart so strangely beat? He pushed his horse as near as possible to the carriage; he rode beside it; he stretched out his hand and touched it. As soon as the nature of the road permitted, he gave an order to make better speed, and his horse began to trot; he thought less of the danger from which he was fleeing than of the place of rest where Veranilda would step down from the carriage, and he would look upon her face.

Under the great white moon, the valley into which they were descending lay revealed in every feature, and the road itself was as well illumined as by daylight. On they sped, as fast as the mules could be driven. Near or far sounded from time to time the howl of a wolf, answered by the fierce bark of dogs in some farm or village; the hooting of owls broke upon the stillness, or the pipe of toads from a marshy hollow. By the wayside would be seen moving stealthily a dark form, which the travellers knew to be a bear, but they met no human being, nor anywhere saw the gleam of a light in human habitation. Coming within view of some temple of the old religion, all crossed themselves and murmured a prayer, for this was the hour when the dethroned demons had power over the bodies and the souls of men.

After a long descent they struck into the Via Latina, still in spite of long neglect almost as good a road as when the legions marched over its wheel-furrowed stones. If the information on which Leander had calculated was correct, some three days' journey by this way would bring them within reach of the Gothic king; but Marcian was now debating with himself at what point he should quit the high road, so as to make certain his escape, in case the Greek horsemen began a chase early on the morrow. To the left lay a mountainous region, with byways and little ancient towns, in old time the country of the Hernici; beyond, a journey of two good days, flowed the river Liris, and there, not far from the town of Arpinum, was Marcian's ancestral villa. Of this he thought, as his horse trotted beside or behind the carriage. It was much out of his way; surely there would be no need to go so far in order to baffle pursuers. Yet still he thought of his villa, islanded in the Liris, and seemed to hear through the night the music of tumbling waters, and said within his heart, 'Could I not there lie safe?'

Safe?—from the Greeks, that is to say, if they persistently searched for him. Safe, until a messenger could reach Totila, and let him know that Veranilda was rescued.

An hour after midnight, one of the mules' traces broke. In the silence of the stoppage, whilst the driver was mending the harness as best he could, Marcian alighted, stepped to the side of the vehicle, laid a hand on the curtain which concealed those within, and spoke in a subdued voice.

'Is all well with you, lady?'

'As well,' came the answer, 'as it can be with one who dreads her unknown fate.'

The soft accents made Marcian tremble. He expected to hear a sweet voice, but this was sweeter far than he could have imagined: its gentleness, its sadness, utterly overcame him, so that he all but wept in his anguish of delight.

'Have no fear,' he whispered eagerly. 'It is freedom that awaits you. I am Marcian—Marcian, the friend of Basil.'

There sounded a low cry of joy; then the two names were repeated, his and that of his friend, and again Marcian quivered.

'You will be no more afraid?' he said, as though laughingly.

'Oh no! The Blessed Virgin be thanked!'

An owl's long hoot wailed through the stillness, seeming to fill with its infinite melancholy the great vault of moonlit heaven. In Marcian it produced a sudden, unaccountable fear. Leaping on to his horse, he cursed the driver for slowness. Another minute, and they were speeding onward.

Marcian watched anxiously the course of the silver orb above them. When it began to descend seaward, the animals were showing signs of weariness; before daybreak he must perforce call a halt. In conversation with the leader of his guard, he told the reason of their hasting on by night (known already to the horseman, a trusted follower of the Bishop of Praeneste), and at length announced his resolve to turn off the Latin Way into the mountains, with the view of gaining the little town Aletrium, whence, he explained, they could cross the hills to the valley of the Liris, and so descend again to the main road. It was the man's business to obey; he let fall a few words, however, concerning the dangers of the track; it was well known that bands of marauders frequented this country, moving onward before the slow advance of the Gothic troops. Marcian reflected, but none the less held to his scheme. The beasts were urged along an upward way, which, just about the setting of the moon, brought them to a poor village with a little church. Marcian set himself to discover the priest, and, when this good man was roused from slumber, spoke in his ear a word which had great effect. With little delay stabling was found, and a place of repose for Marcian's followers; he himself would rest under the priest's roof, whither he conducted Veranilda and a woman servant who sat with her in the carriage. The face which was so troubling his imagination he did not yet see, for Veranilda kept the hood close about her as she passed by candle light up steps to the comfortless and dirty little chamber which was the best she could have.

'Rest in peace,' whispered Marcian as the door closed. 'I guard you.'

For an hour or more he sat talking with his host over a pitcher of wine, found how far he was from Aletrium, and heard with satisfaction that the brigand bands seemed to have gone higher into the mountains. The presbyter asked eagerly for Roman news, and cautiously concerning King Totila, whom it was evident he regarded with no very hostile feeling. As the day broke he stretched himself on his host's bed, there being no other for him, and there dozed for two or three hours, far too agitated to enjoy a sound sleep.

When he arose, he went forth into the already hot sunshine, looked at the poor peasants' cottages, and talked with Sagaris, whose half-smiling face seemed anxious to declare that he knew perfectly well on what business they were engaged. At this hour, in all probability, the horsemen of Pelagius were galloping along the Latin Way, in hope of overtaking the fugitives. It seemed little likely that they would search in this direction, and the chances were that they would turn back when their horses got tired out. Of them, indeed, Marcian thought but carelessly; his hard-set brows betokened another subject of disquiet. Should he, after Aletrium, go down again to the Latin Way, or should he push a few miles further to the valley of the Liris, and to his own villa?

To-day, being the first day of the week, there was a gathering to hear mass. Marcian, though he had that in his mind which little accorded with religious worship, felt himself drawn to the little church, and knelt among the toil-worn folk. Here, as always when he heard the liturgy, his heart melted, his soul was overcome with awe. From earliest childhood he had cherished a peculiar love and reverence for the Eucharistic prayer, which was associated with his noblest feelings, his purest aspirations. As he heard it now, here amid the solitude of the hills, it brought him help such as he needed.

'Vere dignum et justum est, aequum et salutare, nos tibi semper et ubique gratias agere, Domine sancte, Pater omnipotens, aeterne Deus.'

When at the end he rose, these words were still resonant within him. He turned to go forth, and there behind, also just risen from her knees, stood a veiled woman, at the sight of whom he thrilled with astonishment. No peasant she; for her attire, though but little adorned, told of refinement, and the grace of her figure, the simple dignity of her attitude, would alone have marked her out among the girls and women who were leaving the church, their eyes all turned upon her and on the female attendant standing respectfully near. Through the veil which covered her face and hung about her shoulders, Marcian could dimly discern lips and eyebrows.

'Lord Marcian, may I speak with you?'

It was the voice of last night, and again it shook him with an ecstasy which had more of dread than of joy.

'You here?' he replied, speaking very low. 'You have heard the mass?'

'I am a Catholic. My religion is that of Basil.'

'God be thanked!' broke from Marcian. And his exclamation meant more than it conveyed to the listener.

'May you tell me whither we are going?' was the next question from the veiled lips.

The church was now empty, but in the doorway appeared faces curiously peering. Marcian looking in that direction seemed for a moment to find no reply; his lips were parted, and his breath came rapidly; then he whispered:

'Not far from here there is a villa. There you shall rest in safety until Basil comes.'

'He is near?'

'Already I have summoned him.'

'O kind Marcian!' uttered the low, sweet voice. 'Oh, true and brave friend!'

In silence they walked together to the priest's house. Marcian had now put off all irresolution. He gave orders to his guard; as soon as the horses had sufficiently rested, they would push on for Aletrium, and there pass the night. The start was made some two hours after noon. Riding once more beside the carriage, Marcian felt his heart light: passions and fears were all forgotten; the sun flaming amid the pale blue sky, the violet shadows of the mountains, the voice of cicadas made rapture to his senses. It was as though Veranilda's beauty, not even yet beheld, rayed something of itself upon all the visible world. Never had a summer's day shone so gloriously for him; never had he so marked the hues of height and hollow, the shape of hills, the winding of a stream. Where an ascent made the pace slow, he alighted, walked by the vehicle, and exchanged a few words with her who sat behind the curtain.

At length Aletrium came in view, a little town in a strong position on the mountain side, its walls and citadel built in old time, long unused for defence, but resisting ages with their cyclopean force. On arriving, they found a scene of disorder, misery and fear. This morning the place had been attacked by a brigand horde, which had ravaged at will: the church was robbed of its sacred vessels, the beasts of burden were driven away, and, worst of all, wives and daughters of the defenceless townsmen had suffered outrage. Marcian, with that air of authority which he well knew how to assume, commanded the attendance of the leading citizens and spoke with them in private. Finding them eager for the arrival of the Goths, to whom they looked rather than to the distant Greeks for protection against ruinous disorder (already they had despatched messengers to Totila entreating his aid), he made known to them that he was travelling to meet the Gothic outposts, and promised to hasten the king's advance. At present, there seemed to be no more danger, the marauders having gone on into the Apennines; so Marcian obtained lodging for Veranilda and for himself in the priest's house. Only when he was alone did he reflect upon the narrowness of his escape from those fierce plunderers, and horror shook him. There remained but half a day's journey to his villa. He was so impatient to arrive there, and to dismiss the horsemen, that though utterly wearied, he lay awake through many hours of darkness, hearing the footsteps of men who patrolled the streets, and listening with anxious ear for any sound of warning.

He rose in the twilight, and again held conference with those of the townsmen who were stoutest in the Gothic cause. To them he announced that he should travel this day as far as Arpinum (whither he was conducting a lady who desired to enter a convent hard by that city), and thence should proceed in search of Totila, for whom, he assured his hearers, he carried letters of summons from the leading churchmen at Rome. This news greatly cheered the unhappy Aletrians, who had been troubled by the thought that the Goths were heretics. If Roman ecclesiastics closed their eyes to this obstacle, the inhabitants of a little mountain town evidently need nurse no scruples in welcoming the conqueror. With acclamations and good wishes, the crowd saw Marcian and his train set forth along the road over the hills; before the sun had shed its first beam into the westward valley, they had lost sight of Aletrium.

Not a word of the perils escaped had been allowed to reach Veranilda's ear; exhausted by her journeying and her emotions, she had slept soundly through the whole night, and this morning, when Marcian told her how near was their destination, she laughed light-heartedly as a child. But not yet had he looked upon her countenance. At Aletrium he might have done so had he willed, but he withheld himself as if from a dread temptation.

Never had he known such tremours of cowardliness as on this ride over the hills. He strained his eyes in every direction, and constantly imagined an enemy where there was none. The brigands, as he found by inquiry of labouring peasants, had not even passed this way. He would not halt, though the heat of the sun grew terrible. At length, when exhaustion threatened men and beasts, they surmounted a ridge, issued from a forest of chestnut-trees, and all at once, but a little way below them, saw the gleam of the river Liris.

CHAPTER XX
THE ISLAND IN THE LIRIS

Not yet the '*taciturnus amnis*,' which it becomes in the broad, seaward valley far below, the Liris at this point parts into two streams, enclosing a spacious island, and on either side of the island leaps with sound and foam, a river kindred to the mountains which feed its flood. Between the two cataracts, linked to the river banks with great arched bridges, stood Marcian's villa. Never more than a modest country house, during the last fifty years an almost total neglect had made of the greater part an uninhabitable ruin. A score of slaves and peasants looked after what remained of the dwelling and cultivated the land attached to it, garden, oliveyard, vineyard, partly on the island, partly beyond the river in the direction of Arpinum, which historic city, now but sparsely peopled, showed on the hillside a few miles away. Excepting his house in Rome, this was all the property that Marcian possessed. It was dear to him because of the memories of his childhood, and for another reason which sprang out of the depths of his being: on the night after his mother's death (he was then a boy much given to seeing visions) her spirit appeared to him, and foretold that he too should die in this house 'at peace with God.' This phrase, on which he had often brooded, Marcian understood to mean that he should reach old age; and it had long been his settled intention to found in the ruinous villa a little monastery, to which, when his work was over, he could retire to pass the close of life. And now, as he rode down behind the carriage, he was striving to keep his thought fixed on this pious purpose. He resolved that he would not long delay. As soon as Veranilda was safe, he would go on foot, as a pilgrim, to the monastery at Casinum, which were but two or three days' journey, and speak of his intention to the aged and most holy Benedict. Thus fortified, he rode with bright visage down into the valley, and over the bridge, and so to his own gate.

The steward and the housekeeper, who were man and wife, speedily stood before him, and he bade them make ready with all expedition certain chambers long unoccupied, merely saying that a lady would for some days be his guest. Whilst Sagaris guided the horsemen to the stables, and received them hospitably in the servants' quarter, Marcian, using a more formal courtesy than hitherto, conducted his charge into the great hall, and begged her to be seated for a few minutes, until her room was prepared. Seeing that fatigue scarce suffered her to reply, he at once withdrew, leaving her alone with her handmaiden. And yet he had not beheld Veranilda's face.

Himself unable to take repose, he strayed about the purlieus of the villa, in his ears the sound of rushing water, before his eyes a flitting vision which he would not see. He had heard from his steward the latest news of the countryside; it was said in Arpinum that the Gothic forces were at length assembled for the march on Rome; at Aquinum Totila would be welcomed, and what resistance was he likely to meet with all along the Latin Way? When the horsemen had refreshed themselves, Marcian summoned the leader; their services, he said, would no longer be necessary; he bade them depart as early as might be on the morrow, and bear with all speed to their lord the bishop an important letter which he forthwith wrote and gave to the man, together with a generous guerdon. This business despatched, he again wandered hither and thither, incapable of rest, incapable of clear thought, fever in his heart and in his brain.

As the sun sank, fear once more beset him. This house lay open on all sides, its only protection being a couple of dogs, which prowled at large. He thought with dread of the possibility of a brigand attack. But when night had fallen, when all lights except his own were extinguished, when no sound struck against the deep monotone of the cataracts, this emotion yielded before another, which no less harassed his mind. In the hall, in the corridors, in the garden-court, he paced ceaselessly, at times walking in utter darkness, for not yet had the moon risen. When at length its rays fell upon the pillars of the upper gallery where Veranilda slept, he stood looking towards her chamber, and turned away at length with a wild gesture, like that of a demoniac in torment.

The man was torn between spiritual fervour and passions of the flesh. With his aspiration to saintliness blended that love of his friend which was the purest affection he had known in all the years of manhood; yet this very love became, through evil thoughts, an instrument against him, being sullied, poisoned by the basest spirit of jealousy, until it seemed all but to have turned to hate. One moment he felt himself capable of acting nobly, even as he had resolved when at mass in the little mountain church; his bosom glowed with the defiance of every risk; he would guard Veranilda secretly until he could lay her hand in that of Basil. The next, he saw only danger, impossibility, in such a purpose, and was anxious to deliver the beautiful maiden to the king of her own race as soon as might be—lest worse befell. Thus did he strive with himself, thus was he racked and rent under the glowing moon.

At dawn he slept. When he rose the horsemen had long since set forth on their journey home. He inquired which road they had taken. But to this no one had paid heed; he could only learn that they had crossed the river by the westward bridge, and so perhaps had gone back by way of Aletrium, instead of descending the valley to the Latin Way. Even yet Marcian did not feel quite safe from his Greek pursuers. He feared a meeting between them and the Praenestines.

Having bathed (a luxury after waterless Rome), and eaten a morsel of bread with a draught of his own wine, he called his housekeeper, and bade her make known to the lady, his guest, that he begged permission to wait upon her. With but a few minutes' delay Veranilda descended to the room which lay behind the atrium. Marcian, loitering among the ivied plane-trees without, was told of her coming, and at once entered.

She was alone, standing at the back of the room; her hands hanging linked before her, the lower part of the arms white against the folds of a russet-coloured tunic. And Marcian beheld her face.

He took a few rapid steps toward her, checked himself, bowed profoundly, and said in a somewhat abrupt voice:

'Gracious lady, is it by your own wish that you are unattended? Or have my women, by long disuse, so forgotten their duties—'

Veranilda interrupted him.

'I assure you it was my own wish, lord Marcian. We must speak of things which are not for others' hearing.'

In the same unnatural voice, as though he put constraint upon himself for the performance of a disagreeable duty, he begged her to be seated, and Veranilda, not without betraying a slight trouble of surprise, took the chair to which he pointed. But he himself did not sit down. In the middle of the room stood a great bronze candelabrum, many-branched for the suspension of lamps, at its base three figures, Pluto, Neptune, and Proserpine. It was the only work of any value which the villa now contained, and Marcian associated it with the memories of his earliest years. As a little child he had often gazed at those three faces, awed by their noble gravity, and, with a child's diffidence, he had never ventured to ask what beings these were. He fixed his eyes upon them now, to avoid looking at Veranilda. She, timidly glancing at him, said in her soft, low voice, with the simplest sincerity:

'I have not yet found words in which to thank you, lord Marcian.'

'My thanks are due to you, dear lady, for gracing this poor house with your presence.'

His tone was more suavely courteous. For an instant he looked at her, and his lips set themselves in something meant for a smile.

'This is the end of our journey?' she asked.

'For some days—if the place does not displease you.'

'How could I be ill at ease in the house of Basil's friend, and with the promise that Basil will soon come?'

Marcian stared at the face of Proserpine, who seemed to regard him with solemn thoughtfulness.

'Had you any forewarning of your release from the monastery?' he asked of a sudden.

'None. None whatever.'

'You thought you would remain there for long to come?'

'I had not dared to think of that.'

Marcian took a few paces, glanced at the sweet face, the beautiful head with its long golden hair, and came back to his place by the candelabrum, on which he rested a trembling hand.

'Had they spoken of making you a nun?'

A look of dread came upon her countenance, and she whispered, 'Once or twice.'

'You would never have consented?'

'Only if I had known that release was hopeless, or that Basil—'

Her voice failed.

'That Basil—?' echoed Marcian's lips, in an undertone.

'That he was dead.'

'You never feared that he might have forgotten you?'

Again his accents were so hard that Veranilda gazed at him in troubled wonder.

'You never feared that?' he added, with fugitive eyes.

'Had I dreamt of it,' she replied, 'I think I should not live.' Then in a voice of anxious humility, 'Could Basil forget me?'

'Indeed, I should not think it easy,' murmured the other, his eyes cast down. 'And what,' he continued abruptly, 'was said to you when you left the convent? In what words did they take leave of you?'

'With none at all. I was bidden prepare for a journey, and soon after they led me to the gates. I knew nothing, nor did the woman with me.'

'Was the lady Aurelia in the same convent?' Marcian next inquired.

'I never saw her after we had landed from the ship which carried us from Surrentum?'

'You do not know, of course, that Petronilla is dead?'

He told her of that, and of other events such as would interest her, but without uttering the name of Basil. Above all, he spoke of Totila, lauding the victorious king who would soon complete his triumph by the conquest of Rome.

'I had all but forgotten,' were Veranilda's words, when she had listened anxiously. 'I thought only of Basil.'

He turned abruptly from her, seemed to reflect for a moment, and said with formal politeness:

'Permit me now to leave you, lady. This house is yours. I would it offered you worthier accommodation. As soon as I have news, I will again come before you.'

Veranilda rose whilst he was speaking. Her eyes were fixed upon him, wistfully, almost pleadingly, and before he had reached the exit she advanced a step, with lips parted as if to beseech his delay. But he walked too hurriedly, and was gone ere she durst utter a word.

At the same hurried pace, gazing before him and seeing nothing, Marcian left the villa, and walked until he came to the river side. Here was a jutting rock known as the Lover's Leap; story told of a noble maiden, frenzied by unhappy love, who had cast herself into the roaring waterfall. Long he stood on the brink, till his eyes dazzled from the sun-stricken foam. His mind was blasted with shame; he could not hold his head erect. In sorry effort to recover self-respect he reasoned inwardly thus:

'Where Basil may be I know not. If he is still at Asculum many days must pass before a summons from me could bring him hither. He may already be on his way to join the king, as I bade him in my last message. The uncertainty, the danger of this situation, can be met only in one way. On leaving Rome I saw my duty plain before me. A desire to pleasure my friend made me waver, but I was wrong—if Basil is to have Veranilda for his bride he can only receive her from the hands of Totila. Anything else would mean peril to the friend I love, and disrespect, even treachery, to the king I honour. And so it shall be; I will torment myself no more.'

He hastened back into the villa, summoned Sagaris, and bade him be ready in half an hour to set forth on a journey of a day or two. He then wrote a brief letter to the king of the Goths. It was in the Gothic tongue, such Gothic as a few Romans could command for everyday use. Herein he told that Veranilda, intrusted to him by the deacon Leander to be conducted to the king's camp, had arrived in safety at his villa by Arpinum. The country being disturbed, he had thought better to wait here with his charge until he could learn the king's pleasure, which he begged might be made known to him as soon as possible.

'This,' he said, when Sagaris appeared before him equipped for travel, 'you will deliver into the king's own hands. At Aquinum you will be directed to his camp, which cannot be far beyond. Danger there is none between here and there. Make your utmost speed.'

Many were the confidential missions which Sagaris had discharged; yet, looking now into his man's face, the master was troubled by a sudden misgiving. The state of his own mind disposed him to see peril everywhere. At another time he would not have noted so curiously a sort of gleam in the Syrian's eye, a something on the fellow's cunning, sensual lips, which might mean anything or nothing. Did Sagaris divine who the veiled lady was? From the bishop's man he could not have learned it, they themselves, as the bishop had assured Marcian, being totally ignorant in the matter. If he guessed the truth, as was likely enough after all the talk he had heard concerning Veranilda, was it a danger? Had Sagaris any motive for treachery?

'Listen,' continued Marcian, in a tone such as he had never before used with his servant, a tone rather of entreaty than of command. 'Upon the safe and swift delivery of that letter more depends than you can imagine. You will not lack your reward. But not a word to any save the king. Should any one else question you, you will say that you bear only a verbal message, and that you come direct from Rome.'

'My lord shall be obeyed,' answered the slave, 'though I die under torture.'

'Of that,' said Marcian, with a forced laugh, 'you need have no fear. But, hark you!' He hesitated, again searching the man's countenance. 'You might chance to meet some friend of mine who would inquire after me. No matter who it be—were it even the lord Basil—you will answer in the same words, saying that I am still in Rome. You understand me? Were it even lord Basil who asked?'

'It shall be as my lord commands,' replied the slave, his face set in unctuous solemnity.

'Go, then. Lose not a moment.'

Marcian watched him ride away in the blaze of the cloudless sun. The man's head was sheltered with a broad-brimmed hat of the lightest felt, and his horse's with a cluster of vine-leaves. He rode away at a quick trot, the while dust rising in a cloud behind him.

And Marcian lived through the day he knew not how. It was a day of burning sunshine, of heat scarce tolerable even in places the most sheltered. Clad only in a loose tunic, bare-armed, bare-footed, he lay or sauntered wherever shade was dense, as far as possible from the part of the villa consecrated to his guest. Hour after hour crawled by, an eternity of distressful idleness. And, even while wishing for the day's end, he dreaded the coming of the night.

It came; the silent, lonely night, the warm, perfumed night, the season of fierce temptations, of dreadful opportunity. Never had the passionate soul of Marcian been so manifestly lured by the Evil One, never had it fought so desperately in the strength of religious hopes and fears. He knelt, he prayed, his voice breaking upon the stillness with anguish of supplication. Between him and the celestial vision rose that face which he had at length beheld, a face only the more provocative of sensual rage because of its sweet purity, its flawless truth. Then he flung himself upon the stones, bruised his limbs, lay at length exhausted, as if lifeless.

No longer could he strengthen himself by the thought of loyalty in friendship; that he had renounced. Yet he strove to think of Basil, and, in doing so, knew that he still loved him. For Basil he would do anything, suffer anything, lose anything; but when he imaged Basil with Veranilda, at once his love turned to spleen, a sullen madness possessed him, he hated his friend to the death.

By his own order, two watchmen stood below the stairs which led to Veranilda's chamber. Nigh upon midnight he walked in that direction, walked in barefooted stealth, listening for a movement, a voice. Nearer and nearer he approached, till he saw at length the ray of a lantern; but no step, no murmur, told of wakeful guard. Trembling as though with cold, though sweat streamed over his body, he strode forward; there, propped against the wall, sat the two slaves fast asleep. Marcian glanced at the stairs; his face in the dim lantern light was that of a devil. All of a sudden one of the men started, and opened his eyes. Thereupon Marcian caught up a staff that lay beside them, and began to belabour them both with savage blows. Fiercely, frantically, he plied his weapon, until the delinquents, who had fallen to their knees before him, roared for mercy.

'Let me find you sleeping again,' he said in a low voice, 'and your eyes shall be burnt out.'

He stole away into the darkness, and the men whispered to each other that he had gone mad. For Marcian was notably humane with his slaves, never having been known even to inflict a whipping. Perhaps they were even more astonished at this proof that their master seriously guarded the privacy of his guest; last night they had slept for long hours undisturbed, and, on waking, congratulated each other with familiar jests on having done just what was expected of them.

The morn broke dark and stormy. Thunder-clouds purpled before the rising sun, and ere mid-day there fell torrents of rain. Heedless of the sky, Marcian rode forth this morning; rode aimlessly about the hills, for the villa was no longer endurable to him. He talked awhile with a labouring serf, who told him that the plague had broken out in Arpinum, where, during the last week or two, many had died. From his steward he had already heard the same news, but without heeding it; it now alarmed him, and for some hours fear had a wholesome effect upon his thoughts. In the coolness following upon the storm, he enjoyed a long, tranquil sleep. And this day he did not see Veranilda.

A mile or two down the valley was a church, built by Marcian's grandfather, on a spot where he had been saved from great peril; the land attached to it supported two priests and certain acolytes, together with a little colony of serfs. On his ride this morning Marcian had passed within view of the church, and would have gone thither but for his rain drenched clothing. Now, during the second night of temptation, he resolved to visit the priests as soon as it was day and to bring one of them back with him to the villa, to remain as long as Veranilda should be there. Firm in this purpose he rose with the rising sun, called for his horse, and rode to the bridge. There, looking down at the white cataract, stood Veranilda and her attendant.

He alighted. With a timid smile the maiden advanced to meet him.

'Abroad so early?' were his first words, a mere tongue-found phrase.

'I was tempted by the fresh morning. It does not displease you, lord Marcian?'

'Nay, I am glad.'

'It is so long,' continued the gentle voice, 'since I was free to walk under the open sky.'

Marcian forgot that his gaze was fixed upon her, forgot that he was silent, forgot the purpose with which he had ridden forth.

'I hoped I might see you to-day,' she added. 'You have yet no news for me?'

'None.'

The blue eyes drooped sadly.

'To-morrow, perhaps,' she murmured. Then, with an effort to seem cheerful, as if ashamed of her troubled thought, 'I had listened so long to a sound of falling water that I could not resist the desire to see it. How beautiful it is!'

Marcian felt surprise; he himself saw the cataract as an object of beauty, but had seldom heard it so spoken of, and could least of all have expected such words on the lips of a woman, dread seeming to him the more natural impression.

'That on the other side,' he said, pointing across the island, 'is more beautiful still. And there is shade, whilst here the sun grows too hot. But you must not walk so far. My horse has a very even pace. If you would let me lift you to the saddle—'

'Oh, gladly!' she answered, with a little laugh of pleasure.

And it was done. For a moment he held her, for a moment felt the warmth and softness of her flesh; then she sat sideways upon the horse, looking down at Marcian with startled gaiety. He showed her how to hold the reins, and the horse went gently forward.

'It makes me a child again,' she exclaimed. 'I have never ridden since I was a little girl, when my father—'

Her voice died away; her look was averted, and Marcian, remembering the shame that mingled with her memories, began to talk of other things.

By a path that circled the villa, they came to a little wood of ilex, which shadowed the brink of the larger cataract. Marcian had bidden Veranilda's woman follow them, but as they entered the wood, his companion looking eagerly before her, he turned and made a gesture of dismissal, which the servant at once obeyed. In the shadiest spot which offered a view of the plunging river, he asked Veranilda if she would alight.

'Willingly, I would spend an hour here,' she replied. 'The leafage and the water make such a delightful freshness.'

'I have anticipated your thought,' said Marcian. 'The woman is gone to bid them bring seats.'

Veranilda glanced back in surprise and saw that they were alone. She thanked him winsomely, and then, simply as before, accepted his help. Again Marcian held her an instant, her slim, light body trembling when he set her down, as if from a burden which strained his utmost force. She stepped forward to gaze at the fall. He, with an exclamation of alarm, caught her hand and held it.

'You are too rash,' he said in a thick voice. 'The depth, the roar of the waters, will daze you.'

Against his burning palm, her hand was cool as a lily leaf. He did not release it, though he knew that *his* peril from that maidenly touch was greater far than hers from the gulf before them. Veranilda, accepting his protection with the thoughtlessness of a child, leaned forward, uttering her wonder and her admiration. He, the while, watched her lips, fed his eyes upon her cheek, her neck, the golden ripples of her hair. At length she gently offered to draw her hand away. A frenzy urged him to resist, but madness yielded to cunning, and he released her.

'Of course Basil has been here,' she was saying.

'Never.'

'Never? Oh, the joy of showing him this when he comes! Lord Marcian, you do not think it will be long?'

Her eyes seemed as though they would read in the depth of his; again the look of troubled wonder rose to her countenance.

'It will not be more than a few days?' she added, in a timid undertone, scarce audible upon the water's deeper note.

'I fear it may be longer,' replied Marcian.

He heard his own accents as those of another man. He, his very self, willed the utterance of certain words, kind, hopeful, honest; but something else within him commanded his tongue, and, ere he knew it, he had added:

'You have never thought that Basil might forget you?'

Veranilda quivered as though she had been struck.

'Why do you again ask me that question?' she said gently, but no longer timidly. 'Why do you look at me so? Surely,' her voice sank, 'you could not have let me feel so happy if Basil were dead?'

'He lives.'

'Then why do you look so strangely at me? Ah, he is a prisoner?'

'Not so. No man's liberty is less in danger.'

She clasped her hands before her. 'You make me suffer. I was so light of heart, and now—your eyes, your silence. Oh, speak, lord Marcian!'

'I have hidden the truth so long because I knew not how to utter it. Veranilda, Basil is false to you.'

Her hands fell; her eyes grew wider in wonder. She seemed not to understand what she had heard, and to be troubled by incomprehension rather than by a shock of pain.

'False to me?' she murmured. 'How false?'

'He loves another woman, and for her sake has turned to the Greeks.'

Still Veranilda gazed wonderingly.

'Things have come to pass of which you know nothing,' pursued Marcian, forcing his voice to a subdued evenness, a sad gravity. 'Listen whilst I tell you all. Had you remained but a few days longer at Cumae, you would have been seized by the Greeks and sent to Constantinople; for the Emperor Justinian himself had given this command. You came to Surrentum; you plighted troth with Basil; he would have wedded you, and—not only for safety's sake, but because he wished well to the Goths—would have sought the friendship of Totila. But you were carried away; vainly we searched for you; we feared you had been delivered to the Greeks. In Rome, Basil was tempted by a woman, whom he had loved before ever he saw you, a woman beautiful, but evil hearted, her name Heliodora. She won him back to her; she made him faithless to you and to the cause of the Goths. Little by little, I learnt how far he had gone in treachery. He had discovered where you were, but no longer desired to release you that you might become his wife. To satisfy the jealousy of Heliodora, and at the same time to please the Greek commander in Rome, he plotted to convey you to Constantinople. I having discovered this plot, found a way to defeat it. You escaped but narrowly. When I carried you away from Praeneste, pursuers were close behind us, therefore it was that we travelled through the night. Here you are in safety, for King Totila is close at hand, and will guard you against your enemies.'

Veranilda pressed her hands upon her forehead, and stood mute. As his eyes shifted furtively about her, Marcian caught sight of something black and undulant stirring among stones near her feet; at once he grasped her by the arm, and drew her towards him.

'A viper!' he exclaimed, pointing.

'What of that?' was her reply, with a careless glance. 'I would not stir a step to escape its fangs.'

And, burying her face in her hands, she wept.

These tears, this attitude of bewildered grief, were Marcian's encouragement. He had dreaded the innocence of her eyes lest it should turn to distrust and rejection. Had she refused to believe him, he knew not how he would have persisted in his villainy; for, even in concluding his story, it seemed to him that he must betray himself; so perfidious sounded to him the voice which he could hardly believe his own, and so slinking-knavish did he feel the posture of his body, the movements of his limbs. The distress which should have smitten him to the heart restored his baser courage. Again he spoke with the sad gravity of a sympathetic friend.

'Dearest lady, I cannot bid you be comforted, but I entreat you to pardon me, the hapless revealer of your misfortune. Say only that you forgive me.'

'What is there to forgive?' she answered, checking her all but silent sobs. 'You have told what it behoved you to tell. And it may be'—her look changed of a sudden—'that I am too hasty in embracing sorrow. How can I believe that Basil has done this? Are you not misled by some false suspicion? Has not some enemy slandered him to you? What can you say to make me credit a thing so evil?'

'Alas! It were but too easy for me to lengthen a tale which all but choked me in the telling; I could name others who know, but to you they would be only names. That of Heliodora, had you lived in Rome, were more than enough.'

'You say he loved her before?'

'He did, dear lady, and when her husband was yet living. Now that he is dead—'

'Have you yet told me all?' asked Veranilda, gazing fixedly at him. 'Has he married her?'

'Not yet—I think.'

Again she bowed her head. For a moment her tears fell silently, then she looked up once more fighting against her anguish.

'It cannot be true that he would have given me to the Greeks; that he may have forgotten me, that he may have turned to another love, I can perhaps believe—for what am I that Basil should love me? But to scheme my injury, to deliver me to our enemies—Oh, you are deceived, you are deceived!'

Marcian was silent, with eyes cast down. In the branches, cicadas trilled their monotone. The viper, which had been startled away, again showed its lithe blackness among the stones behind Veranilda, and Marcian, catching sight of it, again touched her arm.

'The snake! Come away from this place.'

Veranilda drew her arm back as if his touch stung her.

'I will go,' she said. 'I must be alone—my thoughts are in such confusion I know not what I say.'

'Say but one word,' he pleaded. 'Having rescued you, I knew not how to provide for your security save under ward of the king. Totila is noble and merciful; all Italy will soon be his, and the Gothic rule be re-established. Assure me that I have done well and wisely.'

'I hope you have,' answered Veranilda, regarding him for an instant. 'But I know nothing; I must bear what befalls. Let me go to my chamber, lord Marcian, and sit alone and think.'

He led her back into the villa, and they parted without another word.

CHAPTER XXI
THE BETRAYER BETRAYED

Sagaris, making his best speed, soon arrived at Aquinum. He and his horse were bathed in sweat; the shelter of an inn, where he had dinner, tempted him to linger more than he need have done, and the fierce sun was already declining when he rode forth along the Latin Way. As yet he had seen no Goths. Every one talked of Totila, but he had a difficulty in ascertaining where at this moment the king was to be found; some declared he was as near as Venafrum, others that he lay much further down the valley of the Vulturnus. Arrived at Venafrum, the messenger learnt that he could not have less than another whole day's journey before him, so here be harboured for the night.

His wily and unscrupulous mind had all day long been busy with speculations as to the errand on which he was sent. Knowing that his master wrote to Goths in the Gothic tongue, he was spared temptation to break open the letter he carried; otherwise he would assuredly have done so, for the hatred which Sagaris naturally felt for any one in authority over him was now envenomed by jealousy, and for the last month or two he had only waited an opportunity of injuring Marcian and of advancing, by the same stroke, his own fortunes.

Having started from Rome in ignorance of his master's purpose, the events of the night at Praeneste at once suggested to him the name of the person who was being so cautiously and hurriedly conveyed under Marcian's guard, and by the end of the journey he had no doubt left. Here, at last, was the Gothic maiden who had been sought so persistently by Marcian, by Basil, by Bessas, by Heliodora, and doubtless by many others, since her disappearance from Surrentum. Whither was she now being conducted? Sagaris did not know that among her seekers was King Totila himself; on the other hand, he had much reason for suspecting that Marcian pursued Veranilda with a lover's passion, and when the journey ended at the island villa, when the convoy of horsemen was dismissed, when he himself was sent off to a distance, he saw his suspicion confirmed. By some supreme subtlety, Marcian had got the beautiful maiden into his power, and doubtless the letter he was sending to Totila contained some device for the concealing of what had happened.

Now to the Syrian this would have been a matter of indifference, but for his secret communications with Heliodora and all that had resulted therefrom. Heliodora's talk was of three persons—of Marcian, of Basil, of Veranilda— and Sagaris, reasoning from all the gossip he had heard, and from all he certainly knew, concluded that the Greek lady had once loved Basil, but did so no more, that her love had turned to Marcian, and that she either knew or suspected Marcian to be a rival of Basil for the love of Veranilda. Thus had matters stood (he persuaded himself) until his own entrance on the scene. That a woman might look with ardent eyes on more than one man in the same moment, seemed to Sagaris the simplest of facts; he consequently found it easy to believe that, even whilst loving Marcian, Heliodora should have conceived a tenderness for Marcian's slave. That Heliodora's professions might be mere trickery, he never imagined; his vanity forbade it; at each successive meeting he seemed to himself to have strengthened his hold upon the luxurious woman; each time he came away with a fiercer hatred of Marcian, and a deeper resolve to ruin him. True, as yet, he had fed only on promises, but being the man he was, he could attribute to Heliodora a selfish interest in combination with a lover's desire; what more intelligible than that she should use him to the utmost against those she hated, postponing his reward until he had rendered her substantial service? Thus did Sagaris feel and reason, whilst riding along the Latin Way. His difficulty was to decide how he should act at this juncture; how, with greatest profit to himself, he could do most scathe to Marcian.

Was his master serving the Greeks or the Goths? Uncertainty on this point had long troubled his meditations, and was now a cause of grave embarrassment. Eager to betray, he could not be sure to which side betrayal should direct itself. On the whole he himself favoured Totila, feeling sure that the Goth would bring the war to a triumphant end; and on this account he was disposed to do his errand faithfully. If the king interrogated him, he could draw conclusions from the questions asked, and could answer as seemed best for his own ends. So he decided to push on, and, despite the storm which broke on this second morning, he rode out from Venafrum.

A few hours' travel, and, drenched with the furious rain, he came to Aesernia. This town stood in a strong position on an isolated hill; its massive walls yet compassed it about. On arriving at the gate he found himself unexpectedly challenged by armed men, who, though Italians, he at once suspected to be in the Gothic service. A moment's hesitancy in replying to the questions, 'Whence?' and 'Whither?' sufficed to put him under arrest. He was led to the captain, in whom with relief he recognised Venantius of Nuceria. His doubts being at an end, for he knew that this Roman noble had long since openly joined Totila, he begged that Venantius would hear him in private, and this being granted, began by telling in whose service he was.

'I thought I somehow remembered your face,' said the captain, whose look seemed to add that the face did not particularly please him. 'And where is the lord Marcian?'

'In Rome, Illustrious.'

'You have come straight from Rome, then?'

The answer was affirmative and boldly given.

'And whither are you bound? On what business?'

Sagaris, still obeying his master's injunctions, declared that he carried a verbal message to the King of the Goths, and for him alone. Having reflected for a moment, Venantius called the soldier who stood without the door.

'See to the wants of this messenger. Treat him hospitably, and bring him hither again in an hour's time.'

The captain then walked to a house close by, where, admitted to the atrium, he was at once met by an elderly lady, who bent respectfully before him.

'Has the traveller yet risen?' he began by asking.

'Not yet, my lord. A little while ago his servant told me that he was still sleeping.'

'Good; he will recover from his fatigue. But pray inquire whether he is now awake, for I would speak with him as soon as may be.'

The lady was absent for a minute or two, then brought word that the traveller had just awoke.

'I will go to his bedside,' said Venantius.

He was led to an upper chamber, a small, bare, tiled-floored room, lighted by a foot-square window, on which the shutter was half closed against the rays of the sun. Some aromatic odour hung in the air.

'Do you feel able to talk?' asked the captain as he entered.

'I am quite restored,' was the reply of a man sitting up in the bed. 'The fever has passed.'

'So much for the wisdom of physicians!' exclaimed Venantius with a laugh. 'That owl-eyed Aesernian who swears by Aesculapius that he has studied at Constantinople, Antioch, and I know not where else, whispered to me that you would never behold to-day's sunset. I whispered to *him* that he was an ass, and that if he uttered the word *plague* to any one in the house, I would cut his ears off. Nevertheless, I had you put into this out-of-the-way room, that you might not be disturbed by noises. Who'—he sniffed—'has been burning perfumes?'

'My good fellow Felix. Though travel-worn and wounded, he has sat by me all the time, and would only go to bed when I woke up with a cool forehead.'

'A good fellow, indeed. His face spells honesty. I can't say so much for that of a man I have just been talking with—a messenger of your friend Marcian.'

The listener started as though he would leap out of bed. A rush of colour to his cheeks banished the heavy, wan aspect which had partly disguised him, and restored the comely visage of Basil. A messenger from Marcian? he exclaimed. With news for *him*? And, as if expecting a letter, he stretched forth his hand eagerly.

'He has nothing, that I know of, for you,' said the captain. 'If he tells the truth, he is charged with a message for the king.'

'Is it Sagaris—a Syrian slave?'

'A Syrian, by his looks; one I remember to have seen with Marcian a year ago.'

'Sagaris, to be sure. Then you can trust him. He has the eye of his race, and is a prating braggart, but Marcian has found him honest. I must see him, Venantius. Will you send him to me, dear lord?'

Venantius had seated himself on a chair that was beside the bed; he wore a dubious look, and, before speaking again, glanced keenly at Basil.

'Did you not expect,' he asked, 'to meet Marcian in the king's camp?'

'My last news from him bade me go thither as fast as I could, as he himself was leaving Rome to join the king. I should have gone a little out of my road to visit his villa near Arpinum, on the chance of hearing news of him there; but our encounter with the marauders drove me too far away.'

'So much,' said Venantius, 'I gathered from your talk last night, when you were not quite so clear-headed as you are now. What I want to discover is whether this Syrian has lied to me. He declares that he left Marcian in Rome. Now it happens that some of our men, who were sent for a certain purpose, yesterday, along the Latin Way, came across half a dozen horsemen, riding westward, and as their duty was, learnt all they could from them. These six fellows declared themselves servants of the bishop of Praeneste, and said that they had just been convoying a Roman noble and a lady to a villa not far from Arpinum. And the noble's name—they had it, said they, from his own servants at the villa, where they had passed a night—was Marcian.'

Basil stared; he had gone pale again and haggard.

'What lady was with him?' he asked, under his breath.

'That I cannot tell you. The bishop's men knew nothing about her, and had not seen her face. But'—Venantius smiled—'they left her safely housed with our friend Marcian. How comes this Syrian to say that his master is at Rome?

Does he lie? Or did the horsemen lie? Or are there, perchance, two Marcians?'

'I must speak with him,' said Basil. 'Leave me to find out the truth for you. Send Sagaris here, Venantius, I entreat you.'

The captain appeared to hesitate, but, on Basil's beseeching him not to delay, he agreed and left the room. As soon as he was alone, Basil sprang up and dressed. He was aching from head to foot, and a parched mouth, a hot hand, told of fever in his blood. On receipt of Marcian's last letter, he had not delayed a day before setting forth; all was in readiness for such a summons, and thirty well-mounted, well-armed men, chosen from the slaves and freedmen on his Asculan estate in Picenum, rode after him to join the King of the Goths. The journey was rapidly performed; already they were descending the lower slopes of the westward Apennine, when they had the ill-luck to fall in with that same band of marauders which Marcian so narrowly escaped. Basil's first thought was that the mounted troop coming towards him might hem the Gothic service, but this hope was soon dispelled. Advancing with fierce threats, the robbers commanded him and his men to alight, their chief desire being no doubt to seize the horses and arms. Though outnumbered, Basil shouted defiance; a conflict began, and so stout was the resistance they met that, after several had fallen on either side, the brigands drew off. Not, however, in final retreat; galloping on in hope of succour, Basil found himself pursued, again lost two or three men, and only with the utmost difficulty got clear away.

It was the young Roman's first experience of combat. For this he had been preparing himself during the past months, exercising his body and striving to invigorate his mind, little apt for warlike enterprise. When the trial came, his courage did not fail, but the violent emotions of that day left him so exhausted, so shaken in nerve, that he could scarce continue his journey. He had come out of the fight unwounded, but at nightfall fever fell upon him, and he found no rest. The loss of some half dozen men grieved him to the heart; had the brave fellows fallen in battle with the Greeks, he would have thought less of it; to see them slain, or captured, by mere brigands was more than he could bear. When at length he reached Aesernia, and there unexpectedly met with Venantius, he fell from his horse like a dying man. A draught given by the physician sent him to sleep, and from the second hour after sunset until nearly noon of to-day he had lain unconscious.

What he now learnt from Venantius swept into oblivion all that he had undergone. If it were true that Marcian had travelled in this direction with a lady under his guard, Basil could not doubt for a moment who that lady was. The jest of Venantius did not touch him, for Venantius spoke, it was evident, without a thought of Veranilda, perhaps had forgotten her existence; not the faintest tremor of uneasiness stirred in Basil's mind when he imagined Veranilda at his friend's house; Marcian had discovered her, had rescued her, had brought her thither to rest in safety till her lover could join them—brave Marcian, truest of friends! For this had he sent the summons southward, perhaps not daring to speak more plainly in a letter, perhaps not being yet quite sure of success. This had he so often promised—O gallant Marcian!

Quivering with eagerness, he stood at the door of his chamber. Footsteps sounded; there appeared a slave of the house, and behind him that dark, handsome visage which he was expecting.

'Sagaris! My good Sagaris!' he cried joyously.

The Syrian knelt before him and kissed his hand, but uttered no word. At sight of Basil, for which he was not at all prepared, Sagaris felt a happy shock; he now saw his way before him, and had no more anxiety. But, on rising from the obeisance, he let his head drop; his eyes wandered: one would have said that he shrank from observation.

'Speak low,' said Basil, standing by the open door so as to guard against eavesdropping. 'What message have you for me?'

Sagaris replied that he had none.

'None? Your lord charged you with nothing for me in case you should meet me on your way?'

Again Sagaris murmured a negative, and this time with so manifest an air of confusion that Basil stared at him, suspicious, angry.

'What do you mean? What are you keeping from me?'

The man appeared to stammer incoherencies.

'Listen,' said Basil in a low, friendly voice. 'You know very well that the lord Marcian has no secrets from me. With me you can speak in entire confidence. What has come to you, man? Tell me—did your lord leave Rome before or after you?'

'At the same time.'

No sooner had this reply fallen from his lips than Sagaris seemed stricken with alarm. He entreated pardon, declared he knew not what he was saying, that he was dazed by the weariness of travel.

'I should have said—neither before nor after. My lord remains in the city. I was to return with all speed.'

'He remains in the city?'

Basil reflected. It was possible that Marcian had either purposely concealed his journey from this slave, and had suddenly found himself able to set forth just after Sagaris had started.

'You bear a letter for the king?' he asked.

'A letter, Illustrious,' answered the slave, speaking very low.

'Ah, a letter?'

Sagaris went on to say that he had kept this a secret from Venantius, his master having bidden him speak of it to no one and deliver it into the king's own hand.

'It is in the Gothic tongue,' he added, his head bent, his look more furtive than ever; 'and so urgent that I have scarce rested an hour since leaving the villa.'

A terrible light flashed into Basil's eyes. Then he sprang at the speaker, caught him by the throat, forced him to his knees.

'Scoundrel, you dare to lie to me! So you started from the villa and not from Rome?'

Sagaris cried out for mercy, grovelled on the floor. He would tell everything; but he implored Basil to keep the secret, for, did his master learn what had happened, his punishment would be terrible.

'Fool!' cried Basil fiercely. 'How come you to have forgotten all at once that I am your lord's chosen friend, and that everything concerning him is safe with me. In very deed, I think you have ridden too hard in the sun; your brains must have frizzled. Blockhead! If in haste, the lord Marcian did not speak of me, he took it for granted that, should you meet me—'

Something so like a malicious smile flitted over the slave's countenance that in extremity of wrath he became mute.

'Your Nobility is deceived,' said Sagaris, in the same moment. 'My lord expressly forbade me to tell you the truth, should I see you on my journey.'

Basil stared at him.

'I swear by the holy Cross,' exclaimed the other, 'that this is true. And if I did not dread your anger, I could tell you the reason. I dare not. By all the saints I dare not!'

A strange quiet fell upon Basil. It seemed as if he would ask no more questions; he half turned away, and stood musing. Indeed, it was as though he had already heard all the slave had to tell, and so overcome was he by the revelation that speech, even connected thought, was at first impossible. As he recovered from the stupefying blow, the blood began to boil in his veins. He felt as when, in the fight of two days ago, he saw the first of his men pierced by a javelin. Turning again to Sagaris, he plied him with brief and rapid questions, till he had learnt every detail of Marcian's journey from Rome to the villa. The Syrian spoke of the veiled lady without hesitation as Veranilda, and pretended to have known for some time that she was in a convent at Praeneste; but, when interrogated as to her life at the villa, he affected an affectation of doubt, murmuring that he had beheld nothing with his own eyes, that perhaps the female slaves gossiped idly.

'What do they say?' asked Basil with unnatural self-control.

'They speak of her happy mien and gay talk, of her walking with my lord in private. But I know nothing.'

Basil kept his eyes down for a long minute, then moved like one who has taken a resolve.

'Show me the letter you bear,' he commanded.

Sagaris produced it, and having looked at the seal, Basil silently handed it back again.

'Thrice noble,' pleaded the slave, 'you will not deliver me to my lord's wrath?'

'Have no fear; unless in anything you have lied to me. Follow.'

They descended the stairs, and Basil had himself conducted to the house where Venantius sate at dinner. He spoke with the captain in private.

'This slave has a letter, not merely a message, for the king. He says it is urgent, and so it may be; but, from what I have learnt I doubt whether he is wholly to be trusted. Can you send some one with him?'

'Nothing easier.'

'I,' continued Basil, 'ride straightway for Arpinum. Ask me no questions, Venantius. When I return, if I do return, you shall know what sent me there. I may be back speedily.'

He took food, and in an hour's time was ready to start. Of his followers, he chose ten to accompany him. The rest remained at Aesernia. Felix, worn out by watching and with a slight wound in the side which began to be troublesome, he was reluctantly obliged to leave. Having inquired as to the road over the mountains by which he might reach Arpinum more quickly than by the Latin Way, he rode forth from the town, and was soon spurring at headlong speed in a cloud of dust.

His thoughts far outstripped him; he raged at the prospect of long hours to elapse ere he could reach Marcian's villa. With good luck he might arrive before nightfall. If disappointed in that, a whole night must pass, an eternity of torment, before he came face to face with him he had called his dearest friend, now his abhorred enemy.

What if he did not find him at the villa? Marcian had perhaps no intention of remaining there. Perhaps he had already carried off his victim to some other place.

Seeing their lord post so furiously, the men looked in wonder at each other. Some of them were soon left far behind, and Basil, though merciless in his frenzy, saw at length that his horse was seriously distressed; he slackened pace, allowed his followers to rejoin him, and rode, perforce, at what seemed to him a mere crawl. The sun was a flaming furnace; the earth seemed to be overspread with white fire-ash, which dazed the eyes and choked. But Basil felt only the fire in his heart and brain. Forgetful of all about him, he had not ridden more than a few miles, when he missed the road; his men, ignorant of the country, followed him without hesitation, and so it happened that, on stopping at one of the few farms on their way, to ask how far it still was to Arpinum, he learnt that he must ride back for nearly a couple of hours to regain the track he should have taken. He broke into frantic rage, cursed the countrymen who directed him, and as he spurred his beast, cursed it too because of its stumbling at a stone.

There was now no hope of finishing the journey to-day. His head on his breast, Basil rode more and more slowly. The sun declined, and ere long it would be necessary to seek harbourage. But here among the hills no place of human habitation came in view. Luckily for themselves some of the horsemen had brought provender. Their lord had given thought to no such thing. The sun set; the hills cast a thickening shadow, even Basil began to gaze uneasily ahead. At length there appeared a building, looking in the dusky distance like a solitary country house. It proved to be the ruin of a temple.

'Here we must stop,' said Basil. 'My horse can go no further. Indeed, the darkness would stay us in any case. We must shelter in these walls.'

The men peered at each other, and a whisper went among them. For their part, said one and all, they would rest under the open sky. Basil understood.

'What! you are afraid? Fools, do as you will. These walls shall shelter me though all the devils in hell were my bedfellows.'

What had come to him? asked his followers. Never had Basil been known to speak thus. Spite of their horror of a forsaken temple, two or three entered, and respectfully made offer of such food as they had with them. Basil accepted a piece of bread, bade them see to his horse, and crept into a corner of the building. He desired to be alone and to think; for it seemed to him that he had not yet been able to reflect upon the story told by Sagaris. What was it that lurked there at the back of his mind? A memory, a suggestion of some sort, which would have helped him to understand could he but grasp it. As he munched his bread he tried desperately to think, to remember; but all within him was a passionate misery, capable only of groans and curses. An intolerable weariness possessed his limbs. After sitting for a while with his back against the wall, he could not longer hold himself in this position, but sank down and lay at full length; and even so he ached, ached, from head to foot.

Perhaps an hour had passed, and it was now quite dark within the temple, when two of the men appeared with blazing torches, for they, by means of flint and iron, had lit a fire in a hollow hard by, and meant to keep it up through the night as a protection against wolves. They brought Basil a draught of water in a leather bottle, from a little stream they had found; and he drank gratefully, but without a word. The torchlight showed bare walls and a shattered roof. Having searched all round and discovered neither reptile nor beast, the men made a bed of leaves and bracken, with a folded cloak for a pillow, and invited their master to lie upon it. Basil did so, turned his face away, and bade them leave him alone.

What was that memory at the back of his mind? In the effort to draw it forth he ground his teeth together, dug his nails into his hands. At moments he forgot why he was wretched, and, starting up, strained his eyes into the darkness, until he saw the face of Sagaris and heard him speaking.

For a while he slept; but dreadful dreams soon awoke him, and, remembering where he was, he shook with horror. Low sounds fell upon his ear, movements, he thought, in the black night. He would have shouted to his men, but shame kept him mute. He crossed himself and prayed to the Virgin; then, raising his eyes, he saw through the broken roof a space of sky in which a star shone brilliantly. It brought him comfort; but the next moment he remembered Sagaris, and mental anguish blended with his fears of the invisible.

Again sleep overcame him. He dreamt that an evil spirit, with a face he knew but could not name, was pursuing him over trackless mountains. He fled like the wind; but the spirit was close behind him, and wherever he turned his head, he saw the familiar face grinning a devilish mockery. A precipice lay before him. He leapt wildly, and knew at once that he had leapt into fire, into hell. But the red gleam was that of a torch, and before him, as he opened his eyes, stood one of his faithful attendants who had come to see if all was well with him. He asked for water, and the man fetched him a draught. It was yet long till dawn.

Now he could not lie still, for fever burned him. Though awake, he saw visions, and once sent forth what seemed to him a yell of terror; but in truth it was only a moan, and no one heard. He relived through the fight with the marauders; sickened with dread at the gleam of weapons; flamed into fury, and shouted with savage exultation as he felt his sword cut the neck of an enemy. He was trying to think of Veranilda, but all through the night her image eluded him, and her name left him cold. He was capable only of hatred. At daybreak he slept heavily; the men, approaching him and looking at his haggard face, thought better to let him rest, and only after sunrise did he awake. He was angry that they had not aroused him sooner, got speedily to horse, and rode off almost at the same speed as yesterday. Now, at all events, he drew near to his goal; for a ride of an hour or two he needed not to spare his beast; sternly he called to his men to follow him close.

And all at once, as though his brain were restored by the freshness of the morning, he grasped the thought which had eluded him. Marcian's treachery was no new thing: twice he had been warned against his seeming friend, by Petronilla and by Bessas, and in his folly he had scorned the accusation which time had now so bitterly justified. Forgotten, utterly forgotten, until this moment; yet how blinded he must have been by his faith in Marcian's loyalty not to have reflected upon many circumstances prompting suspicion. Marcian had perhaps been false to him from the very day of Veranilda's disappearance, and how far did his perfidy extend? Had he merely known where she was concealed, or had he seen her, spoken with her, wooed her all along? He had won her; so much was plain; and he could scarce have done so during the brief journey to his villa. O villainous Marcian! O fickle, wanton Veranilda!

So distinct before his fiery imagination shone the image of those two laughing together, walking alone (as Sagaris had reported), that all reasoning, such as a calmer man might have entertained, was utterly forbidden. Not a doubt crossed his mind. And in his heart was no desire but of vengeance.

At length he drew near to Arpinum. Avoiding the town, he questioned a peasant at work in the fields, and learnt his way to the island. Just as he came within view of the eastward waterfall, a girl was crossing the bridge, away from the villa. Basil drew rein, bidding his men do likewise, and let the girl, who had a bundle on her head, draw near. At sight of the horsemen, of whom she was not aware till close by them, the maid uttered a cry of alarm, and would have run back but Basil intercepted her, jumped from his horse, and bade her have no fear, as he only wished to ask a harmless question. Easily he learnt that Marcian was at the villa, that he had arrived a few days ago, and that with him had come a lady.

'What is that lady's name?' he inquired.

The girl did not know. Only one or two of the slaves, she said, had seen her; she was said to be beautiful, with long yellow hair.

'She never goes out?' asked Basil.

The reply was that, only this morning, she had walked in the wood—the wood just across the bridge—with Marcian.

Basil sprang on to his horse, beckoned his troop, and rode forward.

CHAPTER XXII
DOOM

When Marcian parted from Veranilda in the peristyle, and watched her as she ascended to her chamber, he knew that sombre exultation which follows upon triumph in evil. Hesitancies were now at end; no longer could he be distracted between two desires. In his eye, as it pursued the beauty for which he had damned himself, glowed the fire of an unholy joy. Not without inner detriment had Marcian accustomed himself for years to wear a double face; though his purpose had been pure, the habit of assiduous perfidy, of elaborate falsehood, could not leave his soul untainted. A traitor now for his own ends, he found himself moving in no unfamiliar element, and, the irrevocable words once uttered, he thrilled with defiance of rebuke. All the persistency of the man centred itself upon the achievement of this crime, to him a crime no longer from the instant that he had irrevocably willed it.

On fire to his finger-tips, he could yet reason with the coldest clarity of thought. Having betrayed his friend thus far, he must needs betray him to the extremity of traitorhood; must stand face to face with him in the presence of the noble Totila, and accuse him even as he had done to Veranilda. Only thus, as things had come about, could he assure himself against the fear that Totila, in generosity, or policy, or both, might give the Amal-descended maid to Basil. To defeat Basil's love was his prime end, jealousy being more instant with him than fleshly impulse. Yet so strong had this second motive now become, that he all but regretted his message to the king: to hold Veranilda in his power, to gratify his passion sooner or later, by this means or by that, he would perhaps have risked all the danger to which such audacity exposed him. But Marcian was not lust-bitten quite to madness. For the present, enough to ruin the hopes of Basil. This done, the field for his own attempt lay open. By skilful use of his advantages, he might bring it to pass that Totila would grant him a supreme reward—the hand of Veranilda.

Unless, indeed, the young king, young and warm-blooded however noble of mind, should himself look upon Veranilda with a lover's eyes. It was not the first time that Marcian had thought of this. It made him wince. But he reminded himself that herein lay another safeguard against the happiness of Basil, and so was able to disregard the fear.

He would let his victim repose during the heat of the day, and then, towards evening, would summon her to another interview. Not much longer could he hope to be with her in privacy; to-morrow, or the next day at latest, emissaries of the Gothic king would come in response to his letter. But this evening he should speak with her, gaze upon her, for a long, long hour. She was gentle, meek, pious; in everything the exquisite antithesis of such a woman as Heliodora. Out of very humility she allowed herself to believe that Basil had ceased to love her. How persuade her, against the pure loyalty of her heart, that he had even plotted her surrender to an unknown fate? What proof of that could he devise? Did he succeed in overcoming her doubts, would he not have gone far towards winning her gratitude?

She would shed tears again; it gave him a nameless pleasure to see Veranilda weep.

Thinking thus, he strayed aimlessly and unconsciously in courts and corridors. Night would come again, and could he trust himself through the long, still night after long speech with Veranilda? A blacker thought than any he had yet nurtured began to stir in his mind, raising its head like the viper of an hour ago. Were she but his—his irredeemably? He tried to see beyond that, but his vision blurred.

Her nature was gentle, timid; the kind of nature, he thought, which subdues itself to the irreparable. So soft, so sweet, so utterly woman, might she not, thinking herself abandoned by Basil, yield heart and soul to a man whom she saw helpless to resist a passionate love of her? Or, if this hope deceived him, was there no artifice with which to cover his ill-doing, no piece of guile subtle enough to cloak such daring infamy?

He was in the atrium, standing on the spot where first he had talked with her. As then, he gazed at the bronze group of the candelabrum; his eyes were fixed on those of Proserpine.

A slave entered and announced to him a visit from one of the priests whom he was going to see when the meeting at the bridge changed his purpose. The name startled him. Was this man sent by God? He bade introduce the visitor, and in a moment there entered a white-bearded, shoulder-bowed ecclesiastic, perspiring from the sunshine, who greeted him with pleasant cordiality. This priest it was—he bore the name Gaudiosus—who had baptized Marcian, and had given him in childhood religious teaching; a good, but timid man, at all times readier to praise than to reprove, a well-meaning utterer of smooth things, closing his eyes to evil, which confused rather than offended him. From the same newsbearer, who told him of Marcian's arrival at the villa, Gaudiosus had heard of a mysterious lady; but it was far from his thought to meddle with the morals of one whose noble birth and hereditary position of patron inspired him with respect; he came only to gossip about the affairs of the time. They sat down together, Marcian glad of the distraction. But scarce had they been talking for five minutes, when again the servant presented himself.

'What now?' asked his master impatiently.

'My lord, at the gate is the lord Basil.'

Marcian started up.

'Basil? How equipped and attended?'

'Armed, on horseback, and with a number of armed horsemen.'

'Withdraw, and wait outside till I call you.'

Marcian turned to the presbyter. His cheeks were flushed, his eyes strangely bright.

'Here,' he said, in low, hurried tones, 'comes an evil man, a deep-dyed traitor, with the aspect of friendliest integrity. I am glad you are with me. I have no leisure now to tell you the story; you shall hear it afterwards. What I ask of you, reverend father, is to bear me out in all I say, to corroborate, if asked to do so, all I state to him. You may rely upon the truth of every word I shall utter; and may be assured that, in doing this, you serve only the cause of good. Let it not surprise you that I receive the man with open arms. He was my dear friend; I have only of late discovered his infamy, and for the gravest reasons, which you shall learn, I am obliged to mask my knowledge. Beloved father, you will give me your countenance?'

'I will, I will,' replied Gaudiosus nervously. 'You would not deceive me, I well know, dear son.'

'God forbid!'

Marcian summoned the waiting servant, and ordered that the traveller should be straightway admitted. A few minutes passed in absolute silence, then, as the two stood gazing towards the entrance, they saw the gleam of a casque and of a breastplate, and before them stood Basil. His arms extended, Marcian stepped forward.

'So soon, O brave Basil!' he exclaimed. 'What speed you must have made! How long is it since my letter reached you?'

There passed the semblance of an embrace between them. Basil was death pale; he spoke in hollow tones, as though his tongue were parched, and looked with bloodshot eyes from Marcian to the ecclesiastic.

'I am travel-worn. Your hospitality must restore me.'

'That it shall,' replied Marcian. 'Or, better still,' he added, 'the hospitality of my father Gaudiosus.' He touched the priest's arm, as if affectionately. 'For here there is little solace; barely one chamber habitable. You have often heard me describe, O Basil, my poor, ruinous island villa, and now at length you behold it. I did not think you would pass this way, or I would have prepared for your fitting reception. By the greatest chance you find me here; and to-morrow I must be gone. But scarce two thousand paces from here is the dwelling of this reverend man, who will entertain you fittingly, and give you the care you need; for it seems to me, dear Basil, that you are more than wearied.'

The listener nodded, and let himself drop upon a seat near to where Marcian was standing.

'What have you to tell me?' he asked under his breath.

'Nothing good, alas!' was the murmured reply.

'Shall we speak in private?'

'Nay, it is needless. All my secrets lie open to Gaudiosus.'

Again Basil cast a glance at the presbyter, who had seated himself and appeared to be absorbed in thought.

'Do you mean,' he asked, 'that something new has befallen?'

His eyes were upon Marcian, and Marcian's upon those of Proserpine.

'Yes, something new. The deacon of whom you know has left Rome, accompanying the Pope on his journey eastward. And with him he has taken—'

A name was shaped upon the speaker's lips, but whether of purpose, or because his voice failed him, it found no utterance.

'Veranilda?'

As Basil spoke, his eye was caught by the movement of a curtain at the back of the room. The curtain was pushed aside, and there appeared the figure of a maiden, pale, beautiful. Marcian did not see her, nor yet did the priest.

'Veranilda?' repeated Basil, in the same questioning tone. He leaned forward, his hand upon his wrist.

'She—alas!' was Marcian's reply.

'Liar! traitor! devil!'

At each word, Basil's dagger drank blood up to the hilt. With his furious voice blended a yell of terror, of agony, a faint cry of horror from Gaudiosus, and a woman's scream. Then came silence.

The priest dropped to his knees by Marcian's prostrate form. Basil, the stained weapon in his crimson hand, stared at Veranilda, who also had fallen.

'Man! What hast thou done?' gasped Gaudiosus.

The trembling, senile tones wakened Basil as if from a trance. He thrust his dagger into its sheath, stepped to the back of the room, and bent over the white loveliness that lay still.

'Is it death?' he murmured.

'Death! death!' answered the priest, who had just heard Marcian's last sob.

'I speak not of that perjured wretch,' said Basil. 'Come hither.'

Gaudiosus obeyed, and looked with wonder at the unconscious face.

'Who is this?' he asked.

'No matter who. Does she live?'

Basil had knelt, and taken one of the little hands in both his own, staining it with the blood of Marcian.

'I can feel no throb of life,' he said, speaking coldly, mechanically.

The priest bent, and put his cheek to her lips.

'She lives. This is but a swoon. Help me to bear her to the couch.'

But Basil took the slender body in his arms, and carried it like that of a child. When he had laid it down, he looked at Gaudiosus sternly.

'Have you authority in this house?'

'Some little, perhaps. I know not. What is your will?'

Utterly confounded, his eyes dropping moisture, his limbs shaken as if with palsy, the priest babbled his reply.

'Use any power you have,' continued Basil, 'to prevent more bloodshed. Outside the gates are men of mine. Bid the porter admit them to the outer court. Then call thither two servants, and let them bear away *that*—whither you will. After, you shall hear more.'

Like an obedient slave, Gaudiosus sped on his errand. Basil the while stood gazing at Veranilda; but he did not go very near to her, and his look had nothing of tenderness. He saw the priest return, followed by two men, heard him whisper to them, saw them take up and carry away their master's corpse; all this as if it did not regard him. Again he turned his gaze upon Veranilda. It seemed to him that her lips, her eyelids moved. He bent forward, heard a sigh. Then the blue eyes opened, but as yet saw nothing.

Gaudiosus reappeared, and Basil beckoned him.

'You do not know her?' he asked in a low voice.

'I never looked upon her face till now,' was the reply.

At the sound of their voices Veranilda stirred, tried to rouse herself, uttered a sound of distress.

'Speak to her,' said Basil.

Gaudiosus approached the couch, and spoke soothing words.

'What dreadful thought is this?' said Veranilda. 'What have I seen?'

The priest whispered an adjuration to prayer. But she, raising her head, cast terrified glances about the hall. Basil had moved further away, and she did not seem to be aware of his presence.

'How long is it,' he asked, with his eyes upon Gaudiosus, 'since Marcian came from Rome?'

'This is the fourth day. So I have been told. I myself saw him for the first time not an hour—nay, not half an hour ago.'

'You knew not that he brought *her* with him?'

Basil, without looking in that direction, signalled with his head towards Veranilda.

'I had heard of some companion unnamed.'

'He had not spoken of her to you?'

'Not a word.'

On the tesselated floor where Marcian had fallen was a pool of blood. Basil only now perceived it, and all at once a violent shudder went over him.

'Man of God!' he exclaimed in a voice of sudden passion, terribly resonant after the dull, hard accents of his questioning. 'You look upon me with abhorrence, and, perhaps, with fear. Hearken to my vindication. He whom I have slain was the man I held in dearest friendship. I believed him true to the heart's core. Yesterday—was it but yesterday?—O blessed Christ!—it seems to me so long ago—I learned that his heart was foul with treachery. Long, long, he has lied to me, pretending to seek with me for one I had lost, my plighted love. In secret he robbed me of her. Heard you not his answer when, to catch the lie on his very lips, I asked what news he could give me of her. I knew that she was here; his own servant had secretly avowed the truth to me. And you heard him say that she was gone on far travel. Therefore it was that he would not harbour me in his house—me, his friend. In the name of the Crucified, did I not well to lay him low?'

Somewhat recovered from the emotions which had enfeebled him, Gaudiosus held up his head, and made solemn answer.

'Not yours was it to take vengeance. The God to whom you appeal has said: "Thou shalt do no murder."'

'Consider his crime,' returned the other. 'In the moment when he swore falsely I lifted up my eyes, and behold, she herself stood before me. She whom I loved, who had pledged herself to me, who long ago would have been my wife but for the enemy who came between us—she, hidden here with him, become a wanton in his embraces—'

A low cry of anguish interrupted him. He turned. Veranilda had risen and drawn near.

'Basil! You know not what you say.'

'Nor what I *could* say,' he replied, his eyes blazing with scorn. 'You, who were truth itself have you so well learned to lie? Talk on. Tell me that he held you here perforce, and that you passed the days and the nights in weeping. Have I not heard of your smiles and your contentment? Whither did you stray this morning? Did you go into the wood to say your orisons?'

Veranilda turned to the priest.

'Servant of God I Hear me, unhappy that I am!'

With a gesture of entreaty she flung out her hands, and, in doing so, saw that one of them was red. Her woebegone look changed to terror.

'What is this? His blood is upon me—on my hand, my garment. When did I touch him? Holy father, whither has he gone? Does he live? Oh, tell me if he lives!'

'Come hence with me,' said Gaudiosus. 'Come where I may hear you utter the truth before God.'

But Veranilda was as one distraught. She threw herself on to her knees.

'Tell me he lives. He is but sorely hurt? He can speak? Whither have they carried him?'

Confirmed in his damning thought by every syllable she uttered, Basil strode away.

'Lead her where you will,' he shouted. 'I stay under this abhorred roof only till my men have eaten and taken rest.'

Without knowing it, he had stepped into the pool of blood, and a red track was left behind him as he went forth from the hall.

CHAPTER XXIII
THE RED HAND

Resting at length from desire and intrigue, Marcian lay cold upon the bed where he had passed his haunted nights. About his corpse were gathered all the servants of the house; men, with anger on their brows, muttering together, and women wailing low because of fear. The girl who had met the horsemen by the bridge told her story, whence it became evident that Marcian's death was the result of private quarrel; but some of the slaves declared that this armed company came in advance of the Gothic host; and presently the loss of their master was all but forgotten in anxiety as to their own fate at the hands of the Emperor.

This talk was interrupted by the approach of Basil's men, who came to seek a meal for themselves and forage for their horses. Having no choice but to obey, the servants went about the work required of them. A quiet fell upon the house. The strangers talked little, and, when they spoke, subdued their voices. In still chambers and corridors was heard now and then a sound of weeping.

Basil, though he had given orders for departure as soon as the meal was done, knew not whither his journey should be directed. A paralysis of thought and will kept him pacing alone in the courtyard; food he could not touch; of repose he was incapable; and though he constantly lifted up his bloodstained hand, to gaze at it as if in bewildered horror, he did not even think of washing the blood away. At moments he lost consciousness of what he had done, his mind straying to things remote; then the present came back upon him with a shock, seeming, however, to strike on numbed senses, so that he had to say to himself, 'I have slain Marcian,' before he could fully understand his suffering.

Veranilda was now scarce present to his mind at all. Something vaguely outlined hovered in the background; something he durst not look at or think about; the sole thing in the world that had reality for him was the image of Marcian—stabbed, shrieking, falling, dead. Every minute was the fearful scene re-enacted. More than once he checked himself in his walk, seeming to be about to step on Marcian's body.

At length, seeing a shadow draw near, he raised his eyes and beheld Gaudiosus. He tried to speak, but found that his tongue clave to the roof of his mouth. Automatically he crossed himself, then caught the priest's hand, and knelt and kissed it.

'Rise, my son,' said Gaudiosus, 'for I would talk with you.'

On one side of the courtyard was a portico with seats, and thither the old man led.

'Unless,' he began gravely, 'unless the author of all falsehood—who is so powerful over women—has entered into this maiden to baffle and mislead me utterly, I feel assured that she is chaste; not merely unsullied in the flesh, but as pure of heart as her fallen nature may permit a woman to be.'

Basil gazed at him darkly.

'My father, how can you believe it? Did you not hear her lament because the man was dead? It is indeed the devil that beguiles you.'

Gaudiosus bent his head, and pondered anxiously.

'Tell me,' he said at length, 'all her story, that I may compare it with what I have heard from her own lips.'

Slowly at first, and confusedly, with hesitations, repetitions, long pauses, Basil recited the history of Veranilda, so far as he knew it. The priest listened and nodded, and when silence came, continued the narrative. If Veranilda spoke truth she had never seen Marcian until he took her from the convent at Praeneste. Moreover, Marcian had never uttered to her a word of love; in his house she had lived as chastely as among the holy sisters.

'What did she here, then?' asked Basil bitterly. 'Why did he bring her here? You know, O father, that it was not in fulfilment of his promise to me, for you heard his shameless lie when I questioned him.'

'He told her,' replied the priest, 'that she sojourned here only until he could put her under the protection of the Gothic King.'

'Of Totila?' cried Basil. 'Nay, for all I know, he may have thought of that—his passion being appeased.'

Even as he spoke be remembered Sagaris and the letter written in Gothic. Some motive of interest might, indeed, have prompted Marcian to this step. None the less was he Veranilda's lover. Would he otherwise have kept her here with him, alone, and not rather have continued the journey, with all speed, till he reached Totila's camp?

'When I left her,' pursued Gaudiosus, whose confidence in his own judgment was already shaken by the young man's vehemence, 'I spoke in private with certain of the bondswomen, who declared to me that they could avouch the maiden's innocence since her coming hither—until to-day's sunrise.'

Basil laughed with scorn.

'Until to-day's sunrise? And pray, good father, what befell her at that moment? What whisper the Argus-eyed bondswomen?'

'They tell me,' replied the priest, 'that she went forth and met Marcian, and walked with him in a wood, her own woman having been sent back to the villa. This troubled me; but her voice, her countenance—'

'Helped by the devil,' broke in Basil. 'Reverend man, do not seek to deceive yourself, or to solace me with a vain hope. I pray you, did Marcian, when you came to visit him, speak of a lady whose virtue he was sworn to guard? Plainly, not a word fell from him. Yet assuredly he would have spoken had things been as you pretend.'

Gaudiosus, bent double, a hand propping his white-bearded chin, mused for a little with sadded air.

'Lord Basil,' he resumed at length, 'somewhat more have I to say to you. I live far from the world, and hear little of its rumour. Until this day your name was unknown to me, and of good concerning you I have to this hour heard nothing save from your own lips. May I credit this report you make of yourself? Or should I rather believe what Marcian, in brief words, declared to me when he heard that you were at his gate?'

The speaker paused, as if to collect courage.

'He spoke ill of me?' asked Basil.

'He spoke much ill. He accused you of disloyalty in friendship, saying that he had but newly learnt how you had deceived him. More than this he had not time to tell.'

Basil looked into the old man's rheumy eyes.

'You do well to utter this, good father. Tell me one thing more. Yonder maiden, does she breathe the same charge against me?'

'Not so,' replied Gaudiosus. 'Of you she said no evil.'

'Yet I scarce think'—he smiled coldly—'that she made profession of love for me?'

'My son, her speech was maidenly. She spoke of herself as erstwhile your betrothed; no more than that.'

As he uttered these words, the priest rose. He had an uneasy look, as if he feared that infirmity of will and fondness for gossip had betrayed him into some neglect of spiritual obligation.

'It is better,' he said, 'that we should converse no more. I know not what your purposes may be, nor do they concern me I remain here to pray by the dead, and I shall despatch a messenger to my brother presbyter, that we may prepare for the burial. Remember,' he raised his head, and his voice struck a deeper note, 'that the guilt of blood is upon you, and that no plea of earthly passion will avail before the Almighty Judge. Behold your hand—even so, but far more deeply have you stained your soul.'

Basil scarce heard. Numbness had crept over him again; he stared at the doorway by which the priest re-entered the house, and only after some minutes recalled enough of the old man's last words to look upon his defiled hand. Then he called aloud, summoning any slave who might hear him, and when the doorkeeper came timidly from a recess where he had been skulking, bade him bring water. Having cleansed himself, he walked by an outer way to the rear of the villa; for he durst not pass through the atrium.

Here his men were busy over their meal, sitting or sprawling in a shadowed place, the slaves waiting upon them. With a reminder that they must hold themselves ready to ride at any moment, he passed on through a large, wild garden, and at length, where a grove of box-trees surrounded the ruins of a little summer-house, cast himself to the ground.

His breast heaved, his eyes swelled and smarted, but he could not shed tears. Face downwards, like a man who bites the earth in his last agony, he lay quivering. So did an hour or more pass by.

He was roused by the voices of his men, who were searching and calling for him. With an effort, he rose to his feet, and stepped out into the sunshine, when he learnt that a troop of soldiers had just ridden up to the villa, and that their captain, who had already entered, was asking for him by name. Careless what might await him, Basil followed the men as far as the inner court, and there stood Venantius.

'I surprise you,' cried out the genial voice with a cheery laugh. You had five hours start of me. Pray, dear lord, when did you get here?'

Basil could make no reply, and the other, closely observing his strange countenance, went on to explain that, scarcely started from Aesernia on his way to the king, Marcian's messenger had met with Totila himself, who was nearer than had been thought. After reading the letter, Totila had come on rapidly to Aesernia, and had forthwith despatched Venantius to the villa by Arpinum.

'You guess my mission, lord Basil,' he pursued, with bluff good-humour. 'Dullard that I was, the talk of a fair lady travelling in Marcian's charge never brought to my mind that old story of Surrentum. Here is our royal Totila all eagerness to see this maiden—if maiden still she be. What say you on that point, dear lord? Nay, look not so fiercely at me. I am not here to call any one to account, but only to see that the Gothic beauty comes safe to Aesernia as soon as may be.'

'You will find her within,' muttered Basil.

'And Marcian? I might have thought I came inopportunely to this dwelling, but that he himself wrote to the king that the lady was here.'

'You are assured of that?' Basil asked, under his breath.

'I have Totila's word for it, at all events. But you seem indisposed for talk, lord Basil, and my business is with Marcian. The slaves all look scared, and can't or won't answer a plain question. I have no time to waste. Tell me, I pray you, where the lord of the villa may be found.'

Basil summoned one of his followers.

'Conduct the lord Venantius to Marcian's chamber.'

It was done. Basil remained standing in the same spot, his eyes cast down, till a quick step announced the captain's return. Venantius came close up to him, and spoke in a grave but not unfriendly voice:

'The priest has told me what he saw, but will not say more. I ask you nothing, lord Basil. You will make your defence to the king.'

'Be it so.'

'My men must rest for an hour,' continued Venantius. 'We shall ride this afternoon as far as Aquinum, and there pass the night. I go now to speak with Veranilda.'

'As you will.'

Basil withdrew into the portico, sat down, and covered his face with his hands. Fever consumed him, and a dreadful melancholy weighed upon his spirit. At a respectful distance from him, his followers had assembled, ready for departure. The soldiers who had come with Venantius, a score in number, were eating and drinking outside the gates. Within, all was quiet. Half an hour elapsed, and Venantius again came forward. Seeing Basil in the shadow of the portico, he went and sat beside him, and began to speak with rough but well-meaning solace. Why this heaviness? If he surmised aright, Basil had but avenged himself as any man would have done. For his own part, he had never thought enough of any woman to kill a man on her account; but such little troubles were of everyday occurrence, and must not be taken too much to heart. He had seen this Gothic damsel of whom there had been so much rumour, and, by Diana I (if the oath were not inappropriate) her face deserved all that was said of it. His rival being out of the way, why should not Basil pluck up cheer? Totila would not deal harshly in such a matter as this, and more likely than not he would be disposed to give the maiden to a Roman of noble race, his great desire being to win all Romans by generosity.

'Yonder priest tells me,' he added, 'that you were over hasty; that you struck on a mere suspicion. And methinks he may be right. By the Holy Cross, I could well believe this maiden a maiden in very deed. I never looked upon a purer brow, an eye that spoke more innocently. Hark ye, my good Basil, I am told that you have not spoken with her. If you would fain do so before we set forth, I will be no hinderer. Go, if you will, into yonder room'—he pointed to a door near by—' and when she descends (I have but to call), you shall see her undisturbed.'

For a moment Basil sat motionless; then, without a word, he rose and went whither Venantius directed him. But a few minutes passed before he saw Veranilda enter. She was clad for travel, a veil over her face; this, and the shadow in which Basil stood, made her at first unaware of his presence, for Venantius had only requested her to enter this room until the carriage was ready. Standing with bowed head, she sobbed.

'Why do you weep?' demanded an abrupt voice, which made her draw back trembling.

Basil moved a little towards her.

'You weep for *him*?' he added in the same pitiless tone.

'For him, for you, and for myself, alas! alas!'

The subdued anguish of her voice did not touch Basil. He burned with hatred of her and of the dead man.

'Shed no tears for me. I am cured of a long folly. And for you consolation will not be slow in coming. Who knows but you may throw your spell upon Totila himself.'

'You know not what you say,' replied Veranilda; not, as when she used the words before, in accents quivering from a stricken heart, but with sorrowful dignity and self-command. 'Is it Basil who speaks thus? Were it only the wrong done me that I had to bear, I could keep silence, waiting until God restored your justice and your gentleness. But, though in nothing blameworthy, I am the cause of what has come about; for had I not entered that room when I did, you would not have struck the fatal blow. Listen then, O Basil, whilst I make known to you what happened before you came.'

She paused to control herself.

'I must go back to the night when I left the convent. No one had told me I was to go away. In the middle of the night I was aroused and led forth, with me the woman who served me. We had travelled an hour or two, perhaps, when some one standing by the carriage spoke to me, some one who said he was Marcian the friend of Basil, and bade me have no fears, for Basil awaited me at the end of the journey. The next day he spoke to me again, this time face to face, but only a few words. We came to this villa. You have been told, by I know not whom, that I was light of heart. It is true, for I believed what Marcian had said to me, and nothing had befallen to disturb my gladness. I lived with my serving woman privately, in quiet and hope. This morning, yielding, alas! to a wish which I thought harmless, I went forth with my attendant to the waterfall. As I stood gazing at it, the lord Marcian came forth on horseback. He alighted to speak with me, and presently asked if I would go to see another fall of the river, across the island. I consented. As we went, he dismissed my servant, and I did not know what he had done (thinking she still followed), until, when we were in a wood at the water's edge, I could no longer see the woman, and Marcian told me he had bidden her go to fetch seats for us. Then he began to speak, and what he said, how shall I tell you?'

There was another brief silence. Basil did not stir; his eyes were bent sternly upon the veiled visage.

'Was it evil in his heart that shaped such words? Or had he been deceived by some other? He said that Basil had forgotten me; that Basil loved, and would soon wed, a lady in Rome. More than that, he said that Basil was plotting to get me into his power, his purpose being to deliver me to the Greeks, who would take me to Constantinople. But Marcian, so he declared, had rescued me in time, and I was to be guarded by the King of the Goths.'

The listener moved, raising his arm and letting it fall again. But he breathed no word.

'This did he tell me,' she added. 'I went back to the villa to my chamber. I sat thinking, I know not how long; I know not how long. Then, unable to remain any longer alone, driven by my dreadful doubt, I came forth to seek Marcian. I descended the stairs to the atrium. You saw me—alas! alas!'

Basil drew nearer to her.

'He had spoken no word of love?'

'No word. I had no fear of *that*.'

'Why, then, did he frame these lies, these hellish lies?'

'Alas!' cried Veranilda, clasping her hands above her head. 'Did he still live, the truth might be discovered. His first words to me, in the night when he stood beside the carriage, sounded so kind and true; he named himself the friend of Basil, said that Basil awaited me at the journey's end. How could he speak so, if he indeed then thought you what he afterwards said? Oh, were he alive, to stand face to face with me again!'

'It is not enough,' asked Basil harshly, 'that I tell you he lied?'

She did not on the instant reply, and he, possessed with unreasoning bitterness, talked wildly on.

'No! You believed him, and believe him still. I can well fancy that he spoke honestly at first; but when he had looked into your face, when he had talked with you, something tempted him to villainy. Go! Your tears and your lamentations betray you. It is not of me that you think, but of him, him, only him! "Oh, were he alive!" Ay, keep your face bidden; you know too well it could not bear my eyes upon it.'

Veranilda threw back the long veil, and stood looking at him.

'Eyes red with weeping,' he exclaimed, 'and for whom? If you were true to me, would you not rejoice that I had slain my enemy? You say you were joyful in the thought of seeing me again? You see me—and with what countenance?'

'I see not Basil,' she murmured, her hands upon her breast.

'You see a false lover, an ignoble traitor—the Basil shown you by Marcian. What would it avail me to speak in my own defence? His voice is in your ears, its lightest tone outweighing my most solemn oath. "Oh, that he were alive!" That is all you find to say to me.'

'I know you not,' sobbed Veranilda. 'Alas, I know you not!'

'Nor I you. I dreamt of a Veranilda who loved so purely and so constantly that not a thousand slanderers could have touched her heart with a shadow of mistrust. But who are you—you whom the first gross lie of a man lusting for your beauty utterly estranges from your faith? Who are you—who wail for the liar's death, and shrink in horror from the hand that slew him? I ever heard that the daughters of the Goths were chaste and true and fearless. So they may be—all but one, whose birth marked her for faithlessness.'

As though smitten by a brutal blow, Veranilda bowed her head, shuddering. Once more she looked at Basil, for an instant, with wide eyes of fear; then hid herself beneath the veil, and was gone.

CHAPTER XXIV
THE MOUNT OF THE MONK

Basil rode with his own man apart from Venantius and the soldiers who guarded the conveyance in which sat Veranilda. Venantius, for his part, would fain have lightened the way with friendly talk, but finding Basil irresponsive, he left him to his gloomy meditations. And so they came to Aquinum, where they passed the night.

By way of precaution, the captain set a guard before the house in which his fellow-traveller slept, and at daybreak, as soon as he had risen, one of the soldiers thus employed reported to him that the young Roman had fallen into such distemper that it seemed doubtful whether he could continue the journey; a servant who had slept at Basil's door declared that all through the night his master had talked wildly, like one fever-frenzied. Venantius visited the sick man, and found him risen, but plainly in poor case for travel.

'Why, you will never mount your horse,' he opined, after touching Basil's hand, and finding it on fire. 'This is what comes of a queasy conscience. Take heart, man! Are you the first that stuck a false friend between the ribs, or the first to have your love kissed against her will? That it *was* against her will, I take upon myself to swear. You are too fretful, my good lord. Come, now! What are we to do with you?'

'I can ride on,' answered Basil. 'Pay no heed to me, and leave me in peace, I pray you.'

He was helped to horseback, and the cavalcade went forth again along the Latin Way. This morning, no beam of sunrise shone above the mountains; the heavens were sullen, and a hot wind blew from the south. Even Venantius, though he hummed a song to himself, felt the sombre influence of the air, and kept glancing uneasily backwards at the death-pale man, who rode with head upon his breast. Scarcely had they ridden for an hour at foot-pace, when a shout caught the captain's ear; he turned, just in time to see Basil dropping to the ground.

'God's thunder!' he growled. 'I have been expecting this. Well if he dies, it may save the king some trouble.'

He jumped down, and went to Basil's side. At first the sufferer could not speak, but when water had been given him, he gazed at Venantius with a strange smile, and, pointing before him, said faintly:

'Is not yonder Casinum?'

'It is. We will bear you thither for harbourage. Courage, friend!'

'Above, on the mountain,' continued Basil painfully, 'dwells my kinsman Benedict, with his holy men. Could I but reach the monastery!'

'Why, perchance you may,' replied the captain. 'And in truth you would be better cared for there.'

'Help me, good Venantius!' panted Basil, with eyes of entreaty. 'Let me die in the monastery.'

In those days of pestilence, every fever-stricken person was an object of dread to all but the most loving or the most courageous. The stalwart Venantius thought for a moment of carrying Basil before him on his horse, but prudence overcame this humane impulse. Into the carriage, for the same reason (had there been no other), he could not be put; but there was a vacant place beside the driver, and here, supported with cords, he managed to keep his seat until they arrived at Casinum.

Owing to its position on the highroad, trodden by so many barbaric armies, this city had suffered repeated devastation. Its great buildings stood desolate, or had fallen to utter ruin, and the country around, once famous for its fertility, showed but a few poor farms. What inhabitants remained dwelt at the foot of the great hill on whose summit rose the citadel, still united with the town by two great walls. After passing between the tombs on the Latin Way, memorials of citizens long dead, the travellers entered by an unprotected gateway, and here Venantius called a halt. Wishing to make no longer pause than was needful to put the sick man in safety, he despatched a few soldiers through the silent town to seek for means of conveying Basil up to the monastery on the height. By good luck these emissaries came upon a couple of monks, who lost no time in arranging for the conveyance of the sufferer. A light cart drawn by two mules speedily appeared, and on this Basil was laid. One only of his men did Venantius allow to accompany him, the others were bidden ride on with the captain's own soldiers to Aesernia.

'There you will find us all when you are on your legs again,' said Venantius, 'unless by that time we have marched Romewards, in which case you shall have a message. Trust me to look after all you left there; I answer for its safety and for that of your good fellows. Keep up heart, and God make you sound.'

Basil, couched on a bed of dry leaves, raised himself so as to watch the troop as it rode forth again from the ruined gate. Whether she who sat hidden within the carriage had heard of his evil plight he knew not, and could not have brought himself to ask. The last of his own horsemen (some of whom had taken leave of him with tears) having vanished from sight, he fell back, and for a while knew nothing but the burning torment in his brain.

The ascent of the mountain began. It was a rough, narrow road, winding through a thick forest of oak and beech trees, here and there so steep as to try the firm footing of the mules, and in places dangerous because of broken ground on the edge of precipitous declivities. The cart was driven by its owner, a peasant of Casinum, who at times sat sideways on one of the beasts, at times walked by them; behind came the two religious men, cowled, barefooted; and last Basil's attendant on horseback.

From Venantius the monks had learned who their charge was. His noble origin, and still more the fact of his kindred with their beloved Abbot Benedict, inspired in them a special interest. They spoke of him in whispers together, compassionated his sufferings, remarked on the comeliness of his features, and assured each other that they detected in him no symptom of the plague. It being now the third hour, they ceased from worldly talk and together recited their office, whereto the peasant and the horseman gave pious ear.

Basil lay with closed eyes, but at a certain moment he seemed to become aware of what was passing, crossed himself, and then folded his hands upon his breast in the attitude of prayer. Having observed this, one of the monks, his orisons finished, went up to the cart and spoke comfortable words. He was a man in the prime of life, with cheek as fresh as a maid's, and a step that seemed incapable of weariness; his voice sounded a note of gentle kindness which caused the sufferer to smile at him in gratitude.

'This tree,' he said presently, pointing to a noble beech, its bole engraven with a cross, 'marks the middle point of the ascent. A weary climb for the weak, but not without profit to him who thinks as he walks—for, as our dear brother Marcus has said, in those verses we are never tired of repeating:—

"Semper difficili quaeruntur summa labore,
Arctam semper habet vita beata viam."'

The other monk, an older man, who walked less vigorously, echoed the couplet with slow emphasis, as if savouring every word. Then both together, bowing their cowled heads, exclaimed fervently:

'Thanks be to God for the precious gifts of our brother Marcus!'

Basil endeavoured to utter a few words, but he was now so feeble that he could scarce make his voice heard above the creak of the wheels. Again he closed his eyes, and his companions pursued their way in silence. When at length they issued from the forest they overlooked a vast landscape of hill and valley, with heads of greater mountains high above them. Here rose the walls of the citadel, within which Benedict had built his monastery. For some distance around these ancient ramparts the ground was tilled, and flourishing with various crops. At the closed gateway of the old Arx, flanked by a tower, the monks rang, and were at once admitted into the courtyard, where, in a few moments, the prior and all his brethren came forward to greet the strangers. Because of Basil's condition the ceremony usual on such arrivals was in his case curtailed: the prior uttered a brief prayer, gave the kiss of peace, and ordered forthwith the removal of the sick man to a guest-chamber, where he was laid in bed and ministered to by the brother Marcus, whose gifts as a healer were not less notable than his skill in poesy. The horseman, meanwhile, as custom was with all visitors, had been led to the oratory to hear a passage of Holy Scripture; after which the prior poured water upon his hands, and certain of the monks washed his feet.

Before sunset Basil lost consciousness of present things; and many days went by before he again spoke as a sane man. When at length the fever declined, and his head turned upon the pillow in search of a human countenance, he saw standing beside him a venerable figure in the monastic garb, whose visage, though wrinkled with age and thought, had such noble vividness in its look, and wore a smile so like that of youth in its half-playful sweetness, that Basil could but gaze wonderingly, awestruck at once, and charmed by this unexpected apparition.

'My son,' sounded in a voice grave and tender, 'be your first syllables uttered to Him by whose omnipotent will you are restored to the life of this world.'

With the obedience of a child he clasped his thin hands, and murmured the prayer of childhood. Then the gracious figure bent over him. He felt the touch of lips upon his forehead, and in the same moment fell asleep.

It was night when he again woke. A little lamp revealed bare walls of stone, a low, timbered ceiling, a floor of red tiles. Basil's eyes, as soon as they were open, looked for the venerable figure which he remembered. Finding no one, he thought the memory was but of a dream. Feeling wonderfully at ease in body and calm in mind, he lay musing on that vision of the noble countenance, doubting after all whether a dream could have left so distinct an impression, when all at once there fell upon his ear a far sound of chanting, a harmony so sweetly solemn that it melted his heart and filled his eyes with tears. Not long after, when all was silent again, he heard the sound of soft footsteps without, and in the same moment the door of his cell opened. The face which looked in seemed not quite unknown to him, though he could not recall where he had seen it.

'You have slept long, dear brother,' said Marcus, with a happy smile. 'Is all well with you?'

'Well, God be thanked,' was the clear but faint reply.

The poet-physician, a small, nervous, bright-eyed man of some forty years, sat down on a stool by the bedside and began talking cheerfully. He had just come from matins, and was this morning excused from lauds because it behoved him to gather certain herbs, to be used medicinally in the case of a brother who had fallen sick yesterday. Touching a little gold locket which Basil wore round his neck on a gold thread he asked what this contained, and being told that it was a morsel of the Crown of Thorns, he nodded with satisfaction.

'We questioned whether to leave it on you or not, for we could not open it, and there was a fear lest it might contain something'—he smiled and shook his bead and sighed—'much less sacred. The lord abbot, doubtless'—here his voice sank—'after a vision, though of this he spoke not, decided that it should be left. There was no harm, for all that'—his eyes twinked merrily—'in tying this upon the place where you suffered so grievously.'

From amid Basil's long hair he detached what looked like a tiny skein of hemp, which, with an air singularly blended of shrewdness and reverence, he declared to be a portion of a garb of penitence worn by the Holy Martin, to whom the oratory here was dedicated. Presently Basil found strength to ask whether the abbot had been beside him.

'Many times,' was the answer. 'The last, no longer ago than yestereve, ere he went to compline. You would have seen him on the day of your arrival, ere yet you became distraught, but that a heaviness lay upon him because of the loss of a precious manuscript on its way hither from Rome—a manuscript which had been procured for him after much searching, only to be lost by the folly of one to whom it was intrusted; if, indeed, it was not rather whisked away by the Evil One, who, powerless for graver ill against our holy father, at times seeks to discomfort him by small practice of spite. Sorrow for this loss brought on a distemper to which his age is subject.'

Reminded all at once that he had no time to lose, Marcus threw open the shutter, extinguished the lamp, and slipped away, leaving his patient with eyes turned to the pale glimmer of dawn at the tiny window. Now only did there stir in Basil clear recollection of the events which had preceded his coming hither. Marcus's sly word in regard to the locket had awakened his mind, and in a few moments he thought connectedly. But without emotion, unless it were a vague, tender sadness. All seemed to have happened so long ago. It was like a story he had heard in days gone by. He thought of it until his brain began to weary, then again came sleep.

A day or two passed. He had begun to eat with keen appetite, and his strength increased hour by hour. On a Sunday, after the office of the third hour, Marcus cheerily gave him permission to rise. This prompted Basil to inquire whether his man, who had come with him, was still in the monastery. Marcus, with eyes averted, gave a nod. Might he speak with him, Basil asked. Presently, presently, was the answer. Marcus himself aided the convalescent to dress; then having seated him in a great chair of rude wickerwork, used only on occasions such as this, left him to bask in a beam of sunshine. Before long, his meal was brought him, and with it a book, bound in polished wood and metal, which he found to be a Psalter. Herein, when he had eaten, he read for an hour or so, not, however, without much wandering of the thoughts. He had fallen into reverie, when his door opened, and there appeared before him the Abbot Benedict.

Basil started up, stood for a moment in agitation, then sank upon his knees, with head reverently bowed.

'Rise, rise, my son,' spoke the voice which had so moved him in his vision of a week ago, a voice subdued by years, but perfectly steady and distinct. 'Our good brother Marcus assures me that I may talk with you a little while without fear of overtasking your strength—nay, sit where you were, I pray you. Thanks be to God, I need not support for my back.'

So saying, the abbot seated himself on the stool, and gazed at Basil with a smile of infinite benevolence.

'Your face,' he continued, 'speaks to me of a time very far away. I see in it the presentment of your father's father, with whom, when he was much of your age, I often talked. His mother had a villa at Nursia, the home of my youth. Once he turned aside from a journey to visit me when I dwelt at Sublaqueum.'

The reminiscence checked his tongue he kept silence for a moment, musing gravely.

'But these are old stories, my Basil, and you are young. Tell me somewhat of your parents, and of your own life. Did not your good father pass away whilst at Constantinople?'

Thus, with perfect simplicity, with kindliest interest in things human, did Benedict draw the young man into converse. He put no question that touched on the inner life, and Basil uttered not a word concerning his late distress, but they touched for a moment upon public affairs, and Basil learnt, without show of special interest, that Totila still lingered in Campania.

'Your follower, Deodatus,' said the abbot presently, 'begs each day for permission to see you. The good fellow has not lived in idleness; he is a brave worker in wood, and by chance we much needed one of his craft. Not many things of this world give me more pleasure than to watch a cunning craftsman as he smooths timber, and fits the pieces together, and makes of them something that shall serve the needs of men. Is it not, in some sort, to imitate the great Artificer? Would, O Basil, that our country had more makers and fewer who live but to destroy.'

'Would it were so, indeed!' sighed Basil, in a low, fervent voice.

'But the end is not yet,' pursued Benedict, his eyes gazing straight before him, as if they beheld the future. 'Men shall pray for peace, but it will not be granted them, so great are the iniquities of the world which utters the name of Christ, yet knows Him not.'

He paused with troubled brow. Then, as if reminding himself that his hearer had need of more encouraging words, he said cheerfully:

'To-morrow, perchance, you will have strength to leave your room. Deodatus shall come to you in the morning. When you can walk so far, I will pray you to visit me in my tower. You knew not that I inhabit a tower? Even as the watchman who keeps guard over a city. And,' he added more gravely, as if to himself rather than to the listener, 'God grant that my watch be found faithful.'

Thereupon the abbot rose, and gently took his leave; and Basil, through all the rest of the day, thought of him and of every word he had uttered.

Not long after sunrise on the morrow, Deodatus was allowed to enter. This man, whose age was something more than thirty, was the son of a serf on Basil's land, and being of very peaceful disposition, had with some reluctance answered the summons to arm himself and follow his lord to the wars. Life in the monastery thoroughly suited his temper; when Basil encouraged him to talk, he gave a delighted account of the way in which his days were spent; spoke with simple joy of the many religious services he attended, and had no words in which to express his devotion to the abbot.

'Why, Deodatus,' exclaimed his master, smiling, 'you lack but the cowl to be a very monk.'

'My duty is to my lord,' answered the man, bending his head.

'Tell me now whether any news has reached you, in all this time, of those from whom my sickness parted us.'

But Deodatus had heard nothing of his fellows, and nothing of Venantius.

'It may be,' said Basil, 'that I shall send you to tell them how I fare, and to bring back tidings. Your horse is at hand?'

As he spoke he detected a sadness on the man's countenance. Without more words, he dismissed him.

That day he sat in the open air, in a gallery whence he could survey a great part of the monastic buildings, and much of the mountain summit on its western side. For an hour he had the companionship of Marcus, who, pointing to this spot and to that, instructed Basil in the history of what he saw, now and then reciting his own verses on the subject. He told how Benedict, seeking with a little company of pious followers for a retreat from the evil of the world, came to ruined Casinum, and found its few wretched inhabitants fallen away from Christ, worshipping the old gods in groves and high places. Here, on the mountain top, stood temples of Jupiter, of Apollo, and of Venus. The house of Apollo he purified for Christian service, and set under the invocation of the Holy Martin. The other temples he laid low, and having cut down the grove sacred to Apollo, on that spot he raised an oratory in the name of the Baptist. Not without much spiritual strife was all this achieved; for—the good Marcus subdued his voice—Satan himself more than once overthrew what the monks had built, and, together with the demons whom Benedict had driven forth, often assailed the holy band with terrors and torments. Had not the narrator, who gently boasted a part in these beginnings, been once all but killed by a falling column, which indeed must have crushed him, but that he stretched out a hand in which, by happy chance, he was holding a hammer, and this—for a hammer is cruciform—touching the great pillar, turned its fall in another direction. Where stood the temple of Venus was now a vineyard, yielding excellent wine.

'Whereof, surely, you must not drink?' interposed Basil, with a smile.

'Therein, good brother,' replied Marcus, 'you show but little knowledge of our dear lord abbot. He indeed abstains from wine, for such has been the habit of his life, but to us he permits it, for the stomach's sake; being of opinion that labour is a form of worship, and well understanding that labour, whether of body or of mind, can only be performed by one in health. This very day you shall taste of our vintage, which I have hitherto withheld from you, lest it should overheat your languid blood.'

Many other questions did Basil ask concerning the rule of the monastery. He learned that the day was equitably portioned out (worship apart) between manual and mental work. During summer, the cooler hours of morning and afternoon were spent in the field, and the middle of the day in study; winter saw this order reversed. On Sunday the monks laboured not with their hands, and thought only of the Word of God. The hours of the divine office suffered, of course, no change all the year round: their number in the daytime was dictated by that verse of the Psalmist: 'Septies in die laudem dixi tibi'; therefore did the community assemble at lauds, at prime, at the third hour, at mid-day, at the ninth hour, at vespers, and at compline. They arose, moreover, for prayer at midnight, and for matins before dawn. On all this the hearer mused when he was left alone, and with his musing blended a sense of peace such as had never before entered into his heart.

He had returned to his chamber, and was reposing on the bed, when there entered one of the two monks by whom he was conveyed up the mountain.

With happy face, this visitor presented to him a new volume, which, he declared with modest pride, was from beginning to end the work of his own hand.

'But an hour ago I finished the binding,' he added, stroking the calf-skin affectionately. 'And when I laid it before the venerable father, who is always indulgent to those who do their best, he was pleased to speak kind things. "Take it to our noble guest," he said, "that he may see how we use the hours God grants us. And it may be that he would like to read therein."'

The book was a beautiful copy of Augustine's *De Civitate Dei*. Basil did indeed peruse a page or two, but again his thoughts began to wander. He turned the leaves, looking with pleasure at the fine initial letters in red ink. They reminded him of his cousin Decius, whom a noble manuscript would transport with joy. And thought of Decius took him back to Surrentum. He fell into a dream.

On the morrow, at noon, he was well enough to descend to the refectory, where he had a seat at the abbot's table. His meal consisted of a roast pigeon, a plate of vegetables, honey and grapes, with bread which seemed to him better than he had ever tasted, and wine whereof his still weak head bade him partake very modestly. The abbot's dinner, he saw, was much simpler: a bowl of milk, a slice of bread, and a couple of figs. After the kindly greeting with which he was received, there was no conversation, for a monk read aloud during the repast. Basil surveyed with interest the assembly before him. Most of the faces glowed with health, and on all was manifest a simple contentment such as he had hitherto seen only in the eyes of children. Representatives were here of every social rank, but the majority belonged to honourable families: high intelligence marked many countenances, but not one showed the shadow of anxious or weary thought.

These are men, said Basil to himself, who either have never known the burden of life, or have utterly cast it off; they live without a care, without a passion. And then there suddenly flashed upon his mind what seemed an all-sufficient explanation of this calm, this happiness. Here entered no woman. Woman's existence was forgotten, alike by young and old; or, if not forgotten, had lost all its earthly taint, as in the holy affection (of which Marcus had spoken to him) cherished by the abbot for his pious sister Scholastica. Here, he clearly saw, was the supreme triumph of the religious life. But, instead of quieting, the thought disturbed him. He went away thinking thoughts which he would fain have kept at a distance.

The ninth hour found him in the oratory, and later he attended vespers, at which office the monks sang an evening hymn of the holy Ambrosius:—

'O lux, beata Trinitas, et principalis Uuitas,
Jam sol recedit igneus; infunde lumen cordibus.

Te mane laudum carmine, te deprecemur vesperi,
Te nostra supplex gloria per cuncta laudet saecula.'

The long sweet notes lingered in Basil's mind when he lay down to rest. And, as he crossed himself before sleeping, the only prayer he breathed was: '*Infunde lumen cordi meo.*'

CHAPTER XXV
THE ABBOT'S TOWER

On the morrow he rose earlier, talking the while with his servant Deodatus. This good fellow continued to exhibit so deep an affection for the life of the monastery that Basil was at length moved to ask him whether, if he had the choice, he would veritably become a monk. Deodatus looked at his master with eyes of pathetic earnestness, tried in vain to speak, and burst into tears. Instructed by a vocation so manifest, Basil began to read more clearly in his own heart, where, in spite of the sorrows he had borne and of the troublous uncertainties that lay before him, he found no such readiness to quit the world. He could approve the wisdom of those who renounced the flesh, to be rewarded with tranquillity on earth and eternal happiness hereafter; but his will did not ally itself with his intellect. Moreover, was it certain, he asked himself, that all who embraced the religious life were so rewarded? In turning the pages of Augustine's work, he had come upon a passage which arrested his eye and perturbed his thought, a passage which seemed clearly to intimate that the soul's eternal destiny had from the beginning of things been decided by God, some men being created for bliss, more for damnation. Basil did not dwell profoundly on this doubt; his nature inclined not at all to theological scrutiny, nor to spiritual brooding; but it helped to revive in him the energies which sickness had abated, and to throw him back on that simple faith, that Christianity of everyday, in which he had grown up.

Going forth in the mellow sunshine, he turned his steps to a garden of vegetables where he saw monks at work. They gave him gentle greeting, and one, he who had brought the volume yesterday, announced that the abbot invited Basil to visit him after the office of the third hour. Thereupon all worked in silence, he watching them.

When the time came, he was conducted to the abbot's dwelling, which was the tower beside the ancient gateway of the Arx. It contained but two rooms, one above the other; below, the founder of the monastery studied and transacted business; in the upper chamber he prayed and slept. When, in reply to his knock at the study door, the voice, now familiar, but for that no less impressive, bade him come forward, Basil felt his heart beat quickly; and when he stood alone in that venerable presence, all his new-born self-confidence fell away from him. Beholding the aged man seated at a table on which lay books, amid perfect stillness, in the light from a large window; before him a golden cross, and, on either side of it, a bowl of sweet-scented flowers; he seemed only now to remember that this was that Benedict whose fame had gone forth into many lands, whose holiness already numbered him with the blessed saints rather than with mortal men, of whom were recounted things miraculous. Looking upon that face, which time touched only to enhance its calm, only to make yet purer its sweet humanity, he felt himself an idle and wanton child, and his entrance hither a profanation.

'Come and sit by me, son Basil,' said the abbot. 'I am at leisure, and shall be glad to hear you speak of many things. Tell me first, do you love reading?'

Basil answered with simple truth, that of late years he had scarce read at all, his inclination being rather to the active life.

'So I should have surmised. But chancing to look from my upper window not long after sunrise, I saw you walking with a book in your hand. What was it?'

Basil murmured that it was the Book of Psalms.

'Look, then,' said Benedict, 'at what lies before me. Here is a commentary on that book, written by the learned and pious Cassiodorus; written in the religious house which he himself has founded, upon the shore of "ship-wrecking Scylaceum," as saith Virgilius. Not a week ago it came into my hands, a precious gift from the writer, and I have read much in it. On the last of his many journeys, travelling from Ravenna to the south, he climbed hither, and sojourned with us for certain days, and great was my solace in the communing we had together. Perchance you knew him in the world?'

Gladly Basil recounted his memories of the great counsellor. And the abbot listened with an attentive smile.

'I marvel not that you loved him. Reading in these pages, I am delighted by the graces of his mind, and taught by the sanctity of his spirit. At the very beginning, how sweetly does his voice sound. Listen. "Trusting in the Lord's command, I knock at the doors of the heavenly mystery, that He may open to my understanding His flowery abodes, and that, permitted to enter the celestial garden, I may pluck spiritual fruit without the sin of the first man. Verily this book shines like a lamp; it is the salve of a wounded spirit, sweet as honey to the inner man. So much hath it of beauty for the senses, such healing in its balmy words, that to it may be applied the words of Solomon: 'A closed garden, and a fountain sealed, a paradise abounding in all fruits.' For if Paradise be deemed desirable because it is watered by the delightful flow of four rivers, how much more blessed is the mind which is refreshed by the founts of one hundred and fifty psalms!"'

Basil scarce heeded the sense of the passage read to him. He could hear only the soft music of the aged voice, which lulled him into a calm full of faith and trust.

'Is not this better,' asked Benedict gently, whilst his eyes searched the young man's countenance, 'than to live for the service of kings, and to utter worldly counsel?'

'Better far, I cannot doubt,' Basil replied with humility.

'Utter the rest of your thought,' said the abbot, smiling. 'You cannot doubt—and yet? Utter your mind to me, dear son.'

'My father, I obey you, desiring indeed with all my soul to seek your guidance. My heart has been too much in this world, and for one thought given to things eternal, I have bestowed a hundred upon my own sorrows, and on those of Italy.'

His voice faltered, his head drooped.

'I say not,' murmured the listener, 'that you do wrong to love your country.'

'Holy father, I were a hypocrite if I spoke of my country first of all. For all but a year gone by, another love has possessed me. Forgive me that I dare to speak such a word before you.'

The abbot turned his eyes to the window. Upon the sill had settled two doves, which seemed to regard him curiously. He made a soft gesture with his hand, and the birds flew away.

'Speak on,' he said after brief reflection, and with the same indulgence. 'He who tells all speaks not to man but to God.'

And Basil told all; told it with humble simplicity, with entire truthfulness, recounting his history from the day when he first beheld Veranilda to the dreadful hour when Marcian's blood stained his hands. He began in calm, but the revival of emotions which had slept during his sickness and his convalescence soon troubled him profoundly. Not only did the dormant feelings wake up again, but things which he had forgotten rushed into his memory. So, when he came to the last interview with Veranilda, he remembered, for the first time since that day, what he had said to her, and the recollection dismayed him. He burst into tears, overwhelmed at once with misery and shame.

'It may be,' he sobbed, 'that she was innocent. Suffering had driven me mad, and I uttered words such as never should have passed my lips. If she is guiltless, there lives no baser man than I. For I reproached her—my father, how you will scorn me!—I cast at her in reproach her father's treachery.'

The abbot's brow rested upon his hand. It was thus he had listened, unmoving, throughout the story; nor did he now stir, until Basil, having ceased alike from speaking and from tears, had sat for a little while in stillness and reflection. Then at length he turned his eyes upon the young man, and spoke with sad gravity.

'Even so, even so. You gave your heart to a woman, and worshipped at her feet, and behold there has come upon you the guilt of blood. Not, you would protest, through your own fault; your friend was false to you, and in just wrath you slew him. Who made you, O Basil, his judge and his executioner?'

'Father, I seek not to excuse my sin.'

'It is well. And what penance will you lay upon yourself?'

Utterly subdued by awe, oblivious of his own will in the presence of one so much more powerful, Basil murmured that whatever penance the man of God saw fit to impose that would he perform.

'Nay,' said Benedict gently, 'that is too like presumption. Say rather, you would endeavour to perform it. I will believe that if I bade you fast long, or repeat many prayers, you would punctually obey me. But what if I demanded of you that against which not only your flesh, but all the motive of your life, rebelled? It were not too much; yet dare you promise to achieve it?'

Basil looked up fearfully, and answered with tremulous lips:

'Not in my own strength; but perchance with the help of God.'

A grave smile passed over Benedict's countenance.

'It is well, my son; again, it is well. Come now, and let us reason of this your sin. You avow to me that God and His commands have ever been little in your mind, whereas you have thought much of this world and its governance. I might ask you how it is possible to reflect on the weal and woe of human kind without taking count of Him who made the world and rules it; but let me approach you with a narrower inquiry. You tell me that you love your country, and desire its peace. How comes it, then, that you are numbered with the violent, the lawless, with those who renounce their citizenship and dishonour the State? Could not all your worldly meditations preserve you from so gross an incoherence of thought and action?'

'Indeed, it should have done.'

'And would, perchance, had not your spleen overcome your reason. Why, that is the case, O Basil, of all but every man who this day calls himself a Roman citizen. Therefore is it that Italy lies under the wrath of the Most High. Therefore is it that Rome has fallen, and that the breath of pestilence, the sword of the destroyer, yea, earthquake and flood and famine, desolate the land. Yet you here find little time, my son, to meditate the laws of God, being so busied for the welfare of men. Methinks your story has aimed a little wide.'

Basil bent low before this gentle irony, which softened his heart. The abbot mused a moment, gazing upon the golden cross.

'In the days of old,' he continued, 'Romans knew how to subdue their own desires to the good of their country. He who, in self-seeking, wronged the State, was cast forth from its bosom. Therefore was it that Rome grew mighty, the Omnipotent fostering her for ends which the fulness of time should disclose. Such virtue had our ancestors, even though they worshipped darkly at the altars of daemons. But from that pride they fell, for their hearts were hardened; and, at length, when heathendom had wellnigh destroyed the principle whereby they waxed, God revealed Himself unto His chosen, that ancient virtue and new faith might restore the world. To turn your thought upon these things, I sent you the book written long ago by the holy father Augustine, concerning the Divine State. Have you read in it?'

'Some little,' answered Basil, 'but with wandering mind.'

'Therein you will discover, largely expounded, these reasonings I do but touch upon. I would have you trace God's working in the past, and, by musing upon what now is, ripen yourself in that citizenship whereon you have prided yourself, though you neither understood its true meaning nor had the strength to perform its duties. Losing sight of the Heavenly City for that which is on earth, not even in your earthly service were you worthy of the name of Roman; and, inasmuch as you wronged the earthly Rome, even so did you sin against that Eternal State of the Supreme Lord whereof by baptism you were made a citizen. By such as you, O Basil, is the anger of our God prolonged, and lest you should think that, amid a long and bloody war, amid the trampling of armies, the fall of cities, one death more is of no account, I say to you that, in the eyes of the All-seeing, this deed of yours may be of heavier moment than the slaughter of a battlefield. From your own lips it is manifest that you had not even sound assurance of the guilt you professed to punish. It may be that the man had not wronged you as you supposed. A little patience, a little of the calm which becomes a reasoning soul, and you might not only have saved yourself from crime, but have resolved what must now ever be a doubt to your harassed thoughts.'

'Such words did Veranilda herself speak,' exclaimed Basil. 'And I, in my frenzy, thought them only a lamentation for the death of her lover.'

'Call it frenzy; but remember, O my son, that no less a frenzy was every act of your life, and every thought, which led you on the path to that ultimate sin. Frenzy it is to live only for the flesh; frenzy, to imagine that any good can come of aught you purpose without beseeching the divine guidance.'

Much else did the abbot utter in this vein of holy admonition. And Basil would have listened with the acquiescence of a perfect faith, but that there stirred within him the memory of what he had read in Augustine's pages, darkening his spirit. At length he found courage to speak of this, and asked in trembling tones:

'Am I one of those born to sin and to condemnation? Am I of those unhappy beings who strive in vain against a doom predetermined by the Almighty?'

Benedict's countenance fell; not as if in admission of a dread possibility, but rather as in painful surprise.

'You ask me,' he answered solemnly, after a pause, 'what no man should ask even when he communes with his own soul in the stillness of night. The Gospel is preached to all; nowhere in the word of God are any forbidden to hear it, or, hearing, to accept its solace. Think not upon that dark mystery, which even to the understandings God has most enlightened shows but as a formless dread. The sinner shall not brood upon his sin, save to abhor it. Shall he who repents darken repentance with a questioning of God's mercy? Then indeed were there no such thing as turning from wrong to righteousness.'

'When I sent you that book,' he resumed, after observing the relief that came to Basil's face, 'I had in mind only its salutary teaching for such as live too much in man's world, and especially for those who, priding themselves upon the name of Roman, are little given to reflection upon all the evil Rome has wrought. Had I known what lay upon your conscience, I should have withheld from you everything but Holy Writ.'

'My man, Deodatus, had not spoken?' asked Basil.

'Concerning you, not a word. I did not permit him to be questioned, and his talk has been only of his own sins.'

Basil wondered at this discretion in a simple rustic; yet, on a second thought, found it consistent with the character of Deodatus, as lately revealed to him.

'He has been long your faithful attendant?' inquired the abbot.

'Not so. Only by chance was he chosen from my horsemen to accompany me hither. My own servant, Felix, being wounded, lay behind at Aesernia.'

'If he be as honest and God-fearing as this man,' said Benedict, 'whose name, indeed, seems well to become him, then are you fortunate in those who tend upon you. But of this and other such things we will converse hereafter. Listen now, son Basil, to my bidding. You have abstained from the Table of the Lord, and it is well. Today, and every day until I again summon you, you will read aloud in privacy the Seven Penitential Psalms, slowly and with meditation; and may they grave themselves in your heart, to remain there, a purification and a hope, whilst you live.'

Basil bowed his head, and whispered obedience.

'Moreover, so far as your strength will suffer it, you shall go daily into the garden or the field, and there work with the brethren. Alike for soul and for body it is good to labour under God's sky, and above all to till God's earth and make it fruitful. For though upon Adam, in whom we all died, was laid as a punishment that he should eat only that which he had planted in the sweat of his brow, yet mark, O Basil, that the Creator inflicts no earthly punishment which does not in the end bear fruit of healing and of gladness. What perfume is so sweet as that of the new-turned soil? And what so profitable to health? When the Romans of old time began to fall from virtue—such virtue as was permitted to those who knew not God—the first sign of their evil state was the forgotten plough. And never again can Italy be blessed—if it be the will of the Almighty that peace be granted her—until valley and mountain side and many-watered plain are rich with her children's labour. I do not bid you live in silence, for silence is not always a good counsellor; but refrain from merely idle speech, and strive, O Basil, strive with all the force that is in you, that your thoughts be turned upward. Go now, my son. It shall not be long before I again call you to my tower.'

So, with a look of kindness which did not soften to a smile, Benedict dismissed his penitent. When the door had closed, he sat for a few minutes with head bent, then roused himself, glanced at the clepsydra which stood in a corner of the room, and turned a page or two of the volume lying before him. Presently his attention was caught by the sound of fluttering wings; on the window sill had again alighted the two doves, and again they seemed to regard him curiously. The aged face brightened with tenderness.

'Welcome,' he murmured, 'ye whose love is innocent.'

From a little bag that lay on the table he drew grains, and scattered them on the floor. The doves flew down and ate, and, as he watched them, Benedict seemed to forget all the sorrows of the world.

CHAPTER XXVI
VIVAS IN DEO

The telling of his story was to Basil like waking from a state of imperfect consciousness in which dream and reality had indistinguishably mingled. Since the fight with the brigands he had never been himself; the fever in his blood made him incapable of wonted thought or action; restored to health, he looked back upon those days with such an alien sense that he could scarce believe he had done the things he related. Only now did their move in him a natural horror when he thought of the death of Marcian, a natural distress when he remembered his bearing to Veranilda. Only now could he see in the light of reason all that had happened between his talk with Sagaris at Aesernia and his riding away with Venantius from the villa on the island. As he unfolded the story, he marvelled at himself, and was overcome with woe.

There needed not the words of the holy abbot to show him how blindly he had acted. He could see now that, however it might appear, the guilt of Marcian was quite unproved. The Syrian slave might have lied, or else have uttered a mistaken suspicion. It might be true that Marcian had been misled by some calumniator into thinking evil of his friend. And had he not heard the declaration of Veranilda, that she had suffered no wrong at his hands? Basil saw the face of his beloved. Only a man possessed by the Evil Spirit could have answered her as he had done. Was not the fact that Marcian had brought Veranilda to his villa in order to give her into the hands of Totila sufficient proof that he had neither wronged her nor meditated wrong? Ay, but Basil reminded himself that he had accused Veranilda of amorous complicity with Marcian. And at this recollection his brain whirled.

Even were it permitted him ever to behold her again, how could he stand before her? Must she not abhor him, as one whose baseness surpassed all she had thought possible in the vilest slave? Jealousy was pardonable; in its rage, a man might slay and be forgiven. But for the reproach with which he had smitten her—her, pure and innocent—there could be no forgiveness. It was an act of infamy, branding him for ever.

Thoughts such as these intermingled with his reading of the Psalms of penitence. Ever and again grief overwhelmed him, and he wept bitterly. At the hour of the evening meal, he would willingly have remained in his cell, to fast and mourn alone; but this, he felt, would have been to shirk part of his penance; for, though the brothers knew not of his sin, he could not meet their eyes for shame, and such humiliation must needs be salutary. This evening other guests sat at the abbot's table, and he shrank from their notice, for though they were but men of humble estate, pilgrims from Lucania, he felt debased before them. The reading, to which all listened during their meal, was selected from that new volume of Cassiodorus so esteemed by the abbot; it closed with a prayer in which Basil found the very utterance his soul needed.

'O Lord, our Teacher and Guide, our Advocate and Judge, Thou the Bestower and the Admonitor, terrible and clement, Rebuker and Consoler, who givest sight to the blind, who makest possible to the weak that which Thou commandest, who art so good that Thou desirest to be for ever petitioned, so merciful that Thou sufferest no one to despair; grant us that which we ask with Thy approval, and yet more that which in our ignorance we fail to beseech. How weak we are, Thou indeed knowest; by what a foe we are beset, Thou art aware. In the unequal contest, in our mortal infirmity, we turn to Thee, for it is the glory of Thy Majesty when the meek sheep overcomes the roaring lion, when the Evil Spirit is repulsed by feeble flesh. Grant that our enemy, who rejoices in our offending, may be saddened by the sight of human happiness. Amen.'

He rose, for the first time, to attend the midnight office, Deodatus, who was punctual as a monk at all the hours, awaking him from sleep. But Marcus whispered an admonishing word.

'I praise your zeal, good brother; nevertheless, as your physician, I cannot suffer your night's rest to be broken. Descend for lauds, if you will, but not earlier.'

Basil bowed in obedience. Lauds again saw him at prayer. Hitherto, when they were together in the oratory, it had been the habit of Deodatus to kneel behind his master; this morning Basil placed himself by his servant's side. They walked away together in the pearly light of dawn, and Basil led the way to a sequestered spot, whence there was a view over the broad valley of the Liris. Several times of late he had come here, to gaze across the mountainous landscape, wondering where Veranilda might be. Turning to his companion, he laid a hand on the man's shoulder, and addressed him in a voice of much gentleness.

'Did you leave nothing behind you, Deodatus, which would make the thought of never returning to your home a sorrow?'

'Nothing, my dear lord,' was the reply. 'In my lifetime I have seen much grief and little solace. All I loved are dead.'

'But you are young. Could you without a pang say farewell to the world?'

Deodatus answered timidly:

'Here is peace.'

Continuing to question, Basil learnt that for this man the life of the world was a weariness and a dread. Hardships of many kinds had oppressed him from childhood; his was a meek soul, which had no place amid the rudeness and violence of the times; from the first hour, the cloistered life had cast a spell upon him.

'Here is peace,' he repeated. 'Here one can forget everything but to worship God. Could I remain here, I were the happiest of men.'

And Basil mused, understanding, approving, yet unable to utter the same words for himself. His eyes strayed towards the far valley, shimmering in earliest daylight. He, too, had he not suffered dread things whilst living in the world? And could he expect that life in the future would be more kindly to him? None the less did his heart yearn for that valley of human tribulation. He struggled to subdue it.

'Deodatus, pray for me, that I may have strength to do that which I see to be the best.'

It was no forced humility. Very beautiful in Basil's eyes showed the piety and calm which here surrounded him, and his reverence for the founder of this house of peace fell little short of that with which he regarded the Saints in heaven. Never before—unless it were at certain moments when conversing with the Lady Silvia—had he felt the loveliness of a life in which religion was supreme; and never, assuredly, had there stirred within him a spirit so devout. He longed to attain unto righteousness, that entire purity of will, which, it now seemed to him, could be enjoyed only in monastic seclusion. All his life he had heard praise of those who renounced the world; but their merit had been to him a far-off, uncomprehended thing, without relation to himself. Now he understood. A man, a sinner, it behoved him before all else to chasten his soul that he might be pleasing unto God; and behold the way! For one who had sinned so grievously, it might well be that there was no other path of salvation.

This morning he went forth with the monks to labour. Brother Marcus conducted him to a plot of garden ground where there was light work to be done, and there left him. Willingly did Basil set about this task, which broke the monotony of the day, and, more than that, was in itself agreeable to him. He had always found pleasure in the rustic life, and of late, at his Asculan villa, had often wished he could abide in quiet for the rest of his days amid the fields and the vineyards. Working in the mellow sunlight, above him the soft blue sky of early autumn, and all around the silence of mountain and of forest, he felt his health renew itself. When the first drops of sweat stood upon his forehead he wiped them away with earthy fingers, and the mere action—he knew not why—gave him pleasure.

But of a sudden he became aware that he had lost something. From the little finger of his left hand had slipped his signet ring. It must have fallen since he began working, and anxiously he searched for it about the ground. Whilst he was thus occupied, Marcus came towards him, carrying a great basket of vegetables. Not without diffidence, Basil told what had happened.

'You will rebuke me, holy brother, for heeding such a loss. But the ring is very old; it has been worn by many of my ancestors, to them it came, and from one who suffered martyrdom in the times of Diocletian.'

'Then, indeed, I did well,' replied Marcus, 'to leave it on your finger during your sickness. I looked at it and saw that it was a Christian seal. Had it been one of those which are yet seen too often, with the stamp of a daemon, I should have plucked it off, and perhaps have destroyed it. The ring of a blessed martyr! Let us seek, let us seek! But, brother Basil,' he added gravely, 'has there passed through your heart no evil thought? I like not this falling of the ring.'

Basil held up his wasted hand with a smile.

'True, true; you have lost flesh. Be thankful for it, dear brother; so much the easier you combat with him whose ally is this body of death. True, the ring may have fallen simply because your finger was so thin. But be warned, O Basil, against that habit of mind which interprets in an earthly sense things of divine meaning.'

'I had indeed let my thoughts dwell upon worldliness,' Basil admitted.

The monk smiled a satisfied reproof.

'Even so, even so! And look you! In the moment of your avowal my hand falls upon the ring.'

Rejoicing together, they inspected it. In the gold was set an onyx, graven with the monogram of Christ, a wreath, and the motto, 'Vivas in Deo.' Marcus knelt, and pressed the seal to his forehead, murmuring ecstatically:

'The ring of a blessed martyr!'

'I am all unworthy to wear it,' said Basil, sincerely hesitating to replace it on his finger. 'Indeed, I will not do so until I have spoken with the holy father.'

This resolve Marcus commended, and, with a kindly word, he went his way. Basil worked on. To discipline his thoughts he kept murmuring, 'Vivas in Deo,' and reflecting upon the significance of the words; for, often as he had seen them, he had never till now mused upon their meaning. What was the life in God! Did it mean that of the world to come? Ay, but how attain unto eternal blessedness save by striving to anticipate on earth that perfection of hereafter? And so was he brought again to the conclusion that, would he assure life eternal, he must renounce all that lured him in mortality.

The brothers returning from the field at the third hour signalled to him that for to-day he had worked enough. One of them, in passing, gave him a smile, and said good-naturedly:

'Thou shalt eat the labour of thine hands; happy shalt thou be, and it shall be well with thee.'

Weary, but with the sense of healthful fatigue, Basil rested for an hour on his bed. He then took the Psalter and opened it at hazard, and the first words his eyes fell upon were:

'Thou shalt eat the labour of thine hands; happy shalt thou be, and it shall be well with thee.'

'A happy omen,' he thought. But stay; what was this that followed?

'Thy wife shall be as a fruitful vine by the sides of thine house; thy children like olive plants round about thy table.

'Behold, thus shall the man be blessed that feareth the Lord.'

The blood rushed into his cheeks. He sat staring at the open page as though in astonishment. He read and re-read the short psalm of which these verses were part, and if a voice had spoken it to him from above he could scarce have felt more moved by the message. Basil had never been studious of the Scriptures, and, if ever he had known that they contained such matter as this, it had quite faded from his memory. He thought of the Holy Book as hostile to every form of earthly happiness, its promises only for those who lived to mortify their natural desires. Yet here was the very word of God encouraging him in his heart's hope. Were not men wont to use the Bible as their oracle, opening the pages at hazard, even as he had done?

It was long before he could subdue his emotions so as to turn to the reading imposed upon him. He brought himself at length into the fitting mind by remembering that this wondrous promise was not for a sinner, a murderer; and that only could he hope to merit such blessing if he had truly repented, and won forgiveness. Stricken down by this reflection he grew once more humble and sad.

In the afternoon, as he was pacing alone in a little portico near the abbot's tower, the prior approached him. This reverend man had hitherto paid little or no attention to Basil. He walked ever with eyes cast down as if in deep musing, yet it was well known that he observed keenly, and that his duties to the community were discharged with admirable zeal and competence. In the world he would have been a great administrator. In the monastery he seemed to find ample scope for his powers, and never varied from the character of a man who set piety and learning above all else. Drawing nigh to Basil he greeted him gently, and asked whether it would give him pleasure to see the copyists at work. Basil gladly accepted this invitation, and was conducted to a long, well-lit room, where, at great desks, sat some five or six of the brothers, each bent over a parchment which would some day form portion of a volume, writing with slow care, with the zeal of devotees and with the joy of artists. Not a whisper broke upon the silence in which the pen-strokes alone were audible. Stepping softly, the prior led his companion from desk to desk, drawing attention, without a word, to the nature of the book which in each case was being copied. It surprised Basil to see that the monks busied themselves in reproducing not only religious works but also the writings of authors who had lived in pagan times, and of this he spoke when the prior had led him forth again.

'Have you then been taught,' asked the prior, 'that it is sinful to read Virgil and Statius, Livy and Cicero?'

'Not so, reverend father,' he replied modestly, his eyes falling before the good-humoured gaze. 'But I was so ill instructed as to think that to those who had withdrawn from the world it might not be permitted.'

'Father Hieronymus had no such misgiving,' said the prior, 'for he himself, at Bethlehem, taught children to read the ancient poets; not unmindful that the blessed Paul himself, in those writings which are the food of our spirit, takes occasion to cite from more than one poet who knew not Christ. If you would urge the impurity and idolatry which deface so many pages of the ancients, let me answer you in full with a brief passage of the holy Augustine. "For," says he, "as the Egyptians had not only idols to be detested by Israelites, but also precious ornaments of gold and silver, to be carried off by them in flight, so the science of the Gentiles is not only composed of superstitions to be abhorred, but of liberal arts to be used in the service of truth."'

They walked a short distance without further speech, then the prior stopped.

'Many there are,' he said, with a gesture indicating the world below, 'who think that we flee the common life only for our souls' salvation. So, indeed, it has been in former times, and God forbid that we should speak otherwise than with reverence of those who abandoned all and betook themselves to the desert that they might live in purity and holiness. But to us, by the grace bestowed upon our holy father, has another guidance been shown. Know, my son, that, in an evil time, we seek humbly to keep clear, not for ourselves only, but for all men, the paths of righteousness and of understanding. With heaven's blessing we strive to preserve what else might utterly perish, to become not only guardians of God's law but of man's learning.'

Therewith did the prior take his leave, and Basil pondered much on what he had heard. It was a new light to him, for, as his instructor suspected, he shared the common view of coenobite aims, and still but imperfectly understood the law of Benedict. All at once the life of this cloister appeared before him in a wider and nobler aspect. In the silent monks bent over their desks he saw much more than piety and learning. They rose to a dignity surpassing that of consul or praefect. With their pens they warred against the powers of darkness, a grander conflict than any in which men drew sword. He wished he could talk of this with his cousin Decius, for Decius knew so much more than he, and could look so much deeper into the sense of things.

Days passed. Not yet did he receive a summons to the abbot's tower. Rapidly recovering strength, he worked long in the fields, and scrupulously performed his penitential exercises. Only, when he had finished his daily reading of the appointed psalms, he turned to that which begins: 'Blessed is every one that feareth the Lord, that walketh in His ways.' How could he err in dwelling upon the word of God? One day, as he closed the book, his heart was so full of a strange, half-hopeful, half-fearful longing, that it overflowed in tears; and amid his weeping came a memory of Marcian, a tender memory of the days of their friendship: for the first time he bewailed the dead man as one whom he had dearly loved.

Then there sounded a knock at the door of his cell. Commanding himself, and turning away so as to hide his face, he bade enter.

And, looking up, he beheld his servant Felix.

CHAPTER XXVII
THE KING OF THE GOTHS

Transported from grief to joy, Basil sprang forward and clasped Felix in his arms.

'God be thanked,' he exclaimed, 'that I see you alive and well! Whence come you? What is your news?'

With his wonted grave simplicity, Felix told that he had long since recovered from the effects of the wound, but had remained at Aesernia, unable to obtain permission to go in search of his master. The Gothic army was now advancing along the Via Latina; Basil's followers were united with the troop under Venantius; and on their arrival at Casinum, Felix succeeded in getting leave to climb to the monastery. He had been assured that his lord had recovered health, and was still sojourning with the holy men; but by whom this news had been brought he could not say. Doubtless Venantius had held communication with the monastery.

'And you are here alone?' asked Basil, fearing still to utter the question which was foremost in his mind.

'Alone of my lord's men. I followed those that came with the king.'

'The king? Totila is here?'

'It was rumoured,' replied Felix, in a reverent voice, 'that he desired to speak of deep matters with the holy Benedict. They are even now conversing.'

Basil fell into a great agitation. Absorbed in his private griefs, and in thoughts of eternity, he had all but forgotten the purpose with which he crossed the Apennines at the summons of Marcian. The name of Totila revived his interest in the progress of the war, but at the same time struck his heart with a chill misgiving. With what eyes would the king regard Marcian's slayer? Was he more likely to pardon the deed if he knew (as assuredly he must) that it was done in jealous love of Veranilda? The words he had not dared to speak leapt to his lips.

'Felix, know you anything of the Gothic lady—of her whom we lost?'

'The lord Venantius brought her to Aesernia,' was the grave reply, 'and she is now among the wives and daughters of the Gothic lords who move with the army.'

Answering other questions, Felix said that he had not seen Veranilda, and that he knew nothing of her save what he had heard from those of Basil's men who had been at the island villa, and, subsequently, from the gossip of the camp. A story had got abroad that Veranilda was the lost princess of the

Amal line surviving in Italy, and it was commonly thought among the Goths that their king intended to espouse her—the marriage to be celebrated in Rome, when Rome once more acknowledged the Gothic ruler. This did Felix report unwillingly, and only because his master insisted upon knowing all.

'Very like it is true,' commented Basil, forcing a smile. 'You know, my good Felix, that the Emperor would fain have had her adorn his court; and I would rather see her Queen of Italy. But tell me now, last of all, what talk there has been of me. Or has my name been happily forgotten?'

'My dear lord's followers,' replied Felix, 'have not ceased to speak of him among themselves, and to pray for his safety.'

'That I gladly believe. But I see there is more to tell. Out with it all, good fellow. I have suffered worse things than any that can lie before me.'

In sad obedience, the servant made known that he and his fellows had been closely questioned, first by Venantius, later, some two or three of them, by the king himself, regarding their master's course of life since he went into Picenum. They had told the truth, happy in that they could do so without fear and without shame.

'And how did the king bear himself to you?' asked Basil eagerly.

'With that nobleness which became him,' was the fervid answer. 'It is said among the Goths that only a lie or an act of cowardice can move Totila to wrath against one who is in his power; and after speaking face to face with him, I well believe it. He questioned me in few words, but not as a tyrant; and when I had replied as best I could, he dismissed me with a smile.'

Basil's head drooped.

'Yes, Totila is noble,' fell softly from him. 'Let be what will be. He is worthier than I.'

A knock sounded again at the door of the cell, and there entered Marcus. His keen and kindly face betrayed perturbation of spirit, and after looking from Basil to the new comer and then at Basil again, he said in a nervous voice:

'The lord abbot bids you repair at once, my brother, to the prior's room.'

'I go,' was the prompt reply.

As they left the room, Marcus caught Basil's arm and whispered:

'It is the King of the Goths who awaits you. But have courage, dear brother; his face is mild. Despite his error, he has borne himself reverently to our holy father.'

'Know you what has passed between them?' asked Basil, also in a whisper.

'That none may know. But when Totila came forth from the tower, he had the face of one who has heard strange things. Who can say what the Almighty purposes by the power of his servant Benedict? Not unguided, surely, did the feet of the misbelieving warrior turn to climb this mount.'

Leaving the poet monk to nurse his hopes, Basil betook himself with rapid steps to the prior's room. At the door stood three armed men; two had the long flaxen hair which proclaimed them Goths, the third was Venantius. A look of friendly recognition was all that passed between Basil and his countryman, who straightway admitted him to the room, announced his name, and retired. Alone—his attitude that of one who muses—sat the Gothic King. He was bareheaded and wore neither armour nor weapon; his apparel a purple tunic, with a loose, gold-broidered belt, and a white mantle purple seamed. Youth shone in his ruddy countenance, and the vigour of perfect manhood graced his frame. The locks that fell to his shoulders had a darker hue than that common in the Gothic race, being a deep burnished chestnut; but upon his lips and chin the hair gleamed like pale gold. Across his forehead, from temple to temple, ran one deep furrow, and this, together with a slight droop of the eyelids, touched his visage with a cast of melancholy, whereby, perhaps, the comely features became more royal.

Upon Basil, who paused at a respectful distance, he fixed a gaze of meditative intentness, and gazed so long in silence that the Roman could not but at length lift his eyes. Meeting the glance with grave good nature, Totila spoke firmly and frankly.

'Lord Basil, they tell me that you crossed Italy to draw your sword in my cause. Is this the truth?'

'It is the truth, O king.'

'How comes it then that you are laden with the death of one who had long proved himself my faithful servant, one who, when you encountered him, was bound on a mission of great moment?'

'He whom I slew,' answered Basil, 'was the man whom of all men I most loved. I thought him false to me, and struck in a moment of madness.'

'Then you have since learnt that you were deceived?'

Basil paused a moment.

'Gracious lord, that I accused him falsely, I no longer doubt, having had time to reflect upon many things, and to repent of my evil haste. But I am still ignorant of the cause which led him to think ill of me, and so to speak and act in a way which could not but make my heart burn against him.'

'Something of this too I have heard,' said the king, his blue eyes resting upon Basil's countenance with a thoughtful interest. 'You believe, then, that your friend was wholly blameless towards you, in intention and in act?'

'Save inasmuch as credited that strange slander, borne I know not upon what lips.'

'May I hear,' asked Totila, 'what this slander charged upon you?'

Basil raised his head, and put all his courage into a brief reply.

'That I sought to betray the lady Veranilda into the hands of the Greeks.'

'And you think,' said the king slowly, meditatively, his eyes still searching Basil's face, 'that your friend could believe you capable of that?'

'How he could, I know not,' came the sad reply. 'Yet I must needs think it was so.'

'Why?' sounded from the king's lips abruptly, and with a change to unexpected sternness. 'What forbids you the more natural thought that this man, this Marcian, was himself your slanderer?'

'Thinking so, O king, I slew him. Thinking so, I defiled my tongue with base suspicion of Veranilda. Being now again in my right mind, I know that my accusation of *her* was frenzy, and therefore I choose rather to believe that I wronged Marcian than that he could conceive so base a treachery.'

Totila reflected. All but a smile as of satisfaction lurked within his eyes.

'Know you,' he next inquired, 'by what means Marcian obtained charge of the lady Veranilda?'

'Of that I am as ignorant as of how she was first carried into captivity.'

'Yet,' said the king sharply, 'you conversed with her after Marcian's death.'

'Gracious lord,' answered Basil in low tones, 'it were miscalled conversing. With blood upon my hands, I said I scarce knew what, and would not give ear to the words which should have filled me with remorse.'

There was again a brief silence. Totila let his eyes stray for a moment, then spoke again meditatively.

'You sought vainly for this maiden, whilst she was kept in ward. Being your friend, did not Marcian lend his aid to discover her for you?'

'He did so, but fruitlessly. And when at length he found her, his mind to me had changed.'

'Strangely, it must be confessed,' said the king. His eyes were again fixed upon Basil with a look of pleasant interest. 'Some day, perchance, you may learn how that came about; meanwhile, you do well to think good rather than evil. In truth, it would be difficult to do otherwise in this dwelling of piety and peace. Is there imposed upon you some term of penance? I scarce think you have it in mind to turn monk?'

The last words, though not irreverently uttered, marked a change in Totila's demeanour. He seemed to lay aside an unwonted gravity, to become the ruler of men, the warrior, the conqueror. His forehead lost its long wrinkle, as, with eyebrows bent and lips compressed into a rallying half smile, he seemed to challenge all the manhood in him he addressed.

'For that,' Basil replied frankly, 'I lack the calling.'

'Well said. And how tends your inclination as regards the things of this world? Has it changed in aught since you came hither?'

'In nothing, O king,' was the firm response 'I honour the Goth, even as I love my country.'

'Spoken like a man. But I hear that you have passed through a long sickness, and your cheek yet lacks something of its native hue. It might be well if you took your ease yet a little with these good bedesmen.'

'It is true that I have not yet all my strength,' answered Basil. 'Moreover,' he added, lowering his voice, 'I would fain lighten my soul of the sin that burdens it. It may be that, ere long, the holy father will grant me absolution.'

Totila nodded with a grave smile.

'Be it so. When you are sound in flesh and spirit, follow me northward. I shall then have more to say to you.'

The look accompanying these words lent them a significance which put confusion into Basil's mind. He saw the courteous gesture wherewith the king dismissed him; he bowed and withdrew; but when he had left the room he stood as one bewildered, aware of nothing, his eyes turned vacantly upon some one who addressed him. Presently he found himself walking apart with Venantius, who spoke to him of public affairs, apprised him of the course of the war during these past weeks, and uttered the hope that before the end of the year the liberators would enter Rome. It was true that the Emperor had at length charged Belisarius with the task of reconquering Italy, but months must pass before an army could be assembled and transported; by the latest news the great commander was in Illyria, striving to make a force out of fresh-recruited barbarians, and lamenting the avarice of Justinian which grudged him needful supplies. And as he listened to all this, Basil felt a new ardour glow within him. He had ever worshipped the man of heroic virtues; once upon a time it was Belisarius who fired his zeal; now his eyes dazzled with the glory of Totila; he burned to devote a loyal service to this brave and noble king.

Suddenly there sounded a trumpet. Its note broke strangely upon the monastic stillness, and, in a moment, echoed clear from the mountains.

'The king goes forth,' said Venantius. 'I must leave you. Join us speedily yonder.'

He pointed towards Rome. On Basil's lips quivered a word, a question, but before it could be uttered the soldier had stridden away, his casque gleaming in the sun, and his sword clanking beside him.

Again with mind confused, Basil went to his cell, and sat there head on hand, trying to recover the mood, the thoughts, with which he had risen this morning. But everything was changed. He could no longer think of the past; the future called to him, and its voice was like that of the Gothic trumpet, stirring his blood, urging him to activity. At midday some one knocked, and there entered Deodatus.

'Where is Felix?' was Basil's first question.

Felix was gone, but only to the town at the foot of the mountain, where he and two of his fellows would abide until their master left the monastery. With this message Deodatus had been charged by Venantius. He added that Felix had been dismissed, at the abbot's order, during Basil's interview with the king.

'I understand,' said Basil in himself; and during the rest of the day he strove with all the force of his will to recover calm and pious thoughts. In the night that followed he slept little; it was now the image of Veranilda that hovered before him and kept him wakeful, perturbed with a tender longing. God, it might be, would pardon him his offence against the Divine law; but could he look for forgiveness from Veranilda? When he thought of the king's last words he was lured with hope; when he reasoned upon this hope, it turned to a mocking emptiness. And through the next day, and the next again, his struggle still went on. He worked and prayed as usual, and read the Psalms of penitence not once only, but several times in the four-and-twenty hours; that other psalm, to which he had turned for strengthening of the spirit, he no longer dared to open. And all this time he scarce spoke with any one; not that the brethren looked upon him with less kindness, or held him at a distance, but the rebuke of his own conscience kept him mute. He felt that his communion with these holy men was in seeming only, and it shamed him to contrast their quiet service of the Eternal with the turbid worldliness of his own thoughts.

During these days the abbot was not seen. Venturing, at length, when he happened to find himself alone with Marcus, to speak of this, he learnt that the holy father was not in his wonted health; Marcus added that the disorder had resulted from the visit of the king. After Totila's departure, Benedict had passed hours in solitary prayer, until a faintness came upon him, from which he could not yet recover. Basil was turning away sadly, when the monk touched his arm, and said in a troubled voice:

'Many times he has spoken of you, dear brother.'

'Would,' replied Basil, 'that I were worthy of his thoughts.'

'Did he think you unworthy,' said Marcus, 'he would not grieve that you must so soon go from among us.'

'The holy father has said that I must soon leave you?'

Marcus nodded gravely, and walked away.

Another week passed. By stern self-discipline, Basil had fixed his thoughts once more on things spiritual, and the result appeared in a quiet contentment. He waited upon the will of Benedict, which he had come to regard as one with the will of God. And at length the expected summons came. It was on the evening of Saturday, after vespers; the abbot had been present at the office, and, as he went forth from the oratory, he bade Basil follow him. They entered the tower, and Benedict, who walked feebly, sat for some moments silent in his chair, as if he had need of repose before the effort of speaking. Through the window streamed a warm light, illumining the aged face turned thither with eyes which dreamt upon the vanishing day.

'So you are no longer impatient to be gone?' were the abbot's first words, spoken in a voice which had not lost its music, though weakness made it low.

'My father,' answered Basil, 'I have striven with myself and God has helped me.'

He knew that it was needless to say more. The eyes bent upon him read all his thoughts; the confessions, the pleadings, he might have uttered, all lay open before that calm intelligence.'

'It is true, dear son,' said Benedict, 'that you have fought bravely, and your countenance declares that, in some measure, victory has been granted you. That it is not the complete victory of those who put the world for ever beneath their feet, shall not move me to murmur. The Lord of the vineyard biddeth whom He will; not all are called to the same labour; it may be—for in this matter I see but darkly—it may be that the earthly strife to which your heart impels you shall serve the glory of the Highest. As indeed doth every act of man, for how can it be otherwise? But I speak of the thought, the purpose, whereby 'in the end of all things, all must be judged.'

Basil heard these sentences with a deep joy. There was silence, and when the aged voice again spoke, it was in a tone yet more solemn. Benedict had risen.

'Answer me, my son, and speak as in the presence of God, whom I humbly serve. Do you truly repent of the sin whereof you made confession to me?'

Kneeling, Basil declared his penitence. Thereupon, Benedict, looking upwards, opened his lips in prayer.

'Receive, O Lord, our humble supplications, and to me, who above all have need of Thy compassion, graciously give ear. Spare Thou this penitent, that, by Thy mercy, he may escape condemnation in the judgment to come. Let him not know the dread of darkness, nor the pang of fire. Having turned from his way of error into the path of righteousness, be he not again stricken with the wounds of sin, but grant Thou that there abide with him for ever that soul's health which Thy grace hath bestowed and Thy mercy hath established.'

As he listened, Basil's eyes filled with tears, and when bidden to rise he felt as one who has thrown off a burden; rejoicing in his recovered strength of body and soul, he gazed into that venerable face with gratitude too great for words.

'Remember now thy Creator in the days of thy youth.' It was with a parent's tenderness that Benedict now spoke. 'I am old, O Basil, and have but a few more steps to take upon this earth. Looking upon me, you see long promise of life before you. And yet—'

The soft accents were suspended. For a moment Benedict gazed as though into the future; then, with a wave of his hand, passed to another thought.

'To-morrow you will join with us in the Holy Communion. You will pass the day in sober joy among the brethren, not one of whom but shares your gladness and desires your welfare. And at sunrise on the day after, you will go forth from our gates. Whether to return, I know not; be that with the Ruler of All. If again you climb this mount, I shall not be here to bid you welcome. Pray humbly, even as I do, that we may meet in the life eternal.'

After Mass on the morrow, when he had joyfully partaken of the Eucharist, Basil was bidden to the priest's room. This time it was the prior himself who received him, and with an address which indicated the change in the position of the penitent, now become an ordinary guest.

'Lord Basil, your follower, Deodatus, is minded to fulfil the prophecy of his name, and tells me that it would be with your good will. Are you content to deprive yourself of his service, that he may continue to abide with us, and after due preparation, take the vows of our community?'

'Content,' was the reply, 'and more than content. If ever man seemed born for the holy life, it is he. I entreat you, reverend father, to favour his desire.'

'Be it so. I have spoken of this matter with the lord abbot, who has graciously given his consent. Let me now make known to you that, at sunrise tomorrow, your attendants who have been sojourning at Casinum, will await you by the gate of the monastery. I wish you, dear lord, a fair journey. Let your thoughts sometimes turn to us; by us you will ever be remembered.'

Long before the morrow's sunrise, Basil was stirring. By the light of his little lamp, he and Deodatus conversed together, no longer as master and servant, but as loving friends, until the bell called them to matins. The night was chill; under a glistening moon all the valley land was seen to be deep covered with far-spreading mist, whereamid the mount of the monastery and the dark summits round about rose like islands in a still, white sea. When matins and lauds were over, many of the monks embraced and tenderly took leave of the departing guest. The last to do so was Marcus, who led him aside and whispered:

'I see you have again put on your ring, as was right. Let me, I beg of you, once more touch it with my lips.'

Having done so with the utmost reverence, he clasped Basil in his arms, kissed him on either cheek, and said, amid tears:

'Lest we should never meet again, take and keep this; not for its worth, for God knows it has little, but in memory of my love.'

The gift was a little book, a beautifully written copy of all the verses composed by the good Marcus in honour of Benedict and of the Sacred Mount of Casinum.

Holding it against his heart, Basil rode down into the mist.

CHAPTER XXVIII
AT HADRIAN'S VILLA

Rome waited. It was not long to the setting of the Pleiades, and there could be no hope that the new army from the East would enter Italy this year. Belisarius lay on the other side of Hadria; in Italy the Imperial commanders scarce moved from the walls where each had found safety. Already suffering dearth (for Totila now had ships upon the Tyrrhene Sea, hindering the corn vessels that made for Portus), such of her citizens as had hope elsewhere and could escape, making haste to flee, watching the slow advance of the Gothic conqueror, and fearful of the leaguer which must presently begin, Rome waited.

One morning the attention of those who went about the streets was caught by certain written papers which had been fixed during the night on the entrance of public buildings and at other such conspicuous points; they bore a proclamation of the King of the Goths. Reminding the Roman people that nearly the whole of Italy was now his, and urging them to avoid the useless sufferings of a siege, Totila made promise that, were the city surrendered to him, neither hurt nor loss should befall one of the inhabitants; and that under his rule Rome should have the same liberty, the same honour, as in the time of the glorious Theodoric. Before these papers had been torn down, their purport became universally known; everywhere men whispered together; but those who would have welcomed the coming of Totila could not act upon their wish, and the Greeks were confident of relief long ere the city could be taken by storm or brought to extremities. Bessas well knew the numbers of Totila's army; he himself commanded a garrison of three thousand men, and not much larger than this was the force with which, after leaving soldiers to maintain his conquest throughout the land, the king now drew towards Rome. At the proclamation Bessas laughed, for he saw in it a device dictated by weakness.

And now, in these days of late autumn, the Gothic army lay all but in sight. Watchers from the walls pointed eastward, to where on its height, encircled by the foaming Anio, stood the little town of Tibur; this, a stronghold overlooking the Ager Romanus, Totila had turned aside to besiege. The place must soon yield to him. How long before his horsemen came riding along the Tiburtine Way?

Close by Tibur, on a gently rising slope, sheltered by mountains alike from northern winds and from the unwholesome breathing of the south, stood the vast pleasure-house built by the Emperor Hadrian, with its presentment in little of the scenes and architecture which had most impressed him in his travels throughout the Roman world. The lapse of four hundred years had restored to nature his artificial landscape: the Vale of Tempe had forgotten its name; Peneus and Alpheus flowed unnoticed through tracts of wood or wilderness; but upon the multitude of edifices, the dwellings, theatres, hippodromes, galleries, lecture halls, no destroyer's hand had yet fallen. They abounded in things beautiful, in carving and mosaic, in wall-painting and tapestries, in statues which had been the glory of Greece, and in marble portraiture which was the boast of Rome. Here, amid the decay of ancient splendour and the luxuriance of the triumphing earth, King Totila made his momentary abode; with him, in Hadrian's palace, housed the Gothic warrior-nobles, and a number of ladies, their wives and relatives, who made, as it were, a wandering court. Honour, pride, and cheerful courage were the notable characteristics of these Gothic women. What graces they had they owed to nature, not to any cultivation of the mind. Their health Buffered in a nomadic life from the ills of the country, the dangers of the climate, and the children by whom a few were accompanied, showed a degeneracy of blood which threatened the race with extinction.

Foremost in rank among them was Athalfrida, sister to the king, and wife of a brawny lord named Osuin. Though not yet five and twenty years old, Athalfrida had borne seven children, of whom five died in babyhood. A creature of magnificent form, and in earlier life of superb vigour, her paling cheek told of decline that had begun; nevertheless her spirits were undaunted; and her voice, in gay talk, in song or in laughter, sounded constantly about the halls and wild gardens. Merry by choice, she had in her a vein of tenderness which now and then (possibly due to failing health) became excessive, causing her to shed abundant tears with little or no cause, and to be over lavish of endearments with those she loved or merely liked. Athalfrida worshipped her husband; in her brother saw the ideal hero. She was ardent in racial feeling, thought nothing good but what was Gothic, and hated the Italians for their lack of gratitude to the people of Theodoric.

To her the king had intrusted Veranilda. Knowing her origin and history, Athalfrida, in the beginning, could not but look coldly upon her charge. The daughter of a Gothic renegade, the betrothed of a Roman noble, and finally an apostate from the creed of her race-how could such an one expect more than the barest civility from Totila's sister? Yet in a little time it had come to pass that Athalfrida felt her heart soften to the sad and beautiful maiden, who never spoke but gently, who had compassion for all suffering, and willing aid for any one she could serve, whom little children loved as soon as they looked into her eyes, and heard her voice. Though a daughter of the abhorred Ebrimut, Veranilda was of Amal blood, and, despite what seemed her weakness and her errors, it soon appeared that she cherished fervidly the glory of the Gothic name. This contradiction puzzled the wife of Osuin, whose thoughts could follow only the plainest track. She suspected that her charge must be the victim of some enchantment, of some evil spell; and in their talk she questioned her with infinite curiosity concerning her acquaintance with Basil, her life in the convent at Praeneste, her release and the journey with Marcian. Veranilda spoke as one who has nothing to conceal; only, when pressed for the story of that last day at the island villa, she turned away her face, and entreated the questioner's forbearance. All else she told with a sad simplicity. Her religious conversion was the result of teaching she had received from the abbess, a Roman lady of great learning, who spoke of things till then unknown to her, and made so manifest the truth of the Catholic creed that her reason was constrained to accept it. Obeying the king's command, Athalfrida refrained from argument and condemnation, and, as Veranilda herself, when once she had told her story, never again returned to it, the subject was almost forgotten. They lived together on terms as friendly as might be between persons so different. The other ladies, their curiosity once satisfied, scarce paid any heed to her at all; and Veranilda was never more content than when left quite alone, to ply her needle and commune with her thoughts.

Against all expectation, the gates of Tibur remained obstinately closed; three weeks went by, and those who came on to the walls to parley had only words of scorn for the Gothic king, whom they bade beware of the Greek force which would shortly march to their succour. Only a small guard of Isaurians held the town, but it was abundantly provisioned, and strong enough to defy attack for an indefinite time. The Goths had no skill in taking fortresses by assault; when walls held firm against them, they seldom overcame except by blockade; and this it was which, despite his conquest of the greater part of Italy, made Totila thus slow and cautious in his approach to Rome. He remembered that Vitiges, who laid siege to the city with a hundred thousand men, had retreated at last with his troops diminished by more than half, so worn and dispirited that they scarce struck another blow against Belisarius. The Greek commander, Totila well knew, would not sally forth and risk an engagement: to storm the battlements would be an idle, if not a fatal, attempt; and how, with so small an army, could he encompass so vast a wall? To guard the entrance to the river with his ships, and to isolate Rome from every inland district of Italy, seemed to the Gothic king the only sure way of preparing his final triumph. But time pressed; however beset with difficulties, Belisarius would not linger for ever beyond Hadria. The resistance of Tibur excited Totila's impatience, and at length stirred his wrath. Osuin heard a terrible threat fall from his lips, and the same evening whispered it to Athalfrida.

'He will do well,' answered his wife, with brows knit.

On the morrow, Athalfrida and Veranilda sat together in the gardens, or what once had been the gardens, of Hadrian's palace, and looked forth over the vast brown landscape, with that gleam upon its limit, that something pale between earth and air, which was the Tyrrhene Sea. Over the sky hung thin grey clouds, broken with strips of hazy blue, and softly suffused with warmth from the invisible sun.

'O that this weary war would end!' exclaimed the elder lady in the language of the Goths. 'I am sick of wandering, sick of this south, where winter is the same as summer, sick of the name of Rome. I would I were back in Mediolanum. There, when you look from the walls, you see the great white mountains, and a wind blows from them, cold, keen; a wind that sets you running and leaping, and makes you hungry. Here I have no gust for food, and indeed there is none worth eating.'

As she spoke, she raised her hand to the branch of an arbutus just above her head, plucked one of the strawberry-like fruits, bit into it with her white teeth, and threw the half away contemptuously.

'You!' She turned to her companion abruptly. 'Where would you like to live when the war is over?'

Veranilda's eyes rested upon something in the far distance, but less far than the shining horizon.

'Surely not *there*!' pursued the other, watching her. 'I was but once in Rome, and I had not been there a week when I fell sick of fever. King Theodoric knew better than to make his dwelling at Rome, and Totila will never live there. The houses are so big and so close together they scarce leave air to breathe; so old, too, they look as if they would tumble upon your head. I have small liking for Ravenna, where there is hardly dry land to walk upon, and you can't sleep for the frogs. Verona is better. But, best of all, Mediolanum. There, if he will listen to me, my brother shall have his palace and his court—as they say some of the emperors did, I know not how long ago.'

Still gazing at the far distance, Veranilda murmured:

'I never saw the city nearer than this.'

'I would no one might ever look upon it again!' cried Athalfrida, her blue eyes dark with anger and her cheeks hot. 'I would that the pestilence, which haunts its streets, might make it desolate, and that the muddy river, which ever and again turns it into a swamp, would hide its highest palace under an eternal flood.'

Veranilda averted her face and kept silence. Thereupon the other seemed to repent of having spoken so vehemently.

'Well, that's how I feel sometimes,' she said, in a voice suddenly gentle. 'But I forgot—or I wouldn't have said it.'

'I well understand, dear lady,' replied her companion. 'Rome has never been loyal to the Goths. And yet some Romans have.'

'How many? To be sure, you know one, and in your thought he stands for a multitude. Come, you must not be angry with me, child. Nay, vexed, then. Nay then, hurt and sad. I am not myself to-day. I dreamt last night of the snowy mountains, and this warmth oppresses me. In truth, I often fear I shall fall sick. Feel my hand, how hot it is. Where are the children? Let us walk.'

Not far away she discovered three little boys, two of them her own, who were playing at battles and sieges upon stairs which descended from this terrace to the hippodrome below. After watching them awhile, with laughter and applause, she threw an arm round Veranilda's waist, and drew her on to a curved portico where, in a niche, stood a statue of Antinous.

'Is that one of their gods, or an emperor?' asked Athalfrida. 'I have seen his face again and again since we came here.'

'Indeed, I know not,' answered her companion. 'But surely he is too beautiful for a man.'

'Beautiful? Never say that, child; for if it be as you think, it is the beauty of a devil, and has led who knows how many into the eternal fire. Had I a hammer here, I would splinter the evil face. I would not have my boys look at it and think it beautiful.'

A heavy footstep sounded on the terrace. Turning, they saw Osuin, an armed giant, with flowing locks, and thick, tawny beard.

'Wife, a word with you,' he shouted, beckoning from some twenty paces away.

They talked together; then the lady returned, a troubled smile on her face, and said softly to Veranilda:

'Some one wishes to speak with you—some one who comes with the king's good-will.'

Veranilda looked towards Osuin.

'You cannot mean—?' she faltered.

'No other,' replied Athalfrida, nodding gaily. 'Are you at leisure? Some other day, perhaps? I will say you would be private—that you cannot now give audience.'

This pleasantry brought only the faintest smile to the listener's face.

'Is it hither that he would come?' she asked, again looking anxiously towards the ruddy giant, who stamped with a beginning of impatience.

'If so it please you, little one,' answered Athalfrida, changing all at once to her softest mood. 'The king leaves all to my discretion, and I ask nothing better than to do you kindness. Shall it be here, or within?'

Veranilda whispered 'Here'; whereupon Osuin received a sign, and stalked off. A few minutes passed, and Athalfrida, who, after caresses and tender words, had drawn apart, as if to watch her children playing, beheld the expected visitor. Her curiosity was not indiscreet; she would have glimpsed the graceful figure, the comely visage, and then have turned away; but at this moment the new comer paused, looked about him in hesitation, and at length advanced towards her. She had every excuse for looking him straight in the face, and it needed not the pleasant note of his speech to dispose her kindly towards him.

'Gracious lady, I seek the lady Veranilda, and was bidden come hither along the terrace.'

Totila's sister had but little of the Latin tongue; now, for perhaps the first time in her life, she regretted this deficiency. Smiling, she pointed to a group of cypresses which hid part of the portico, and her questioner, with a courtly bow, went on. He wore the ordinary dress of a Roman noble, and had not even a dagger at his waist. As soon as he had passed the cypresses, he saw, within the shadow of the portico, the figure his eyes had sought; then he stood still, and spoke with manly submissiveness.

'It is much that you suffer me to come into your presence, for of all men, O Veranilda, I am least worthy to do so.'

'How shall I answer you?' she replied, with a sad, simple dignity. 'I know not of what unworthiness you accuse yourself. That you are most unhappy, I know too well.'

She dared not raise her eyes to him; but in the moment of his appearance before her, it had gladdened her to see him attired as when she first knew him. Had he worn the soldierly garb in which he presented himself at Marcian's villa, the revival of a dread memory would have pierced her heart. Even as in outward man he was the Basil she had loved, so did his voice recall that brighter day.

'Unhappy most of all,' he continued, 'in what I least dare speak of. I have no ground to plead for pardon. What I did, and still more what I uttered, judge it at the worst. I should but add to my baseness if I urged excuses.'

'Let us not remember that, I entreat you,' said Veranilda. 'But tell me, if you will, what has befallen you since?'

'You know nothing of me since then?'

'Nothing.'

'And I nothing of you, save that you were with the Gothic army, and honourably entertained. The king himself spoke to me of you, when, after long sickness, I came to his camp. He asked if it was my wish to see you; but I could not yet dare to stand before your face, and so I answered him. "It is well," said Totila. "Prove yourself in some service to the Goths and to your country, then I will speak with you again." And straightway he charged me with a duty which I the more gladly undertook because it had some taste of danger. He bade me enter Rome, and spread through the city a proclamation to the Roman people—'

'It was you who did that?' interrupted the listener. 'We heard of its being done, but not by what hand.'

'With a servant whom I can trust, disguised, he and I, as peasants bringing food to market, I entered Rome, and remained for two days within the gates; then returned to Totila. He next sent me to learn the strength of the Greek garrisons in Spoletium and Assisium, and how those cities were provisioned; this task also, by good hap, I discharged so as to win some praise. Then the king again spoke to me of you. And as, before, I had not dared to approach you, so now I did not dare to wait longer before making known to you my shame and my repentance.'

'Of what sickness did you speak just now?' asked Veranilda, after a silence.

He narrated to her his sojourn at the monastery, told of the penance he had done, of the absolution granted him by Benedict; whereupon a light came into Veranilda's eyes.

'There lives,' she exclaimed, 'no holier man!'

'None holier lived,' was Basil's grave answer. 'Returning from Assisium, I met a wandering anchorite, who told me of Benedict's death.'

'Alas!'

'But is he reverenced by those of your creed?' asked Basil in surprise.

'Of my creed? My faith is that of the Catholic Church.'

For the first time their eyes met. Basil drew a step nearer; his face shone with joy, which for a moment held him mute.

'It was in the convent,' added Veranilda, 'that I learnt the truth. They whom I called my enemies wrought this good to me.'

Basil besought her to tell him how she had been carried away from Surrentum, and all that had befallen her whilst she was a prisoner; he declared his ignorance of everything between their last meeting in the Anician villa and the dreadful day which next brought them face to face. As he said this, it seemed to him that Veranilda's countenance betrayed surprise.

'I forget,' he added, his head again falling, 'that your mind has been filled with doubt of me. How can I convince you that I speak truly? O Veranilda!' he exclaimed passionately, 'can you look at me, can you hear me speak, and still believe that I was ever capable of betraying you?'

'That I never believed,' she answered in a subdued voice.

'Yet I saw in your eyes some doubt, some hesitation.'

'Then it was despite myself. The thought that you planned evil against me I have ever cast out and abhorred. Why it was said of you, alas, I know not.'

'What proof was given?' asked Basil, gazing fixedly at her.

'None.'

Her accent did not satisfy him; it seemed to falter.

'Was nothing said,' he urged, 'to make credible so black an untruth?'

Veranilda stood motionless and silent.

'Speak, I beseech you!' cried Basil, his hands clasped upon his breast. 'Something there is which shadows your faith in my sincerity. God knows, I have no right to question you thus—I, who let my heart be poisoned against you by a breath, a nothing. Rebuke me as you will; call me by the name I merit; utter all the disdain you must needs feel for a man so weak and false—'

His speech was checked upon that word. Veranilda had arrested him with a sudden look, a look of pain, of fear.

'False?' fell from her lips.

'Can *you* forget it, O Veranilda? Would that I could!'

'In your anger,' she said, 'as when perchance you were already distraught with fever, you spoke I know not what. Therein you were not false to me.'

'False to myself; I should have said. To you, never, never! False to my faith in you, false to my own heart which knew you faithful; but false as men are called who—'

Again his voice sank. A memory flashed across him, troubling his brow.

'What else were you told?' he asked abruptly. 'Can it be a woman's name was spoken? You are silent. Will you not say that this thought, also, you abhorred and rejected?'

The simple honesty of Veranilda's nature would not allow her to disguise what she thought. Urging question after question, with ardour irresistible, Basil learnt all she had been told by Marcian concerning Heliodora, and, having learnt it, confessed the whole truth in utter frankness, in the plain, blunt words dictated by his loathing of the Greek woman with whom he had once played at love. And, as she listened, Veranilda's heart grew light; for the time before her meeting with Basil seemed very far away, and the tremulous passion in his voice assured her of all she cared to know, that his troth pledged to her had never suffered wrong. Basil spoke on and on, told of his misery in Rome whilst vainly seeking her; how he was baffled and misled; how at length, in despair, he left the city and went to his estate by Asculum. Then of the message received from Marcian, and how eagerly he set forth to cross the Apennines, resolved that, if he could not find Veranilda, at least he would join himself with her people and fight for their king; of his encounter with the marauding troop, his arrival, worn and fevered, at Aesernia, his meeting with Sagaris, their interview, and what followed upon it.

'To this hour I know not whether the man told me what he believed, or coldly lied to me. He has the face of a villain and may well have behaved as one—who knows with what end in view? Could I but lay hands upon him, I would have the truth out of his tongue by torture. He is in Rome. I saw him come forth from Marcian's house, when I was there on the king's service; but, of course, I could not speak with him.'

Veranilda had seated herself within the portico. Basil stood before her, ever and again meeting her eyes as she looked up.

'Just as little,' he resumed after a pause of troubled thought, 'can I know whether Marcian believed me a traitor, or himself had a traitorous mind. The more I think, the less do I understand him. I hope, I hope with all my heart, that he was innocent, and daily I pray for his eternal welfare.'

'That is well done, O Basil,' said the listener, for the first time uttering his name. 'My prayers, too, he shall have. That he was so willing to credit ill of you, I marvel; and therein he proved himself no staunch friend. But of all else, he was guiltless.'

'So shall he ever live in my memory,' said Basil. 'Of him I always found it easier to believe good than evil, for many were the proofs he had given me of his affection. Had it been otherwise, I should long before have doubted him; for, when I was seeking you in Rome, more than once did a finger point to Marcian, as to one who knew more than he would say. I heard the accusation with scorn, knowing well that they who breathed it desired to confound me.'

This turned his thoughts again to the beginning of their sorrows; and again he gently asked of Veranilda that she would relate that part of her story which remained unknown to him. She, no longer saddened by the past, looked frankly up into his face, and smiled as she began. Now first did Basil hear of the anchoret Sisinnius, and how Aurelia was beguiled into the wood, where capture awaited her. Of the embarkment at Surrentum, Veranilda had only a confused recollection: fear and distress re-awoke in her as she tried to describe the setting forth to sea, and the voyage that followed. Sisinnius and his monkish follower were in the ship, but held no speech with their captives. After a day or two of sailing, they landed at nightfall, but in what place she had never learnt. Still conducted by the anchorets, they were taken to pass the night in a large house, where they had good entertainment, but saw only the female slaves who waited upon them. The next day began a journey by road; and thus, after more than one weary day, they arrived at the house of religious women which was to be Veranilda's home for nearly a twelvemonth.

'I knew not where I was, and no one would answer me that question, though otherwise I had gentle and kindly usage. Aurelia I saw no more; we had not even taken leave of each other, for we did not dream on entering the house that we were to be parted. Whether she remained under that roof I never learnt. During our journey, she suffered much, often weeping bitterly, often all but distraught with anger and despair. Before leaving the ship we were told that, if either of us tried to escape, we should be fettered, and only the fear of that indignity kept Aurelia still. Her face, as I remember its last look, was dreadful, so white and anguished. I have often feared that, if she were long kept prisoner, she would lose her senses.'

Basil having heard the story to an end without speaking, made known the thoughts it stirred in him. They talked of Petronilla and of the deacon Leander, and sought explanations of Veranilda's release. And, as thus they conversed, they forgot all that had come between them; their constraint insensibly passed away; till at length Basil was sitting by Veranilda's side, and holding her hand, and their eyes met in a long gaze of love and trust and hope.

'Can you forgive?' murmured Basil, upon whom, in the fulness of his joy, came the memory of what he deemed his least pardonable sin.

'How can I talk of forgiveness,' she returned, 'when not yours was the blame, but mine? For I believed—or all but believed—that you had forgotten me.'

'Beloved, I was guilty of worse than faithlessness. I dread to think, and still more to speak, of it; yet if I am silent, I spare myself; and seem, perhaps, to make light of baseness for which there are no words of fitting scorn. That too, be assured, O Veranilda, I confessed to the holy Benedict.'

Her bowed head and flushing cheek told him that she understood.

'Basil,' she whispered, 'it was not you, not you.'

'Gladly would I give myself that comfort. When I think, indeed, that this hand was raised to take my friend's life, I shake with horror and say, "Not *I* did that!" Even so would I refuse to charge my very self with those words that my lips uttered. But to you they were spoken; you heard them; you fled before them—'

'Basil! Basil!'

She had hidden her face with her hands. Basil threw himself upon his knees beside her.

'Though I spoke in madness, can you ever forget? God Himself, I know, will sooner blot out my sin of murder than this wound I inflicted upon your pure and gentle heart!'

Veranilda caught his hand and pressed her lips upon it, whilst her tears fell softly.

'Listen, dearest Basil,' she said. 'To think that I guard this in my memory against you would be to do me wrong. Remember how first I spoke to you about it, when we first knew that we loved each other. Did I not tell you that this was a thing which could never be quite forgotten? Did I not know that, if ever I sinned, or seemed to sin, *this* would be the first rebuke upon the lips of those I angered? Believing me faithless—nay, not you, beloved, but your fevered brain—how could you but think that thought? And, even had you not spoken it, must I not have read it in your face? Never ask me to forgive what you could not help. Rather, O Basil, will I entreat you, even as I did before, to bear with the shame inseparable from my being. If it lessen not your love, have I not cause enough for thankfulness?'

Hearing such words as these, in the sweetest, tenderest voice that ever caressed a lover's senses, Basil knew not how to word all that was in his heart. Passion spoke for him, and not in vain; for in a few moments Veranilda's tears were dry, or lingered only to glisten amid the happy light which beamed from her eyes. Side by side, forgetful of all but their recovered peace, they talked sweet nothings, until there sounded from far a woman's voice, calling the name of Veranilda.

'That is Athalfrida,' she said, starting up. 'I must not delay.'

One whisper, one kiss, and she was gone. When Basil, after brief despondency came forth on to the open terrace, he saw her at a distance, standing with Athalfrida and Osuin. Their looks invited him to approach, and, when he was near, Veranilda stepped towards him.

'It will not be long,' she said calmly, 'before we again meet. The lord Osuin promises, and he speaks for the king.'

Basil bowed in silence. The great-limbed warrior and his fair wife had their eyes upon him, and were smiling good-naturedly. Then Osuin spoke in thick-throated Latin.

'Shall we be gone, lord Basil?'

From the end of the terrace, Basil looked back. Athalfrida stood with her arm about the maiden's waist; both gazed towards him, and Veranilda waved her hand.

CHAPTER XXIX
ROME BELEAGUERED

A few days later the guards at the Tiburtine Gate of Rome were hailed, before dawn, by a number of Greek soldiers in the disarray of flight. It was a portion of the garrison of Tibur: the town had been betrayed at sunset, by certain of its inhabitants who watched at one of the gates. The soldiers fought their way through and most of them escaped, and had fled hither through the darkness. Before the end of the day came news more terrible. A peasant from a neighbouring farm declared that all the people of Tibur, men, women, and children, had perished under the Gothic sword, not even ministers of religion having found mercy. And very soon this report, at first doubted, was fully confirmed. The event excited no less astonishment than horror, contrasting as it did with Totila's humanity throughout the war. Some offered as explanation the fact that many Goths lived at Tibur, whose indifference or hostility had angered the king; others surmised that this was Totila's warning after the failure of his proclamation to the Romans. Whatever the meaning of such unwonted severity, its effect upon the Romans was unfavourable to the Gothic cause. Just about this time there happened to arrive two captains, sent by Belisarius with a small troop for the reinforcement of Bessas. The addition to the strength of the garrison was inconsiderable, but it served to put the city in heart once more. The Patricius himself would not be long in coming, and when did the name of Belisarius sound anything but victory?

This confidence increased when Totila, instead of marching upon Rome, as all had expected, turned in the opposite direction, and led his forces across the Apennines. The gates were thrown open; the citizens resumed their ordinary life, saying to each other that all fear of a siege was at an end; and when certain ships from Sicily, having by good luck escaped the Gothic galleys, landed a good supply of corn, there was great exultation. True, only a scanty measure of this food reached the populace, and that chiefly by the good offices of the archdeacon Pelagius, now become as dear to the people as Pope Vigilius was hateful; the granaries were held by Bessas, who first of all fed his soldiers, and then sold at a great price. As winter went on, the Romans suffered much. And with the spring came disquieting news of Totila's successes northwards: the towns of Picenum had yielded to him; he was moving once more in this direction; he captured Spoletium, Assisium, and still came on.

Belisarius, meanwhile, had crossed to Italy, and was encamped at Ravenna. Why, asked the Romans, impatiently, anxiously, did he not march to meet the Gothic king? But the better informed knew that his army was miserably insufficient; they heard of his ceaseless appeals to Byzantium, of his all but despair in finding himself without money, without men, in the land which but a few years ago had seen his glory. Would the Emperor take no thought for Italy, for Rome? Bessas, with granaries well stored, and his palace heaped with Roman riches, shrugged when the nobles spoke disrespectfully of Justinian; his only loyalty was to himself.

At high summertide, the Gothic camp was pitched before Rome, and the siege anticipated for so many months had at length begun. For whatever reason, Totila had never attempted to possess himself of Portus, which guarded the mouth of the river Tiber on the north bank and alone made possible the provisioning of the city. Fearing that this stronghold would now be attacked, Bessas despatched a body of soldiers to strengthen its garrison; but they fell into a Gothic ambush, and were cut to pieces. Opposite Portus, and separated from it by a desert island, on either side of which Tiber flowed to the sea, lay the ancient town of Ostia, once the port of the world's traffic, now ruinous and scarce inhabited. Here Totila established an outpost; but he did not otherwise threaten the harbour on the other side. His purpose evidently was to avoid all conflict which would risk a reduction of the Gothic army, and by patient blockade to starve the Romans into surrender.

He could not surround the city, with its circuit of twelve miles; he could not keep ceaseless watch upon the sixteen gates and the numerous posterns. King Vitiges, in his attempt to do so, had suffered terrible losses. It was inevitable that folk should pass in and out of Rome. But from inland no supplies could be expected by the besieged, and any ship sailing up to Portus would have little chance of landing its cargo safely. Before long, indeed, this was put to proof. The Pope, whose indecision still kept him lingering in Sicily, nearly a twelvemonth after his departure from Rome for Constantinople, freighted a vessel with corn for the relief of the city, and its voyage was uninterrupted as far as the Tiber's mouth. There it became an object of interest, not only to the Greeks on the walls of Portus, but to the Gothic soldiers at. Ostia, who forthwith crossed in little boats, and lay awaiting the ship at the entrance to the haven. Observant of this stratagem, the garrison, by all manner of signalling, tried to warn the sailors of the danger awaiting them; but their signals were misunderstood, being taken for gestures of eager welcome; and the ship came on. With that lack of courage which characterised them, the Greeks did nothing more than wave arms and shout: under their very eyes, the corn-ship was boarded by the Goths, and taken into Ostia.

Of courage, indeed, as of all other soldierly virtues, little enough was exhibited, at this stage of the war, on either side. The Imperial troops scattered about Italy, ill-paid, and often starving mercenaries from a score of Oriental countries, saw no one ready to lead them to battle, and the one Byzantine general capable of commanding called vainly for an army. Wearied by marchings and counter-marchings, the Gothic warriors were more disposed to rest awhile after their easy conquests than to make a vigorous effort for the capture of Rome. Totila himself, heroic redeemer of his nation, turned anxious glances towards Ravenna, hoping, rather than resolving, to hold his state upon the Palatine before Belisarius could advance against him. He felt the fatigue of those about him, and it was doubtless under the stress of such a situation, bearing himself the whole burden of the war, that he had ordered, or permitted, barbarous revenge upon the city of Tibur. For this reason he would not, even now, centre all his attention upon the great siege; he knew what a long, dispiriting business it was likely to be, and feared to fall into that comparative idleness. Soon after the incident of the Sicilian corn-ship, he was once more commanding in the north, where a few cities yet held out against him. Dreadful stories were told concerning the siege of Placentia, whose inhabitants were said to have eaten the bodies of their dead ere they yielded to the Goth. So stern a spirit of resistance was found only in places where religious zeal and national sentiment both existed in their utmost vigour, and Totila well knew that, of these two forces ever threatening to make his conquests vain, it was from religion that he had most to fear. In vain was the history of Gothic tolerance known throughout Italy; it created no corresponding virtue in the bosom of Catholicism; the barbaric origin of the Goths might be forgotten or forgiven, their heresy—never.

Totila, whose qualities of heart and mind would have made him, could he but have ruled in peace, a worthy successor of the great Theodoric, had reflected much on this question of the hostile creeds; he had talked of it with ministers of his own faith and with those of the orthodox church; and it was on this account that he had sought an interview with the far-famed monk of Casinum. Understanding the futility of any hope that the Italians might be won to Arianism, and having sufficient largeness of intellect to perceive how idle was a debate concerning the 'substance' of the Father and of the Son, Totila must at times have felt willing enough to renounce the heretical name, and so win favour of the Italians, the greater part of whom would assuredly have preferred his rule to that of the Emperor Justinian. But he knew the religious obstinacy of his own people; to imagine their following him in a conversion to Catholicism was but to dream. Pondering thus, he naturally regarded with indulgence the beautiful and gentle Gothic maiden delivered into his power by a scheming Roman ecclesiastic. After his conversations with Veranilda, he had a pensive air; and certain persons who observed him remarked on it to each other, whence arose the rumour that Totila purposed taking to wife this last descendant of the Amals. Whatever his temptations, he quickly overcame them. If ever he thought of marriage, policy and ambition turned his mind towards the royal Franks; but the time for that had not yet come. Meanwhile, having spoken with the young Roman whom Veranilda loved, he saw in Basil a useful instrument, and resolved, if his loyalty to the Goths bore every test, to reward him with Veranilda's hand.

The marriage would be of good example, and might, if the Gothic arms remained triumphant, lead to other such.

After the meeting at Hadrian's villa which he granted to the lovers, Totila summoned Basil to his presence. Regarding him with a good-natured smile, he said pleasantly:

'Your face has a less doleful cast than when I first saw it.'

'That,' answered Basil, 'is due in no small degree to the gracious favour of my king.'

'Continue to merit my esteem, lord Basil, and proof of my good-will shall not be wanting. But the time for repose and solace is not yet. To-morrow you will go with Venantius to Capua, and thence, it may be, into Apulia.'

Basil bowed in silence. He had hoped that the siege of Rome was now to be undertaken, and that this would ensure his remaining near to Veranilda. But the loyalty he professed to Totila was no less in his heart than on his lips, and after a moment's struggle he looked up with calm countenance.

'Have you aught to ask of me?' added Totila, after observing his face.

'This only, O king: that if occasion offer, I may send written news of myself to her I love.'

'That is a little thing,' was the answer, 'and I grant it willingly.'

Totila paused a moment; then, his blue eyes shining with a vehement thought, added gravely:

'When we speak together within the walls of Rome, ask more, and it shall not be refused.'

So Basil rode southward, and happily was far away when Tibur opened its gates to the Goth. For more than half a year he and Venantius were busy in maintaining the Gothic rule throughout Lucania and Apulia, where certain Roman nobles endeavoured to raise an army of the peasantry in aid of the Greek invasion constantly expected upon the Adriatic shore. When at length he was recalled, the siege of Rome had begun. The Gothic ladies now resided at Tibur, where a garrison was established; there Basil and Veranilda again met, and again only for an hour. But their hopes were high, and scarce could they repine at the necessity of parting so soon. Already in a letter, Basil had spoken of the king's promise; he now repeated it, whilst Veranilda flushed with happiness.

'And you remain before Rome?' she asked.

'Alas, no! I am sent to Ravenna, to spy out the strength of Belisarius.'

But Rome was besieged, and so hateful had Bessas made himself to the Roman people that it could not be long ere some plot among them delivered the city.

'Then,' cried Basil exultantly, 'I shall ask my reward.'

CHAPTER XXX
✦ ✦ ✦ ✦

On a winter's day, at the hour of sundown, Heliodora sat in her great house on the Quirinal, musing sullenly. Beside her a brazier of charcoal glowed in the dusk, casting a warm glimmer upon the sculptured forms which were her only companions; she was wrapped in a scarlet cloak, with a hood which shadowed her face. All day the sun had shone brilliantly, but it glistened afar on snowy summits, and scarce softened the mountain wind which blew through the streets of Rome.

To divert a hungry populace, now six months besieged, Bessas was offering entertainments such as suited the Saturnalian season. To-day he had invited Rome to the Circus Maximus, where, because no spectacle could be provided imposing enough to fill the whole vast space, half a dozen shows were presented simultaneously; the spectators grouped here and there, in number not a fiftieth part of that assembly which thundered at the chariots in olden time. Here they sat along the crumbling, grass-grown, and, as their nature was, gladly forgot their country's ruin, their own sufferings, and the doom which menaced them. Equestrians, contortionists, mimes, singers, were readily found in the city, where a brave or an honest man had become rare indeed. What a performance lacked in art, he supplied by shamelessness; and nowhere was laughter so hearty, or the crowd so dense, as in that part of the circus where comic singers and dancers vied with the grossest traditions of the pagan theatre.

Heliodora could not miss such an opportunity of enjoyment and of display. She sat amid her like, the feline ladies and the young nobles, half brute, half fop, who though already most of them fasted without the merit of piety, still prided themselves on being the flower of Roman fashion. During one of the pauses of the festival, when places were changed, and limbs stretched, some one whispered to her that she was invited to step towards that place of honour where sat the Emperor's representative. An invitation of Bessas could not lightly be declined, nor had Heliodora any reluctance to obey such a summons. More than a year had gone by since her vain attempt, on Marcian's suggestion, to enslave the avaricious Thracian, and, since then, the hapless Muscula had had more than one successor. Roman gossip, always busy with the fair Greek, told many a strange story to account for her rigour towards the master of Rome, who was well known to have made advances to her. So when to-day they were seen sitting side by side, conversing vivaciously, curiosity went on tiptoe. The entertainment over, Heliodora was carried home in her litter, no friend accompanying her. Few nowadays were the persons in Rome who bade guests to their table; even the richest had no great superfluity of viands. After sunset, the city became a dark and silent desert, save when watch-fires glared and soldiers guarded the walls.

As was the case with all Romans who not long ago had commanded a multitude of slaves and freedmen, Heliodora's household was much reduced. Even before the siege began, many of the serving class stole away to the Goths, who always received them with a welcome; and since the closing of the gates this desertion had been of daily occurrence, the fugitives having little difficulty in making their escape from so vast a city so sparsely populated. No longer did the child from far-off Anglia ride about on his mistress's errands; a female slave, punished for boxing his ears, had stifled him as he slept, and fled that night with five or six others who were tired of the lady's caprices and feared her cruelty. Her aviary was empty. Having wearied of that whim, she had let the birds loose; a generosity she regretted now that toothsome morsels were rare. In her strong box there remained little money, and the estate she owned in a distant part of Italy might as well have been sunk in the sea for all the profit it could yield her. True, she had objects of value, such as were daily accepted by Bessas in exchange for corn and pork; but, if it came to that extremity, could not better use be made of the tough-skinned commander? Heliodora had no mind to support herself on bread and pork whilst food more appetising might still be got.

It was all but dark. She rang a hand-bell and was answered by a maidservant.

'Has Sagaris returned yet?' she asked impatiently.

'Lady, not yet.'

Heliodora kept silence for a moment, then bade the girl bring her a lamp. A very small lamp was set upon the table, and as she glanced at its poor flame, Heliodora remembered that the store of oil was nearly at an end.

Again she had sat alone for nearly half an hour, scarcely stirring, so intent was she on the subject of her thoughts, when a light footfall sounded without, and the curtain at the door was raised. She turned and saw a dark countenance, which smiled upon her coldly.

'Where have you been?' broke angrily from her lips.

'Hither and thither,' was the softly insolent reply, as Sagaris let the curtain fall behind him and stepped forward to the brazier, over which he held out his hands to warm them.

By his apparel, he might have been mistaken for a noble.

Nominally he had for a year held the office of steward to Heliodora. That his functions were not, as a matter of fact, all comprised under that name was well known to all in the house, and to some beyond its walls.

'Were you at the Circus?' she next inquired, using the large hood to avoid his gaze without seeming to do so.

'I was there, gracious lady. Not, of course, in such an exalted place as that in which I saw *you*.'

'I did not choose that place,' said Heliodora, her voice almost conciliatory. 'Being sent for, I could not refuse to go.'

Sagaris set a stool near to his mistress, seated himself, and looked up into her face. She, for an instant, bore it impatiently, but of a sudden her countenance changed, and she met the gaze with a half-mocking smile.

'Is this one of your jealous days?' she asked, with what was meant for playfulness, though the shining of her eyes and teeth in the lamplight gave the words rather an effect of menace.

'Perhaps it is,' answered the Syrian. 'What did Bessas say to you?'

'Many things. He ended by asking me to sup at the palace. You will own that the invitation was tempting.'

Sagaris glared fiercely at her, and drew upon himself a look no less fierce.

'Fool!' she exclaimed, once more speaking in a natural voice. 'How shall we live a month hence? Have you a mind to steal away to the Goths? If you do so, you can't expect me to starve here alone. Thick-willed slave! Can you see no further than the invitation to sup with that thievish brute?—which I should have accepted, had I not foreseen the necessity of explaining to your dulness all that might follow upon it.'

Esteeming himself the shrewdest of mankind, Sagaris deeply resented these insults, not for the first time thrown at him by the woman whom he regarded with an Oriental passion and contempt.

'Of course I know what you mean,' he replied disdainfully. 'I know, too, that you will be no match for the Thracian robber.'

Heliodora caught his arm.

'What if I can make him believe that Belisarius has the Emperor's command to send him in chains to Constantinople! Would he not rather come to terms with Totila, who, as I know well, long ago offered to let him carry off half his plunder?'

'You know that? How?'

'Clod-pate! Have you forgotten your master whom Basil slew? Did I not worm out of him, love-sick simpleton that he was, all the secrets of his traffic with Greeks and Goths?'

Again they glanced at each other like wild creatures before the leap.

'Choose,' said Heliodora. 'Leave me free to make your fortune, for Totila is generous to those who serve him well; or stay here and spy upon me till your belly pinches, and the great opportunity of your life is lost.'

There was a silence. The Syrian's features showed how his mind was rocking this way and that.

'You have not cunning for this,' he snarled. 'The Thracian will use you and laugh at you. And when you think to come back to me....'

He touched the dagger at his waist.

In that moment there came confused sounds from without the room. Suddenly the curtain was pulled aside, and there appeared the face of a frightened woman, who exclaimed: 'Soldiers, lady, soldiers are in the house!'

Heliodora started up. Sagaris, whose hand was still on the dagger's hilt, grasped her by the mantle, his look and attitude so like that of a man about to strike that she sprang away from him with a loud cry. Again the curtain was raised, and there entered hurriedly several armed men. Their leader looked with a meaning grin at the lady and her companion, who now stood apart from each other.

'Pardon our hasty entrance, fair Heliodora,' he said in Greek. 'The commander has need of you—on pressing business.'

'The commander must wait my leisure,' she replied with a note of indignation over-emphasised.

'Nay, that he cannot,' returned the officer, leering at Sagaris. 'He is even now at supper, and will take it ill if you be not there when he rises from table. A litter waits.'

Not without much show of wrath did Heliodora yield. As she left the room, her eyes turned to Sagaris, who had shrunk into a corner, coward fear and furious passion distorting his face. The lady having been borne away, a few soldiers remained in the house, where they passed the night. On the morrow Bessas himself paid a visit to that famous museum of sculpture, and after an inspection, which left no possible hiding-place unsearched, sent away to the Palatine everything that seemed to him worth laying hands upon.

Meanwhile the domestics had all been held under guard. Sagaris, who heard his relations with Heliodora jested over by the slaves and soldiers, passed a night of terror, and when he knew of the commander's arrival, scarce had strength to stand. To his surprise, nothing ill befell him. During the pillage of the house he was disregarded, and when Bessas had gone he only had to bear the scoffs of his fellow-slaves. These unfortunates lived together as long as the scant provisions lasted, then scattered in search of sustenance. The great house on the Quirinal stood silent, left to its denizens of marble and of bronze.

Sagaris, who suspected himself to have been tricked by Heliodora in the matter of her removal to the Palatine, and had not the least faith in her power to beguile Bessas, swore by all the saints that the day of his revenge should come; but for the present he had to think of how to keep himself alive. Money he had none; it was idle to hope of attaching himself to another household, and unless he escaped to the Goths, there was no resource but to beg from one or other of those few persons who, out of compassion and for their souls' sake, gave alms to the indigent. Wandering in a venomous humour, he chanced to approach the Via Lata, and out of curiosity turned to the house of Marcian. Not knowing whether it was still inhabited, he knocked at the door, and was surprised to hear a dog's bark, for nearly all the dogs in Rome had already been killed and eaten. The wicket opened, and a voice spoke which he well remembered.

'You alive still, old Stephanus? Who feeds you? Open and teach me the art of living on nothing.'

He who opened looked indeed the image of Famine—a fleshless, tottering creature, with scarce strength left to turn the key in the door. His only companions in the house were his daughter and the dog. Till not long ago there had been also the daughter's child, whom she had borne to Marcian, but this boy was dead.

'I'm glad to see you,' said Stephanus mysteriously, drawing his visitor into the atrium, and speaking as if the house were full of people who might overhear him. 'Your coming to-day is a strange thing. Have you, perchance, had a dream?'

'What dream should I have had?' answered Sagaris, his superstition at once stirring.

The old man related that last night, for the third time, he had dreamt that a treasure lay buried in this house. Where he could not say, but in his dream he seemed to descend stairs, and to reach a door which, when he opened it, showed him a pile of gold, shining in so brilliant a light that he fell back blinded, whereupon the door closed in his face. To this the Syrian listened very curiously. Cellars there were below the house, as he well knew, and hidden treasure was no uncommon thing in Rome. Having bidden Stephanus light a torch, he went exploring, but though they searched long, they could find no trace of a door long unopened, or of a walled-up entrance.

'You should have more wit in your dreaming, old scarecrow,' said Sagaris. 'If I had had a dream such as that a second time, not to speak of a third, do you think I should not have learnt the way. But you were always a clod-pate.'

Thus did he revenge himself for the contumely he had suffered from Heliodora. As he spoke they were joined by the old man's daughter, who, after begging at many houses, returned with a pocketful of lentils. The girl had been pretty, but was now emaciated and fever-burnt; she looked with ill-will at Sagaris, whom she believed, as did others of his acquaintance, to have murdered Marcian, and to have invented the story of his death at the hands of Basil. Well understanding this, Sagaris amused himself with jesting on the loss of her beauty; why did she not go to the Palatine, where handsome women were always welcome? Having driven her away with his brutality, he advised Stephanus to keep silent about the treasure, and promised to come again ere long.

He now turned his steps to the other side of Tiber, and, after passing through poor streets, where some show of industries was still kept up by a few craftsmen, though for the most part folk sat or lay about in sullen idleness, came to those grinding-mills on the slope of the Janiculum which were driven by Trajan's aqueduct. Day and night the wheels made their clapping noise, seeming to clamour for the corn which did not come. At the door of one of the mills, a spot warmed by the noonday sun, sat a middle-aged man, wretchedly garbed, who with a burnt stick was drawing what seemed to be diagrams on the stone beside him. At the sound of a footstep, rare in that place, he hastily smeared out his designs, and looking up showed a visage which bore a racial resemblance to that of Sagaris. Recognising the visitor, he smiled, pointed to the ground in invitation, and when Sagaris had placed himself near by, began talking in the tongue of their own Eastern land. This man, who called himself Apollonius, had for some years enjoyed reputation in Rome as an astrologer, thereby gaining much money; and even in these dark days he found people who were willing to pay him, either in coin or food, for his counsel and prophecies. Fearful of drawing attention upon himself, as one who had wealth in store, he had come to live like a beggar in this out-of-the-way place, where his money was securely buried, and with it a provision of corn, peas, and lentils which would keep him alive for a long time. Apollonius was the only man living whom Sagaris, out of reverence and awe, would have hesitated to rob, and the only man to whom he did not lie. For beside being learned in the stars, an interpreter of dreams, a prophet of human fate, Apollonius spoke to those he could trust of a religion, of sacred mysteries, much older, he said, and vastly more efficacious for the soul's weal than the faith in Christ. To this religion Sagaris also inclined, for it was associated with memories of his childhood in the East; if he saw the rising of the sun, and was unobserved, he bowed himself before it, with various other observances of which he had forgotten the meaning.

His purpose in coming hither was to speak of Stephanus's dream. The astrologer listened very attentively, and, after long brooding, consented to use his art for the investigation of the matter.

* * * *

Milton Keynes UK
Ingram Content Group UK Ltd.
UKHW032232011124
450424UK00008B/909